6th Edition

Understanding

SOCIAL
POLICY

MICHAEL HILL

First published 1980 by Blackwell Publishers Ltd and Martin Robertson & Co. Ltd

Second edition 1983
Reprinted 1985, 1986, 1987

Third edition 1988
Reprinted 1989, 1992

Fourth edition 1993
Reprinted 1993, 1994, 1995, 1996

Fifth edition 1997
Reprinted 1997, 1998

Sixth edition 2000

2 4 6 8 10 9 7 5 3 1

Blackwell Publishers Ltd
108 Cowley Road
Oxford OX4 1JF, UK

Blackwell Publishers Inc.
350 Main Street
Malden, Massachusetts 02148
USA

British Library Cataloguing in Publication Data

A CIP catalogue record for this book is available from the British Library.

Library of Congress Cataloging-in-Publication Data
Hill, Michael J. (Michael James), 1937–
    Understanding social policy / Michael Hill. — 6th ed.
        p. cm.
    Includes bibliographical references and index.
    ISBN 0–631–21686–3 (alk. paper) — ISBN 0–631–21687–1 (alk. paper)
    1. Great Britain — Social policy. 2. Welfare state. 3. Welfare economics. I. Title.
HN390 .H52 2000
361.6′1′0941—dc21   99-049424

Typeset in 10.5/12 pt Sabon
by SetSystems Ltd, Saffron Walden, Essex
Printed in Great Britain by MPG Books Ltd, Bodmin, Cornwall

This book is printed on acid-free paper.

Contents

Preface

This book is an introduction to the study of social policy. It is based on the view that those who study this subject need to consider the way in which policy is made and implemented, as well as to learn about the main policies and their limitations. It has been written for people who have had no previous training in the social sciences, with the needs of social workers, health visitors and other social policy 'practitioners' very much in mind, as well as those of undergraduates.

The preparation of the sixth edition of this book has involved a substantial revision to take into account the impact of the election in 1997 of a Labour government led by Tony Blair. That government claims to be engaged in a radical reform programme led by a philosophy which departs, in a 'third way', from the positions adopted by both the old Left and the new Right. In examining, and setting out the details, of the innovations which are occurring in almost all areas of social policy, this book critically examines that claim. It shows that much that is changing can only be explained in terms of the way in which the government is building on previous policy. It also suggests that some of the boldest claims made by the government, particularly those which concern the new role labour market participation is expected to play in social welfare, need to viewed with considerable scepticism.

At this stage in the history of a textbook, it is impossible to acknowledge satisfactorily all the people who have helped to shape the author's approach. However, I have been particularly grateful for the very active editorial stance taken by Jill Landeryou, assisted by Sarah Falkus, at Blackwell Publishers.

The book remains dedicated to my wife Betty who, when she was a health visitor student, first helped me to identify the gap in the market. As usual, she has helped with the preparation of the book, collecting relevant material and reading drafts.

Acknowledgements

Office for National Statistics 1998a: *Regional Trends*, Office for National Statistics. © Crown Copyright 1999.

Office for National Statistics 1998b: *Labour Force Survey*, Office for National Statistics. © Crown Copyright 1999.

Office for National Statistics 1999a: *Labour Market Trends*, Office for National Statistics. © Crown Copyright 1999.

Office for National Statistics 1999b: *Social Trends*, Office for National Statistics. © Crown Copyright 1999.

Department of Health 1998b: *Health and Personal Social Services Statistics for England, 1997, edition.* Crown copyright is reproduced with the permission of the Controller of Her Majesty's Stationery Office.

Department of Social Security 1997: *Social Security Statistics*, Department of Social Security, London. Crown copyright is reproduced with the permission of the Controller of Her Majesty's Stationery Office.

Acheson, D. 1988: *Inequalities and Health*, London: HMSO. Crown copyright is reproduced with the permission of the Controller of Her Majesty's Stationery Office.

Wilcox, S. 1998: *Housing Finance Review*, York: Joseph Rowntree Foundation.

Chapter 1

WHAT IS SOCIAL POLICY?

- Introduction
- Which policies?
- Conclusions: Studying social policy

- Suggestions for further reading

Introduction

This is a book about British social policy. Social policy may be defined as policy activities which influence welfare. While non-state bodies may be described as having 'policies', a generic expression like 'social policy' is primarily used to define the role of the state in relation to the welfare of its citizens. That is how it is used in this book.

However, this usage raises two key questions:

1 Since the welfare of citizens is affected by their own actions and by the actions of others, what is it about the role of the state in relation to welfare that is different?
2 What are the kinds of actions which have an impact on welfare?

One, perhaps simpler, way to answer the question 'What is social policy?' is to provide a list of the areas of public policy included under that heading. This simpler approach will be adopted here. However, the issues identified above cannot be ignored altogether. It is necessary to look a little at the rationale for the policy areas chosen. In doing so, this chapter will also throw some light on some of the main concerns of the study of social policy.

Which Policies?

The policy areas covered in this book are set out in the titles of chapters 5–10. The first three of those chapters deal with policy areas that everyone seems to include within their definition of social policy – social security, health and the personal social services. Chapter 9 looks at employment policy, and in doing so considers not just government programmes for unemployed people but also some of the ways in which interventions in social policy and interventions in the labour market relate to each other. Chapter 9 raises issues, seldom far away in any discussion of social policy, about the impact of economic policy and the relevance of economic and commercial considerations. That is also the case in chapter 10, which looks at housing policy. Most books and courses on social policy deal with housing, though with some uncertainty about the extent to which they are concerned with the private sector. There are important questions in relation to housing policy that concern the extent to which a free market can operate, in relation to the private sector, and the extent to which housing which is publicly subsidized can be managed as if it were a private business concern. While employment and housing are two policy areas where social and economic issues are particularly mingled together, they are not alone; social issues arise, for example, in relation to many aspects of environment policy and transport policy.

A chapter on education policy is included in this book (chapter 8). Often, this is not examined by social policy texts. The fact that it is difficult to find reasons either for including it or for excluding it tells us something about the peculiarly arbitrary process involved in categorizing policies as 'social'. Clearly, the field of education is one in which there is a considerable amount of public expenditure on services that contribute to public welfare. So, is the hallmark of social policy expenditure its contribution to public welfare, and what does this really mean? If education policy is included, why not also include leisure policy or environment policy? In fact, the inclusion of education, and the exclusion of leisure and the environment, is the consequence of a comparatively arbitrary decision based on a conventional view of the limits to social policy which is clearly open to challenge; see Cahill (1994) for such a challenge.

In the introduction, one of the problems about a straightforward definition of social policy which equates it with state activity to influence public welfare was mentioned: namely, that it is important not to let this lead to the false assumption that it is *only* state activity which influences or promotes welfare. However, there is another problem. To see policies as having objectives involves confusing the character of the policies with the motives and purposes of the people who advocate, adopt and implement them. Policies proclaimed to be 'social' may advance welfare; but they may also be instruments for securing other objectives, which may be detrimental to people's well-being.

Several influential discussions of social policy have suggested that welfare policies are promulgated not from humanitarian concerns to meet need, but as responses to social unrest. Piven and Cloward, for example, argue about social security policies (Piven and Cloward, 1972, p. xiii):

> The key to an understanding of relief-giving is in the functions it serves for the larger economic and political order, for relief is a secondary and supportive institution. Historical evidence suggests that relief arrangements are initiated or expanded during the occasional outbreaks of civil disorder produced by mass unemployment, and are then abolished or contracted when political stability is restored. . . . this view clearly belies the popular supposition that government social policies, including relief policies, are becoming progressively more responsible, humane and generous.

Piven and Cloward are primarily concerned to explain relief policies in the USA, but they draw on English data too, and they clearly intend their analysis to apply to other countries. Other writers have analysed British policies in similar terms. In particular, Marxists have argued that advanced capitalist societies require an infrastructure of welfare policies to help in maintaining order, buying off working-class protest and securing a work-force with acceptable standards of health and education; see, for example, O'Connor (1973) and Gough (1979). Other radical analyses of social policy have seen social policy as sustaining not only class-based patterns of domination, but also patriarchy and racial inequality (Williams, 1989).

Clearly, perspectives like these give a very different meaning to 'welfare'. Policies that promote welfare are explained in terms of social control; they are measures to combat disorder and crime, just like police and penal policies, or measures to legitimize and prop up the capitalist system. It is not necessary to accept totally this interpretation of public policy to agree that there may be circumstances under which social control motives mingle with humanitarian motives in creating what we describe as 'social policies'. Moreover, the more extreme interpretations of the origins of social policies that have been mentioned do not exhaust the range of possibilities. Contemporary studies of both policy making and policy implementation suggest that we need to give attention to some very complex relationships between the mixed goals of those able to influence policies and the varied consequences of their interventions. Outcomes may be the unintended results of policy inputs. Most policy is incremental in character, involving marginal adjustments to what has gone before and being motivated to correct what are seen as undesirable consequences of previous policies. Accordingly, social policy need not be interpreted in terms either of the continual evolution of a welfare state inspired by humanitarian ideals or of a conspiracy to manipulate a powerless proletariat. Yet the rejection of these interpretations need not imply either that individuals with altruistic motives play no part in the evolution of policy, or that manipulative and social control-motivated actions are not involved in the policy process.

This discussion implies three things for the definition of social policy:

1 The policies that are identified as 'social' should not be interpreted as if they were conceived and implemented with only the welfare of the public in mind.
2 Other policies, not conventionally identified as social policies, may make a comparable, or even greater, contribution to welfare.
3 Public policy should be seen as a whole in which social policies are significantly interlinked with other policies.

Just because it is convenient to single out some policies for special attention, and just because there are courses on social policy that require the study of a specific and limited range of public policies, we should not therefore fall into the trap of seeing these as the main government contributions to welfare, or the 'general good'. Let us look at the implications of these arguments a little more by examining the implications, for welfare and for social policy, of policy developments in those important policy areas that no one defines as social policy: foreign and defence policy, and economic policy.

It is important to recognize that the origins of the modern nation-state lie in the achievement of a monopoly of force within a given territory. The central policy preoccupations of the government of any insecure nation are with the defence of its boundaries, the recognition of its integrity by other nations, and the maintenance of order within its territories. It is only too easy for British students of public policy to lose sight of the importance of these issues. They are the daily fare of our news bulletins, but we rarely stop to think about their relevance for our own state. Incomprehension over events in Northern Ireland and a propensity to underestimate the intensity of the feelings of some people in Scotland on the issue of devolution stem from a tendency to take the integrity and security of the nation for granted. Yet, without a secure nation-state the scope for development of what is conventionally identified as social policy is severely limited.

These facts have three implications for the study of social policy:

1 Social policy expenditure has to compete with other public expenditure dedicated to the defence of the realm. The case against heavy defence expenditure cannot rest simply on arguments that some of that money would be better spent on social policy; it is necessary to prove that some of that expenditure is inappropriate or irrelevant, or to face the argument that, without it, no social policy would be secure.

2 The forms of this defence expenditure have a wide range of social effects in creating employment, disrupting family life and so on. Readers may like to think about the type of policy interactions involved by asking themselves what would be the effects on social life and social policy of the reintroduction of a two-year period of compulsory national service. The important effects they should be able to identify will nevertheless be insignificant by comparison with the effects of mobilization for war itself.

3 While social policies do not have much of an impact on relations with other states, it is important not to lose sight of the contribution they make to integration and harmony within the nation. It is this that has led students of social policy to draw attention to the significant impact of war on policy. Thus Titmuss (1958, p. 86). argued: 'The aims and content of social policy, both in peace and in war, are thus determined – at least to a substantial extent – by how far the co-operation of the masses is essential to the successful prosecution of war'.

The development of the role of the British state in the nineteenth and twentieth centuries is often portrayed as the establishment of 'the welfare state'. To present it in this way is to emphasize social policy developments. However, it is perhaps more important to give attention to the growth of the British economy over that period, and to the role played by government in relation to that economy. Two apparently conflicting political interpretations of these events lead us to ask some broadly similar questions about the relationship between social policy and economic policy.

To the followers of the 'classical economists', who argued that the economy would make the greatest possible contribution to public welfare if competition were to remain unshackled, the period between the middle of the nineteenth century and the present day has been marked by extensive government interference with the economy. Some of this interference has been seen as necessary, where competition has been impossible or illogical. Some of it has been seen as justifiable, because it seeks to ensure competition and prevent monopoly. Much of it has been regarded as stemming from forces eager to interfere with and undermine the market economy, shifting the locus of decision from the market-place to the political arena.

Theorists influenced by Marxism, on the other hand, interpret the same evidence the other way round. They argue that as the industrial economy has grown, so the 'contradictions of capitalism' have increased. Government intervention has been prompted in their view by a desire to save capitalism, not by a desire to undermine it. Regulation has been introduced to prevent the logic of competition from destroying the system. State interventions to protect the working class have been designed, according to this view, to stave off revolution and to help the capitalist system to survive. Late capitalist society, it is argued, experiences a form of 'welfare capitalism' in which those who originally gained so much from competitive industry are still dominant in our society.

Both these views of the relationship between government and the economy stress the extent to which social policy should be seen as dependent on, or even a derivative of, economic policy. The key internal political issues of our age are who controls our economy, and how the rewards that stem from our industrial achievements are to be distributed. These are the implications for social policy:

1 The main determinants of welfare are economic.
2 The government's role in diverting resources into social policies must be seen to be closely interrelated with – even dependent on – the role it plays in the management of the economy.
3 Social policies will be determined by views about the way the economy does, or should, operate. Specific social policies need, therefore, to be understood in terms of their relationships to economic policies.

Here are some examples of important questions frequently asked about social policy which are essentially about the relationship between social and economic policy:

- Are social security policies redistributive?
- How far do the redistributive effects of social security operate beyond minimal insurance limits?
- How does any redistribution by this mechanism compare with redistribution that occurs through other economic mechanisms – the effects of competition, the impact of unemployment and the results of wage bargaining, for example?
- How do social policies, particularly social security policies, affect the labour market?
- What are the effects of public housing on the housing market?
- How far are market forces in this area more influential than state intervention in determining who lives in what housing?

It is important to take a wide view of social policy development, relating it to economic policy. Social policy expenditure amounts to about two-thirds of all public expenditure; see chapter 11. To what extent are there limits to the growth of public expenditure in a mixed economy, and therefore what impact may such limits (or the belief that there are such limits) have on social policy expenditure? Similarly, what is the impact on the economy, and also on the whole political system, of the pattern of employment that has emerged as social policy has become 'big business'? Unlike those stressed above, these are questions about the impact of social policy on economic policy, rather than the other way round. Nevertheless, the key decisions about resources for the social policy sector will be regarded as economic policy decisions.

It has been suggested, then, that, while certain policy areas, subject to a few difficult boundary problems, are defined as social policy, any proper understanding of the forces that determine outcomes in these areas must rest on considerations of other policies not included within the conventional social policy rubric.

However, the introductory comment on the definition of social policy also indicated that the state is not the only body which may have 'policies', and that social welfare depends on much more than state action. Our welfare depends also on our own actions, our job opportunities, the support we enjoy from families and friends, and on the activities of a range of non-state institutions (churches, charities, community organizations, trade unions and so on). An examination of *state* social policy, as in this book, must have regard to the things the state does to support or interfere with these other sources of social welfare. Much ideological debate about social policy is about what the state should or should not do to influence the activities of individuals as economic actors, to affect the roles played by families or to alter the legal framework within which voluntary organizations operate. While the ideological 'colour' of much of that debate derives from alternative views about the management of the economy, considerations regarding the implications of policies (or their absence) for gender and ethnic divisions in society are also important.

Conclusions: Studying social policy

Social policy may be studied in a number of ways. We may merely set out to determine the main policies in the areas in which we are interested; for example:

- What is the system of social security?
- What benefits does the health service provide?
- How has the government intervened in the housing market?

These and similar questions need to be answered by those who want to understand social policy. They can also be related to many other points about the way the services are organized and administered. Hence, the simplest approach to the study of social policy is to describe the policies and institutions that together comprise the system of social services.

Many accounts of the system of social policy include comments on the strengths and weaknesses of specific policies. They relate what there is to what, in the authors' views, there ought to be. The study of social policy, as it has developed in Britain, has been concerned to examine the extent to which the welfare state meets people's needs. Often, indeed, students of social policy go further, and explicitly analyse the extent to which it contributes to social equality. In this sense, an academic discipline has been developed with an explicitly political stance. Social policy is seen as concerned with the alleviation of social ills; its objectives are accepted at face value; and it is analysed in terms of its success in achieving them. Many who have written about social policy have done so from the standpoint of Fabian socialism, concerned with incremental social change to create a more equal society. Few challenged this perspective until the 1980s, when Conservative political thinking shifted sharply to the 'right', to express much more directly suspicion of the claims of the state to regulate many aspects of our lives and to portray welfare policy as a threat to economic enterprise.

In this new edition of this textbook, considerable attention will be given to the impact of the return of a Labour government in 1997. It will be shown to be developing an approach to social policy that does not involve a return to the Fabian perspective. Many Conservative initiatives from the 1980s are being modified, but not entirely transformed. Is this new Labourism another version of 'new right' thinking, or is a distinctive 'third way' being developed which is taking British social policy into hitherto uncharted territory? It is difficult to answer this question at this stage, but the discussion of the various new initiatives in social policy will provide some of the data needed to provide an answer.

There has been an extensive debate among social scientists about the extent to which the analysis of society and of social institutions can be 'value-free'. Broadly, there is today a consensus that there are limits to the extent to which those who study and write about society can set aside their own commitments and prejudices. Some go on to argue, however, that value-freedom within the social sciences as a whole may be achieved by the interplay of arguments and evidence, each biased in different ways but contributing to the advancement of unbiased knowledge as a whole. Others are more sceptical about the extent to which a body of systematic unbiased knowledge can be created, and argue that the value problem is ubiquitous. The study of social policy has been particularly conspicuous for the specific political or value commitments of those who write about it.

The strong normative bias in the study of social policy has led at times to a greater preoccupation with criticism of policies than with attempts to discover why they take the forms they do. In practice, if one believes that policies are wrong or ineffective, it is important to understand why this is so, particularly if one's objective is to change them. The view that it is sufficient to point out that policies are 'wrong' is often linked with a view of policy making according to which men and women of good will are believed to be responsible and anxious to rectify the unwitting mistakes made in the past. This approach to the understanding of the policy system was criticized on pages 3–4.

At this stage, as an author who is arguing that the study of social policy in Britain has been strong on criticism and value-judgement, but weak on analysis, I should make my position clear. Since I believe that students may be aided in drawing their own conclusions if writers make their own value biases explicit, it is particularly important to do this. Broadly, I am deeply concerned about the content of social policy, and have contributed (particularly on social security and housing policies and on measures for the unemployed) to the 'Fabian' critique of policy outlined on page 8. I should not pretend that my personal motivation in studying social policy is not linked with a commitment to non-revolutionary movement towards social equality. However, I feel strongly that a concern to influence the content of social policy must be supported by an understanding of how social policy is made. In this book, therefore, I am concerned with what social policy is, how it was created and how it was implemented, as well as with its weaknesses and arguments about what it should be. I think it very important to see social policy in its political environment. These considerations lead me to be sceptical about 'new Labour', but to have some sympathy for the constraints facing the government as it sets out to tackle social policy issues.

An understanding of the factors that influence the character of social policy must rest on several foundations. Some attention must be given to the social and economic conditions that create the need for social policies. This is a difficult chicken-and-egg issue. One cannot simply look at the kinds of problems found in particular social structures and economic situations and analyse policies as responses to those problems, since policies themselves influence the character of the societies in which they are adopted. For example, government provision of housing may be seen as a response to the inadequacies of the market as a provider of houses, but it has also transformed the character of that market. Interactions between policies and society are complex. It is important, therefore, to draw on economics and sociology to help with the understanding of what occurs. It is also necessary to keep in mind the historical dimensions to these issues.

Social policy making must also be seen as a political process. It has already been stressed that social policy cannot be analysed on its own, without reference to other activities of the state. Policies must be understood as products of politics, and attention must be given to the policy creation roles of politicians, civil servants, pressure groups and the electorate. Policies must also be seen as, to a considerable extent, products of other policies. There is a cumulative process to be analysed in which policies create needs for other policies, opportunities for other policies, and new social situations for further political responses. It will be clear that to understand social policy, considerable attention must be given to the findings of political science.

An often neglected part of the study of policy is the examination of its implementation. The actual impact of any policy on the public will depend on how it is interpreted and put into practice. The implementation process throws light on the strengths and weaknesses of a policy, and experience at the implementation end (by junior officials and the public) is fed back into the policy process to influence future policy change. An understanding of these issues requires the student of social policy to give some attention to organization theory and to the study of administrative law.

A particular characteristic of a state in which extensive social policies have been adopted is that it tends to be bureaucratic. The organizational complexity of such a state necessarily complicates the implementation process. Recent interventions in British social policy have involved the design of new approaches to policy delivery which aim to break out of the traditional bureaucratic approach, creating more flexible organizations and new kinds of public/private partnerships.

The portrait of the study of social policy as presented in the last few paragraphs shows that it is a subject that draws on a number of different academic disciplines. The problem of defining the extent to which it is necessary to delve into these disciplines is like the problem discussed earlier of ascertaining the boundaries between social policy and other kinds of public policy. There is a need to make what we can of an essentially applied subject, hoping that we can gain what is required from other disciplines without going too deeply into them. The boundaries between all the social sciences are unclear. Sometimes, this is a necessary feature of subjects that put some parts of the human experience under the microscope and must abstract this from other parts. In other cases, it is a result of historical accidents in the development of the disciplines, and if the study of society were to be initiated all over again, it would surely be divided rather differently. The study of social policy particularly hives off a specific area of social activity in a way that must violate subject boundaries. If it is important to understand a number of practical policies, because of a concern about their effects on society, it is necessary to accept studies that cannot be defined in terms of a discrete intellectual discipline.

In setting out to examine what social policy is, and how it may be studied, some answers have been suggested to the question, 'Why study it?' Many who are required to study social policy are, or expect to be, involved in its implementation. The part of a social policy course that is concerned with describing and analysing policies and the institutions responsible for them has a clear face value to the social policy 'practitioner'. Equally, it is important for such a person to understand something of the way in which social policy works, and the internal and external forces that shape policies.

It may also help to understand other agencies to which a 'practitioner' has to relate, particularly as a great deal of policy depends, or is intended to depend, on successful co-operation between organizations. It has been stressed that no policy area is discrete, that policies in one area affect those in others. This is particularly true of social policies, whose impact on the public depends on the way they interrelate. Successful treatment of the sick requires attention to their housing and income maintenance problems; the care of the neglected child depends on co-operation between health service workers, personal social services staff and schoolteachers; the homeless often face income maintenance problems as well as housing problems; and so on – the examples are legion.

Hence, the most obvious case for studying social policy is a need for the staff of the various social services to understand the system in which they operate, but that is not all. A characteristic of many of the people who are drawn to work in the social services is a strong commitment to those services. Therefore, it is not surprising that the study of social policy has been deeply concerned with the improvement of policies. Many staff care considerably about the inadequacies of the policies they administer. Yet, achieving policy change is never an easy process, particularly if one is a comparatively junior participant in a large organization. To make a contribution towards this end requires not only knowledge of alternatives and commitment to putting them into practice, but also an understanding of how social policy is made and implemented.

These arguments for studying social policy have been addressed to people likely to be employed in delivering benefits and services. I say 'employed'. However, recent changes to social policy have increased the extent to which private and voluntary organizations are involved in the delivery of social policy. As noted on page 7, they have also made it evident that many social welfare services are not delivered by state agencies, but are left to the slender resources of families, neighbourhoods and communities. Hence this is a book for all concerned citizens who want to influence social policy. Its underlying justification is that participation in policy making, for a group of services of considerable importance to us all, must rest on understanding: understanding of what the policies are, of how they are made and implemented, and of the implications of the many prevailing suggestions on how to change those policies.

Suggestions for further reading

A deeper exploration of the rather arid debate regarding the boundaries of this subject is not recommended. However, Cahill's *The New Social Policy* (1994) offers a valuable survey of the ways in which the traditional concerns of social policy analysis might be widened.

A good introduction to the key issues about social policy is to investigate the various ideological perspectives on its role in society. George and Wilding's *Welfare and Ideology* (1994) offers an excellent overview of this subject. Lois Bryson's *Welfare and the State* (1992) and Fiona Williams's *Social Policy* (1989) offer introductions to the ideological debate, with a strong emphasis on the need to take into account issues about gender, class and race.

An overview of the whole field of social policy is offered in an edited volume by Alcock, Erskine and May *The Student's Companion to Social Policy* (1998). The same editors are now working on an Encyclopaedia.

Chapter 2

THE HISTORY OF
SOCIAL POLICY

Introduction

This chapter deals with some of the key events in the development of British social policy, relating them to social, economic and political trends in our society. To understand the character of British social policy today, it is important to have a historical perspective, particularly on the relationship between social and political change.

At one level, the story is simple. The growth of state involvement with the social welfare of its citizens can be related to the development of an industrial society, and its subsequent maturation, or perhaps decline, into what some writers have described as 'post-industrialism' or 'post-modernism'. Alongside this industrial development are political developments, associated with the extension of the suffrage, involving citizens more thoroughly in the activities of the state. Accompanying these are changes to social life, particularly family life; and changing views of the respective responsibilities of the individual, the family and the state for remedies to social problems. The result is a package of developments – of the state's role, the character of the economy, the nature of political processes and of ideologies – which those without a dogmatic belief about the motive forces in political development find difficult to disentangle in cause–effect terms.

This version of the story of the development of the state's role in social welfare can be applied to a number of industrialized nations – to the USA, to most of the other countries of western and northern Europe and to Australasia – as much as to Britain; this theme has been widely analysed (Ashford, 1986; Esping-Andersen, 1990; Hill, 1996). However, while these 'broad brush' features of the story must not be forgotten, it is important also to try to single out characteristics of Britain's development that help to explain the particular shape of its own social policies. A proper understanding of this subject requires consideration of the general factors, which may apply to a distinct group of nations; the special factors, which are perhaps unique to one nation; and, furthermore, a number of factors that do not fall neatly into either of these categories. Included in this last group is, for example, the 'insurance principle' in social security, adopted in a variety of ways by various governments who clearly attempted to learn from each other's experiences (Heclo, 1974; Baldwin, 1990).

Developments before the Twentieth Century

In dealing with the relationship between past events and contemporary policies, it is always difficult to know how far back to go in time. To understand British social policies, some consideration of the history of the poor-law, with its roots in Elizabethan legislation, is necessary. The Tudor age saw considerable population movements, with changes in agriculture, the growth of towns and some rudimentary developments in manufacturing. The government found it necessary to try to impose a centrally determined framework on what had hitherto been entirely local, and often monastic, charitable initiatives. It placed responsibility for the poor on each parish, with the requirement, under the Acts of Settlement, that the itinerant poor should be returned, if necessary, to their parishes of origin. The parishes were required to levy taxes on property known as 'rates' to provide for the relief of the poor.

The history of the poor-law between the sixteenth and twentieth centuries was one of attempts to make this work – for local initiative with broad guidelines laid down centrally – despite social changes. As Britain became industrialized and urbanized, this strictly local system of administration came under strain. Population movements gradually rendered the Acts of Settlement obsolete. The tasks of the poor-law became more complex as parishes had to cope with, for example, trade recessions and outbreaks of infectious diseases, each affecting large numbers of people in the new towns and cities. By the middle of the nineteenth century, developments in medicine offered a new challenge to the parish 'guardians' who had previously provided only the most rudimentary care to the sick.

The most significant nineteenth-century attempt to modernize the poor-law was the Poor Law Amendment Act of 1834. This set up a national Poor Law Commission to superintend the system, and formed the parishes into groups known as poor-law unions. This important step towards the development of a national system was only a limited success. However, its main contributions to the development of policy were the 'workhouse test' and the doctrine of 'less eligibility'. The aims of these were to curb indiscriminate 'outdoor' relief, i.e. outside institutions. If the poor were not sufficiently desperate to enter the workhouse, they could not be really in need. The system was intended to ensure that those who received help were worse off ('less eligible') than the poorest people in work. In practice, many poor-law unions did not strictly enforce the workhouse test and, as the years passed, the elderly and the sick were increasingly given outdoor relief. Nevertheless, the elimination of the workhouse – and the abolition of the means test adopted to confine relief-giving – became an important preoccupation of twentieth-century critics of the poor-law. The principle of less eligibility continues to influence decisions about relief today.

While the basic nineteenth-century response to poverty was to try to strengthen older institutions, some of the consequences of urbanization and industrialization posed problems for which entirely new responses were necessary. Measures were taken to curb the hours worked by women and children in factories, and to improve safety and working conditions. This significant development in state intervention in the economy seems to have come about as a result of a mixture of growing humanitarian concern and embryonic working-class pressure. The enforcement of this legislation was put into the hands of a central government inspectorate, the first of a number of such inspectorates to be set up in the nineteenth century and to operate, according to Roberts (1960), as an important source of pressure for further social reform.

The rapid spread of infection in areas where people were crowded together was – like the exploitation of child labour – not a new phenomenon but, in an increasingly urbanized society, it took new forms which were more apparent to political opinion, and more threatening to life and industry; and there were many more large populous areas devoid of the most elementary arrangements for disposing of waste or supplying pure water. Furthermore, it was only in the nineteenth century that scientific advance identified the main links between insanitary conditions and disease. In a few areas, local government agencies took some steps to tackle this problem, but real progress did not come until central government gave local authorities powers to act effectively, and also required them to take such action.

Here, then, was an important area of government intervention, pushing local authorities to tackle some of the problems of their own areas. The local government system of the time had been given some shape by the Municipal Corporations Act of 1835, but it was not until the end of the century that it acquired a structure that would enable it to take on the range of functions it carries out today. In the nineteenth century, therefore, some reforms required local authorities to take action and to employ professional staff, such as the medical officers of health required by an Act of 1871. Others, however, set up *ad hoc* authorities to take on functions delegated by central government.

The evolution of state education during the nineteenth century provides a good example of a series of *ad hoc* responses. Religious societies had begun to become involved in the provision of cheap basic education for the children of the poor early in the century. By 1833, they had persuaded the government to provide a small grant towards this work. In 1839, the government set up an inspectorate to provide central supervision of the way the growing state aid was being spent. It was not until 1870, however, that the government moved effectively into the provision of primary education. Motivated, it is widely believed, by a concern about the illiteracy of the growing electorate (the franchise had been considerably widened in 1867), but also undoubtedly by a recognition of a need for a better educated work-force, Parliament provided that school boards, to set up state-financed schools, could be established where there was a clear educational need and the voluntary schools were insufficient in number. In 1880, a further Education Act made schooling compulsory for children between the ages of five and ten, and, in the 1890s, it was established that most elementary education should be free. During the last years of the century, some of the school boards even became involved in secondary education, producing a confused pattern of educational growth that was to prompt government action at the beginning of the twentieth century.

Reference has already been made to the way in which developments in medicine began, in the late nineteenth century, to render inadequate the traditional poor-law approach to the care of the sick. Alongside the development of poor-law hospitals, many voluntary hospitals, assisted by charitable funds that enabled them to provide cheap or free services to the poor, were founded, or grew in strength from their earlier origins. The local authorities were also given powers to establish hospitals to fulfil their duties to contain infectious diseases, and to care for mentally ill people. Medical care outside the hospitals grew in importance in the second half of the century, becoming more than the prerogative of the rich. This was partly a poor-law development, partly the extension of the services of the voluntary hospitals, and partly an aspect of the growth of insurance against misfortune widely practised by the more prosperous of the working classes. In all, a mixed package of health care measures was evolving. This complex mixture, dominated by a powerful medical profession firmly established during the nineteenth century, posed problems for subsequent attempts to rationalize the health services, and therefore influenced the shape the National Health Service (NHS) eventually achieved.

At the end of the nineteenth century, the verdict of the legal philosopher Dicey (1905) was that *laissez-faire* had given way to collectivism; that government had begun to assume a role in society that had taken Britain well on the way to becoming a socialist state. The factory legislation, and the government intervention in the cause of health and safety, implied important changes in the role of the state. The educational system at the primary (or, as it was known then, the elementary) level had received a crucial injection of public provision. The poor-law, on the other hand, had been changed but little. A need for new policies in that area was just beginning to become apparent at the end of the century, as scientific surveys (Booth, 1889; Rowntree, 1901) and journalistic investigations charted the existence of severe problems of poverty caused by factors – in particular sickness and old age – largely outside individual control.

It was stated earlier that the agencies set up during the nineteenth century to implement social policies were often *ad hoc* bodies. While local government was responsible for public health, and for the rudimentary planning, housing and hospital functions required to help to achieve more sanitary urban areas, education was made the responsibility of separately elected school boards. The poor-law came under yet another kind of authority, the boards of guardians, descendants of the former parish officials. However, legislation late in the century provided a new local government structure much better able to take on a wide range of functions. Local Government Acts in 1888 and 1894 set up a system of local authorities that was to remain almost unchanged until the 1970s. They gave a shape to local government, with a split between the highly urbanized areas and the rest of the country, which dominates local politics to this day. The less-urbanized areas acquired a two-tier system of county government, accompanied by lower-tier urban and rural districts. In many urban areas, county boroughs were set up as single all-purpose authorities. London acquired a special two-tier system of its own.

It is convenient, for the presentation of historical accounts, when a specific date can be identified as a watershed. It further adds neatness when that date is the beginning of a century. While there is always an arbitrary aspect to the choice of such dates, particularly in social history, the dividing point between the nineteenth and twentieth centuries seems a particularly significant one. At this time, the large working-class male element added to the electorate in 1885 was just beginning to influence political thinking. The Labour Representation Committee was set up in 1899 to try to elect more working men to Parliament. This body was to turn itself into the Labour Party in 1906. The major political parties, the Conservatives and the Liberals, were increasingly aware of the need to compete for working-class support. For the Conservatives, the formula was an interesting blend of imperialism and social reform (Semmel, 1961). The Liberals had a radical wing, temporarily disadvantaged by the conflict over home rule for Ireland and the jingoism of the Boer War, but ready to push the party towards acceptance of a package of new social measures.

Late in the nineteenth century, Britain had begun to discover that an advanced industrial nation is vulnerable to alarming economic fluctuations, owing to the uncoordinated nature of much business decision making and the international complications of the trade cycle. New competitors had also emerged as other nations – particularly Germany and the USA – industrialized rapidly. The Empire still looked secure, but the competition for new trading outlets was increasing dramatically. At the same time as doubts were beginning to be felt about Britain's economic vulnerability, working people were increasingly organizing in trade unions to try to secure, or guarantee, their share of the progress. The political price of economic failure was being raised. New initiatives to preserve the unity of the nation were required.

1900–1914

The period immediately before World War I was dominated by a series of reforms adopted by the Liberal government after 1906. However, before those reforms are considered, two earlier events require comment. In 1902, the Conservative government passed an important Education Act. This shifted the responsibility for state education from the school boards to the county and county borough councils, and devised a formula for the financial support of the church schools that preserved a measure of voluntary control. The other important feature of this Act was that it legitimized expenditure on secondary and technical schools, and thereby stimulated the growth of this element of state education.

The other significant event was the Boer War. This rather inglorious episode in British imperial history had a considerable significance for social policy. In general, it led to a concern to examine what was wrong with *Great* Britain that she should have been unable to fight effectively against apparently fragile opposition. In particular, politicians, in this age when Britain's imperial success was believed to have been based on racial superiority, sought to examine why so many volunteers to fight had been found to be unfit to do so.

An Interdepartmental Committee on Physical Deterioration was set up. It reported in 1904, urging the establishment of a school medical service and the provision of school meals within the public education system. Both these measures were adopted by the Liberals and implemented soon after they came to power.

Before they lost office, the Conservatives also responded to the growing evidence on the extent of poverty, and the inadequacies of existing measures, by setting up a Royal Commission on the Poor Laws in 1905. The report of this body, which did not appear until 1909, contains a most thorough discussion of British social policy at that time. There was both a majority and a minority report, and the latter provided a well-argued critique of the system. However, without waiting for the Royal Commission, the Liberal government decided to promote two pieces of legislation that significantly modified the role of the poor-law in the provision of social security, the Old Age Pensions Act of 1908 and the National Insurance Act of 1911.

These two measures provide interesting contrasts in approaches to the provision of social security. The old age pension was non-contributory and based on a simple test of means. It was an extension of the outdoor relief given by some boards of guardians, but its means test was a personal and not a family one. The national insurance (NI) scheme, on the other hand, was contributory but not means-tested. It provided cover against sickness and unemployment for some, initially limited, categories of workers. The contributions were to come jointly from employees, employers and the state. The sickness scheme provided not just cash benefits but also medical treatment from a 'panel' doctor who was remunerated on a 'capitation basis' in terms of the number of patients on his or her panel. The Friendly Societies and insurance companies, who were already involved in the provision of sickness cover for many working people, were allowed to participate as agents for the scheme and providers of additional benefits. The scheme protected only employees themselves, not any members of their families.

The National Insurance Act is most important for introducing the 'insurance principle' into British social security legislation. A number of European countries had adopted state or municipal insurance schemes during the last years of the nineteenth century. The British policy makers were particularly aware of the German scheme. Heclo (1974, p. 81) provides an interesting account of the role played by Beveridge, one of the architects of the new scheme, in introducing insurance ideas:

> In his first column for the *Morning Post*, February 16, 1906, he had dismissed contributory social insurance on the German pattern, as had all British investigating committees, with the standard view that it would require an 'un-British' amount of regulation of the individual. Beveridge, however, studied the German experiment more closely during the next year and concluded that the contributory insurance principle could not only reduce costs; it could also eliminate reliance on means tests.

See also Harris (1977) on Beveridge's role.

The idea of social insurance had been adopted in the conservative society of Bismarck's Germany because it offered a low-cost mechanism to meet some social needs while committing workers, as contributors to their own benefits, to the social and economic *status quo*.

This adoption of the insurance principle had important consequences for the development of social policy. In various measures after 1911, governments extended benefits in ways that undermined the *true* insurance basis of the scheme. However, the contributory principle remained an important political symbol and, from time to time, attempts were made to return the scheme closer to its roots. It is always difficult to combine the hard-headed actuarial principles of insurance with a concern for effective and comprehensive social security; yet, as Beveridge recognized, when the only viable political alternative is means testing, the contributory principle has a great appeal.

The 1911 National Insurance Act had implications for more than social security policy, in two ways. The provision of medical services under the sickness benefit scheme used a model for the state payment of general practitioners (GPs) that has continued in the National Health Service to the present day. Abel-Smith (1976, ch. 2) has pointed out that, before 1911, the doctors were in conflict with the Friendly Societies about the conditions under which they were hired to care for members. Hence they were predisposed to secure contracts under the state scheme which preserved their freedom. This right to operate as independent contractors rather than as salaried servants of the state has been zealously preserved by GPs.

It is also important to recognize the National Insurance Act as the kind of response to the problem of unemployment that became dominant in Britain. The early years of the twentieth century saw a number of small experiments in combating unemployment by providing publicly subsidized work. Yet these did not achieve any scale, perhaps because of suspicions of their implications for state involvement in the economy. There was however one measure, adopted in 1908, the Labour Exchange Act, that came to assume importance. The National Insurance Act gave the newly set-up exchanges the role of administering the system of unemployment benefit. This was the activity with which they came to be most closely identified. The hallmark of the British response to defects in the working of the labour market became the provision of relief to the unemployed, and not the creation of special work programmes or measures to facilitate movements of workers between jobs (Harris, 1972).

The Liberal government could, of course, have developed their social security measures to redistribute incomes without either means tests or contributions. Neither then, nor later, have social security measures involved the wholesale redistribution of resources. However, both of the early schemes required quite large subventions from taxation. It is important, therefore, to bear in mind the significance of the budget that Lloyd George introduced in 1909 to finance both social welfare reforms and increased government expenditure on other matters such as defence, by increasing taxation and making it more redistributive. This seems to have been the first occasion on which a British government's annual budget was presented, or perceived, as an instrument for the redistribution of income.

The events of 1909–11 have been given comparatively lengthy attention. The political balance in Britain tipped quite markedly at that time, with important implications for social policy. Such was the ferment of the times throughout Europe, and such was the rising volume of political controversy within Britain (rising political movements on the Left, the women's campaign for votes and the conflict over the future of Ireland), that a more dramatic tipping of the balance than actually occurred in the next few years might have been expected. Certainly many new social policies were shortly to come, but these did little to disrupt the *status quo*; indeed, many must be seen as designed to preserve it.

1914–1939

It is important not to regard the early development of social policy in Britain as simply involving two dramatic jumps forward in the periods 1906–11 and 1944–9. Between these, a great deal happened to influence policies and to give them a character they often retain.

In World War I, Britain experienced conscription for the first time, and the mobilization not only of the whole male work-force but also of many women, hitherto not in employment, to assist the war effort. The war economy produced many domestic shortages. Initially, the government was reluctant to impose controls and rationing, but its desire to curb wage rises and industrial unrest forced it to intervene. In general then, the 'collectivist state' advanced considerably during the war. Civil servants learnt to carry out, and members of the public came to expect, government policies in areas of life never before influenced by state action. This was the general impact of war on public policy. Its specific impact on social policy was more limited. The imposition of controls on private rents in 1915 was a rare, but significant, example of social policy innovation in this period.

However, during and at the end of the war, the government made many promises for a better future. Even before the war ended, an Education Act was passed which recognized the case for state support for free education up to the age of fourteen. At the end of the war Lloyd George promised 'homes fit for heroes', and one of the first pieces of post-war legislation was a Housing Act that provided government subsidies to local authorities to build houses 'for the working classes'. This Act, known as the Addison Act after its sponsor, the Minister of Health, while not the first legislation to allow local authority house building, was the first to subsidize it. It effectively initiated a programme of council-house building that continued, albeit subject to regular modification as governments changed the subsidy arrangements, until the late 1970s. After the Addison Act, both of the minority Labour governments, in power in 1924 and in 1929–31, extended the local authority house-building programme by means of further subsidies. In the 1930s, there was a shift in housing policy, with the government encouraging local authorities to put their emphasis in house provision on clearing the slums. The strict rent control, introduced in the war to protect private tenants, was partly lifted during the inter-war period. However, with this, as with council-house building, no real attempt was made – until the 1980s – to turn back the clock on processes that were ultimately to transform totally the character of Britain's housing market.

The evolution of relief policies for the unemployed in the inter-war years is an interesting story. Unemployment was a recurrent problem throughout this period. Immediately after the war, the government mismanaged the discharge of servicemen back into civilian life, and unemployment rose rapidly. Then the economy picked up and the problem abated, but this proved to be a temporary respite and, by 1921, registered unemployment was over two million. It remained over a million throughout the inter-war period, falling back a bit in the middle 1920s but then rising steeply in 1930. By 1931, it was over two million again, and it did not fall below two million until 1936.

The 1911 National Insurance Act provided unemployment benefit only for workers in a limited number of trades, which were not liable to extensive or prolonged unemployment. It also contained strict rules to protect the insurance fund. Benefits were dependent on past contributions, and the duration of weekly payments to individuals was limited. The scheme was not designed to provide widespread relief in a period of mass unemployment. Gilbert, in his detailed study of social policy in this period, has shown that politicians were alarmed by the reports they received of unrest and agitation among the ranks of the unemployed (Gilbert, 1970). They were particularly conscious of the expectation by ex-soldiers that they would receive generous treatment from the government. Hence the government faced a dilemma. They resolved it by breaching the strict insurance principles and extending the scope of the unemployment benefit scheme.

It would be inappropriate here to set out all the convolutions in public policy on relief for the unemployed in this period. What a whole succession of ministers and official committees had to try to resolve was the conflict between the demand for economy in government expenditure and the rising cost of an insurance benefit scheme no longer entirely restrained by insurance rules. Broadly, the compromise reached was extended but not unlimited insurance benefits, the operation of strict and quite unrealistic tests to ensure that people were 'genuinely seeking work' (a measure particularly aimed at unemployed females) (Deacon, 1976), the use of additional means-tested benefits known then as 'doles', and acceptance that the poor-law authorities would give extensive 'outdoor' relief to the unemployed. Eventually rationalization came, in 1934, when a unified national means-test scheme for benefits additional to insurance benefits was devised, to be administered by the Unemployment Assistance Board (UAB). This new organization was the forerunner of the National Assistance Board set up in 1948. The UAB provided a model that enabled central government to take over the functions of the poor-law agencies. It transferred responsibility for means-tested benefits for the unemployed to this national organization in 1934, added similar benefits for elderly people to its responsibilities in 1940, and most other means-tested cash aid in 1941. By 1948, when it was finally killed, the poor-law was all but dead already.

The demise of the poor-law was also assisted by another piece of legislation in this period: the Local Government Act of 1929. This handed over responsibility for the poor-law from the boards of guardians to the local authorities. As far as the administration of relief was concerned this made little difference; the public assistance committees of the local authorities could be regarded as broadly the guardians under another name. However, the handover of powers brought the institutions that had evolved from the old workhouses into the hands of authorities that could more effectively bring them up to date. This was particularly important for the hospitals, since now a unified public service could be provided. This was a step towards a National Health Service, though in practice few authorities did much to modernize their facilities. Instead, the transformation of the hospital service awaited the special arrangements that were made to co-ordinate their activities with those of the voluntary hospitals during World War II.

While little attempt was made to alter the character of the patchwork of health services available in the inter-war period, all the parties that were to be involved in their transformation in the 1940s were beginning to examine the weaknesses of the existing provision and to formulate alternatives. In view of the importance of medical acquiescence in the system eventually adopted, it was probably necessary for many doctors to become aware of the need for change.

Education services similarly went through a phase of detailed examination of their weaknesses and future potential during the inter-war period. Here, however, the roles given to the local authorities by the Acts of 1902 and 1918 left scope for innovation where money allowed. The teaching profession grew in strength at this time, developing a formal system of training to replace the nineteenth-century pupil–teacher system. Education beyond the primary stage grew in various ways, and this part of the system was ready for rationalization by the end of the 1930s.

This section has described the inter-war period as a period of consolidation in social policy. However, at least one really significant innovation occurred – the development of a public housing sector – and the inroads made into poor-law were of considerable significance for the future. One other element of this that deserves a brief outline was the adoption, in 1925, of a contributory pension scheme to run alongside the non-contributory one.

This period is often thought of as one of failure in British politics, of failure to cope with the rise of Hitler and Mussolini abroad, and failure to deal with unemployment at home. It was, however, also a period when complete adult suffrage was achieved, and in which a political consensus was generated that enabled the Labour Party to establish itself alongside the older parties, so that an element of working-class power developed without turning into a revolutionary force. The key Conservative politicians of that age, Baldwin and Chamberlain, were very much men of the 'consensus', eager to promote cautious innovation in social policy. The Labour leader, Ramsay MacDonald, however, was equally eager to occupy the middle ground. Some historians of the period regard this consensus politics as another of the failures of this age, urging that the compromises by the Left prevented radical change from occurring. Its significance, though, for social policies, was that it created a platform for changes to occur in the 1940s, changes that secured widespread social and political acceptance.

The 1940s

The government was much more ready to mobilize all the nation's resources in World War II than it had been in World War I. Regulation and rationing were not adopted reluctantly but as measures essential to the war effort. Politically, at least after Churchill replaced Chamberlain as Prime Minister in 1940, the nation was more united. The Labour Party regained its self-confidence, shattered by having being deserted by its leaders – who formed a National Government and then heavily defeated Labour in a general election in 1931. It regarded attention to social policies as one of the conditions of its involvement in a coalition government. Although Churchill sometimes appeared to be unhappy about it, planning for the peace was widely accepted as a legitimate political task during the war. Before looking at the two most important examples of planning for peace – the Beveridge Report and the Butler Education Act of 1944 – it is important to note a number of ways in which peacetime policy changes were foreshadowed by *ad hoc* wartime measures. In the last section, reference was made to the way in which the UAB, which was renamed the Assistance Board in 1940, took over various functions from the public assistance committees in the early part of the war. Mention was also made of the integration of the hospital services during the war, under the Emergency Hospital Scheme. The evacuation of children called for the development of special services, foreshadowing developments in child care practice after the war. Rents were again strictly controlled, and empty houses were requisitioned. Price controls and food rationing, together with the full employment which followed from the enormous state investment in the war effort, also made important contributions to welfare. The wartime state had many of the characteristics of the 'welfare state', which is popularly regarded as having been created after the war.

The Beveridge Report was the report of a committee, chaired by one of the architects of the 1911 Insurance Act, on *Social Insurance and Allied Services* (Beveridge, 1942). This recommended the adoption of a contributory social security system which improved on the existing system by protecting all citizens against poverty at times of sickness or unemployment, and in old age. The new system should, it was argued, include family allowances, maternity benefits and provision for widows. The contribution principles should be insurance ones, involving the employee, the employer and the state as before, but the coverage of the scheme should be universal and therefore involve a national pooling of risks. In the arrangements for dependants and widows, there were, inevitably, certain assumptions built into the scheme – about the male breadwinner and his relationship to the family unit – which have left a difficult legacy for attempts to balance the interests of men and women in our own age.

Beveridge argued that other social policies were necessary to underpin his insurance scheme. Support for children would be necessary through a universal 'family allowance' scheme. A system of means-tested assistance would be necessary as a 'safety-net' for the minority whose needs were not adequately covered by the scheme. The maintenance of full employment would be essential to enable social insurance to work properly. A universal health service should take over the provision for medical care in the old insurance scheme and effectively underpin the new one.

Beveridge's insurance scheme was broadly put into legislation. Family allowances were provided by one of the last measures of the coalition government. Most of the rest was enacted by the post-war Labour government, though there was a crucial departure from the insurance principle in that the qualifying period for a full pension was very short. This deviation from Beveridge's plan made the scheme expensive to general taxation, and probably tended to prevent the adoption of benefit levels sufficient to provide subsistence incomes to those with no other resources and to inhibit subsequent increases to keep abreast with the cost of living.

The Education Act passed in 1944 and often identified by the name of the minister responsible, R. A. Butler, provided the framework for the education system until 1988. The Butler Act provided for universal free state secondary education, but did not specify the form it should take or rule on whether there should be selective schools.

At the end of the war, the coalition broke up. In the ensuing general election, both parties promised substantial social policy reforms, but the electorate swung strongly towards the Labour Party, rejecting the old war-leader Churchill in favour of Labour's clearer commitment to a vision of the 'welfare state'. The social security reforms embodied by the Labour Party in the National Insurance Act of 1946 and the National Assistance Act of 1948 have already been mentioned. With the adoption of these measures came the abolition of the poor-law, its income-maintenance responsibilities going to the National Assistance Board and its responsibilities for residential care and other welfare services going to local authority welfare departments.

In 1948, the creation of the National Health Service provided another crucial innovation in social policy. GPs and hospital services were provided free for everyone, in a complex structure designed to unify the hospital sector, while leaving GPs as independent contractors and other community services in the control of the local authorities. This structure was achieved after hard bargaining between the minister, Aneurin Bevan, and the doctors, who were deeply suspicious of state medicine (Eckstein, 1960; Pater, 1981). The scheme was funded out of general taxation, though an element of payment for the health service remained in the NI contribution, creating a confusing illusion that this was what paid for the service. The notion of a totally free service did not last for long. Very soon, Chancellors of the Exchequer, exploiting concern that demand for services was much greater than expected, secured first small payments for spectacles and dental treatment, and then prescription charges, as ways of raising revenue.

Among these widely publicized social policy reforms came another measure, with much less impact on the general public but nevertheless with important implications: the Children Act of 1948. The origins of this reform of the services for deprived children seem to have been in a child care scandal – the O'Neill case – which led to the setting up of the Curtis Committee to investigate contemporary practice (Packman, 1975, ch. 1). The Children Act consolidated the existing child care legislation, and created departments in which professional social work practice would develop in child care and, in due course, in work with families.

The Labour government of 1945–51 did not alter the system of subsidizing local authority housing developed in the inter-war period, but it did, by the Housing Act of 1949, substantially extend the subsidies available. The Act formally removed the limitation confining local authority provision to housing for the 'working classes'. The government's concern throughout the late 1940s was to stimulate building to make up the deficiencies in housing stock arising from bomb damage and the wartime standstill in house building. However, post-war shortages of materials made it difficult to accelerate new building. The Labour government laid its emphasis on local authority housing rather than on private building for sale. It also involved itself, as no government ever had before, in an attempt to secure effective land-use planning and to curb land speculation. The Town and Country Planning Act of 1947 provided a grand design for this purpose, though one of limited success, which was subsequently dismantled by the Conservatives. Another crucial planning innovation, with major implications for the provision of public housing, was the New Towns Act of 1946. This provided jobs and houses in new communities for people from overcrowded cities and run-down industrial areas.

Government involvement in the planning of the use of national resources, which had been one of the necessities of wartime, was continued by the Labour government as a matter of principle. This, in itself, was important in enlarging the involvement of government with many aspects of life in Britain. The continuation of the wartime system of food subsidies and the slow phasing out of rationing protected poor people from the full rigour of market forces. There was a commitment to the maintenance of full employment, with the Keynesian doctrine (Keynes, 1936) that budgetary management could achieve this now a matter of economic orthodoxy. In the 1940s, such economic management was slightly inflationary, but this was broadly seen as a reasonable price to pay for full employment and economic growth. In retrospect, it is difficult to judge the extent to which the success of this policy – and, despite all the worries it caused at the time, it was a success by comparison with the economic management disasters of either the 1920s and 1930s or the 1970s and 1980s – was due to good management, and the extent to which it was due to external and internal economic factors outside government control, in particular to the post-war recovery and the stimulus provided by the continuing military activity of the 'cold war' (Cairncross, 1985).

The 1940s were, in both war and peace, crucial years for the building of the system of social policy Britain has today. However, it has been shown that few of the innovations of this period were without precedent in the policies of earlier years, and that much of the crucial thinking about the form these new institutions should take had been done in the inter-war period. Continuity is also evident in the behaviour of the two major political parties. The Butler Education Act and the Family Allowances Act were both measures of the Conservative-dominated wartime coalition. Preliminary work had also been done during the war on the ideas for the social security scheme, and plans had begun to be drafted for a health service.

The political continuity is also apparent in the fact that the Conservatives did comparatively little, on returning to power in 1951, to dismantle the 'welfare state'. The Labour Party policies that they did contest, and partly reverse, were its nationalization policies, not its social welfare ones. Otherwise, they shifted the house-building emphasis from public to private building but by no means eliminated a substantial public element from their enlarged building programme; they were marginally more ready to increase health service charges; and they were, perhaps, rather slow to raise social security benefits. In the later 1950s, they encouraged education services to flourish; and some local authorities began to innovate in this policy area in ways that, in due course, came to be regarded as radical and politically contentious.

Since the 1940s

The presentation of policies in this section will be sketchy because wherever they are still relevant they are covered more fully in the appropriate detailed chapter later in the book. The aim here is to give the flavour of the key developments in this period as part of the history of social policy.

Broadly the period 1951–99 can be divided into four parts:

1 1951–64 was a period of comparatively little social policy innovation which may be regarded as a time of consolidation or stagnation, according to one's political viewpoint.

2   1964–74 was a period of fairly intense policy change stimulated
     by both political parties, in which considerable difficulties were
     experienced in translating aspirations into practice.
3   1974–79 was a period in which rapid inflation, rising unemploy-
     ment and government by the Labour Party without a parliamen-
     tary majority administered a severe shock to the political and
     social system, and to all who believed that there was still a need
     for developments in social policy.
4   During 1979–97, much more explicitly anti-welfare state Conser-
     vative administrations reinforced that shock by deliberately treat-
     ing inflation as more deserving of its attention than
     unemployment, attacking public services which were seen as
     inhibiting economic recovery and seeking ways to 'privatize'
     public services. In 1997, Labour returned to power, but with a
     stance on public expenditure control that (as far as can be judged
     at the time of writing) limits its capacity to end this period of
     restraint for social policy.

Bearing these points in mind, this section will look at developments in each of the main policy areas over the whole period. The
many changes since 1979 could have been made the subject of a
separate section. However, that would have detached them from the
discussion of related policy changes occurring immediately before.
Instead, therefore, a separate section – called 'the emergence of a
crisis for British social policy' – will sum up the recent period, with
reference to the dramatic economic and political changes which
occurred. These have been seen by some as creating a 'crisis' for
social policy and the demise of the British welfare state.

Housing

The period 1951–64 was a boom period for house-building, both
private and public. It was during this time that two kinds of tenure
began to dominate in Britain: owner-occupation and local authority
tenancy. The decline in the size of the privately rented sector was
rapid and, towards the later part of this period, it was accelerated by
slum clearance. In 1957, the government, believing that the private
rental market could be revived if rent controls were removed, passed
a Rent Act that allowed some decontrol. The main impact of this
measure was that many landlords used the freedom to evict which
was allowed under decontrol to sell previously let properties for
owner-occupation. In the 1960s, the Labour government legislated

to restore security of tenure and to allow rent levels to rise only to levels that fell short of market prices.

When Labour returned to power, they were committed to reversing the emphasis on building for owner-occupation within the building boom, but they also wanted to produce even more houses per annum. The use of restraints on building investment as an economic regulator to prevent excess domestic demand made it difficult for them to achieve their targets. By the end of the 1970s, the additions to the housing stock had been so considerable that arguments were increasingly heard that Britain had enough houses. What complicated this debate was the question of whether there were enough houses of the right kind in the right places. Certainly some of the earlier building activity may have been misplaced effort. In particular, many local authorities produced poor-quality industrially built high-rise flats which were difficult to let (Dunleavy, 1981).

Politicians of both parties became, by the late 1960s, increasingly concerned to stimulate owner-occupation. Tax relief was used to assist borrowing. In the 1980s, changes to financial markets led to growth in the availability of finance for buyers. The growth of house prices fed a belief that there was little risk in mortgage borrowing. Then, at the end of that decade and in the early 1990s, the combination of a new recession and government efforts to combat inflation (including a reduction in tax relief on mortgages) led to a fall in house prices. Many buyers, particularly those who lost jobs, found themselves in 'negative equity' situations in which their houses had fallen in value and their mortgage repayments were difficult to meet.

When they came to power in 1970, the Conservatives decided that public expenditure on local authority housing needed to be curbed. Their Housing Finance Act of 1972 set out to adapt the 'fair rent' principle, which Labour had applied to private rents in the 1960s, to the local authority sector. They linked this with a national rent rebate scheme, rationalizing the variety of local schemes that had been set up over the previous decade, to offset the costs to poorer tenants. This Act was designed to reduce the general subsidy to council tenants; it was linked to changes in the system of national subsidies to local authorities designated to phase out indiscriminate help of this kind in due course. Labour opposed this measure and limited its impact but, on returning to power in 1979, the Conservatives – by reducing new expenditure on public housing, modifying the subsidy formula and encouraging rents to rise – set out to eliminate most subsidies to public housing other than means-tested benefits (housing benefit) for individual occupiers. Measures at the end of the 1980s prevented local government subsidy of council housing and accelerated the rate at which central subsidies were withdrawn.

In addition, legislation enacted in 1980 to give local authority and housing association tenants a 'right to buy' also made extensive inroads into the system of public housing. An Act passed in 1988 sought further to dismantle the system of local authority owned public housing. It aimed to replace it by a mixture of housing associations, tenants co-ownership schemes and private landlords. In practice, the government faced difficulties in implementing this legislation. Tenants and local authorities were often resistant to change, and private capital was not particularly eager to move in. However, subsequently, local authority difficulties in raising capital to enable them to improve their decaying stock encouraged the exploration of ways of effecting the voluntary transfer of local authority houses to housing associations.

Social security and employment policy

The Conservatives did little to change the social security system in the period 1951–64. Towards the end of the period, the two parties began to produce competing plans to superimpose an earnings-related pensions scheme on top of the inadequate flat-rate system. In 1959, the Conservatives introduced a limited graduated pension scheme. In 1964, the Labour Party came to power committed to a much more comprehensive scheme. However, they failed to complete the preparation of this before they lost office in 1970. The Conservatives then took up the idea in a slightly more limited way, but Labour returned to power and put their own scheme on the statute book in 1975. This scheme provided for a mixed scheme of public and private pensions, with many of the better paid and more secure groups of workers able to 'contract out' into private schemes so long as they were at least as good as the State Earnings Related Pensions scheme (SERPS). Conservative legislation in 1986 extended the scope for contracting out, allowing schemes which did not necessarily compete favourably with the state scheme and also reducing the benefits available under SERPS. This encouraged a rapid growth of private pension schemes, including some which were poorly protected. The collapse of some of these led, in the early 1990s, to further regulatory legislation. The new Labour government is unwilling to take on the cost burden that would follow from a return to the strong version of SERPS enacted in 1975. It is adapting instead to a new public/

private partnership approach to this topic involving what are called 'stakeholder pensions'.

In the early 1960s, a number of academic studies were published showing that the 'welfare state' had by no means abolished poverty (Cole and Utting, 1962; Lynes, 1962; Abel-Smith and Townsend, 1965). This 'rediscovery of poverty' would seem to be partly a function of an academic and political interest that had emerged, concerned to look at the adequacy of social policies. The emphasis on the weaknesses of existing social security policies for the relief of poverty led to a reappraisal of those policies.

The Labour government of 1964–70 made a number of changes to social security, therefore. Some of the changes raised some people's incomes, and there were a number of increases in benefit rates. However, inflation was increasing, and public resources were, as ever, limited and in great demand for a wide range of policy objectives. The main policy change in this period was the introduction in 1965 of earnings-related supplements to sickness and unemployment benefits and of a redundancy payments scheme. Also, in 1966 'national assistance' was replaced by 'supplementary benefits'. This reform was designed to remove the stigma of assistance by making rights to these means-tested benefits much clearer, particularly for pensioners.

One particular focus of attention in the debate about poverty was family poverty and, particularly, the problems faced by the low-wage earner. The principle, adopted in 1834, that wages should not be subsidized had been carried forward in social security legislation, but the margin between the income of those in work and those out of work sometimes made the principle of 'less eligibility' appear under threat. The Child Poverty Action Group (CPAG), a pressure group set up in the 1960s, urged governments to deal with this problem by increasing family allowances. These had fallen in value, in real terms, since little effort had been made to update them properly. However, the conventional political view at that time was that family allowances were an unpopular and indiscriminate handout. The CPAG sought to persuade the government that family allowances could be increased at the expense of child tax allowances. This approach was gradually accepted, though not before inflation had reduced the tax threshold so low that most poor wage earners were also benefiting from the tax allowances. In the 1970s, the Conservatives floated an alternative approach, a form of negative income tax called 'tax credits' (HMSO, 1972) and implemented a means-tested benefit for poor wage earners, 'family income supplement'. Labour, on return to power in 1974, decided to press on with the development of a new family allowance scheme, called 'child benefit', designed to replace the older allowance, extend it to the first child in each family, and offset it against the abolition of tax allowances; see McCarthy (1986) for a discussion of these developments. However, it did not abolish family income supplement.

On first returning to power in 1979, the Conservatives set out to make piecemeal adjustments to the social security system. They reduced the value of contributory benefits by altering the procedure for inflation-related increases, and by extending the taxation of benefits. They eliminated earnings-related additions to sickness and unemployment benefits. They then shifted the responsibility for provision for sickness absence for the first 28 weeks from the NI scheme to a statutory sick pay scheme to be run by employers. They attempted also to rationalize the burgeoning supplementary benefit scheme by developing a stronger rule-based structure, and introduced a housing benefit scheme.

However, in 1983, they decided that a more radical reform of social security was necessary. It was an element in public expenditure which they were finding very difficult to control, not surprisingly in the face of an ageing population, rapidly rising unemployment and government measures designed to shift the subsidy of housing on to the social security scheme. Proclaiming themselves to be engaged in the most radical review of social security since Beveridge, they set up a number of ministerially dominated committees to explore options for reform. The eventual outcome was the 1986 Social Security Act. This legislation modified SERPS (in the way outlined on page 33), replaced supplementary benefits by 'income support' and family income supplement by 'family credit'. These two schemes operated with simpler rule structures than had supplementary benefits. Housing benefit was altered to bring it in line with these other two benefits. Some anomalies which had been arising as a result of the previous piecemeal evolution of means-tested benefits were eliminated. The maternity grant and the death grant, two universal benefits initiated in the 1940s but not properly updated in line with inflation, were abolished, to be replaced by means-test related benefits for the very poor. The system of single payments – available to help people who are on supplementary benefits with specific needs – was replaced by a much more limited system, known as the 'social fund', under which all that most people could be given were loans.

Alongside these major structural changes, the Conservatives substantially weakened the benefits designed to protect the unemployed, making support for under-eighteen-year-olds conditional on undergoing training and sharply reducing the amount of help available to other young unemployed people. Penalties for refusing to undergo training and for leaving jobs were made very severe.

This last was an issue to which they returned with further legislation in 1995, to rename unemployment benefit 'job seeker's allowance', to emphasize the behaviour required, and make it means-tested for all after the first six months. At about the same time, the Conservatives changed invalidity benefit to incapacity benefit, aiming to force all but the severely handicapped below pension age to become job seekers.

Another feature of Conservative social security policy in the 1990s was efforts to reduce state support to single parent families. A complex piece of legislation designed to secure increased contributions from 'absent' parents, the Child Support Act of 1991, ran into implementation difficulties and was revised in 1995. At the time of writing, it is still in difficulties and the new government has published a consultative paper foreshadowing further changes, making the scheme simpler.

In many respects, the Beveridge design for social security had been undermined before 1979 by failures to update insurance benefits adequately, by rising unemployment and by the need to provide means-tested benefits for the increasing number of single parent families. The policy changes of the 1980s continued that process, ensuring that means-tested benefits were increasingly of key importance for the relief of poverty. In particular, the 1986 Act extended and rationalized means tests but it did not take social security in the radical new direction that 'negative income tax' or 'social dividend' advocates were suggesting.

The new Labour government has proclaimed 'we will be the party of welfare reform' but the combination of the commitment to a stable public expenditure programme and the tendency of social security costs to rise regardless of policy change limits their room for manoeuvre. They see the solution of that dilemma in increased employment, and see the stimulation of labour market participation by single parents and the disabled as well as the unemployed as central to their social security policy strategy. The key policy innovations involve transforming the family credit into a tax credit (back to the 1970 Conservative agenda!) and devising a similar credit for disabled people.

While in the body of the book (chapter 9) employment policy is considered separately, a brief comment is appropriate here on this issue, which is so closely linked to social security policy. Early in this chapter, it was pointed out that, at the beginning of the century, British governments adopted an approach to the relief of unemployment that largely ruled out the creation of specific employment opportunities. In the early 1970s, interest was awakened in Britain in the case for the development of 'active labour market policies' of the kind adopted in Sweden (Mukherjee, 1972). These involved such things as assisting labour mobility, expanding training when unemployment rises, and creating special work projects for the unemployed. Their appeal was that they were believed to alleviate unemployment, in a largely fully employed economy, without creating inflation.

Their adoption in Britain occurred at a time of high unemployment. Accordingly, instead of serving the economic function for which they were originally advocated, they were modified to serve the political function of reducing the number of unemployed while minimizing intervention in the economy as a whole. There was a particular concentration on measures for young people to the extent that many who leave school at sixteen can expect up to two years in government schemes which combine work experience with training. Indeed, at the end of the 1980s, the government adopted a strategy for employment policy which largely abandoned other job creation measures but strongly emphasized training (Department of Employment, 1988a, b). A similar strong emphasis on training is present in what the new Labour government see as its most important social policy initiative: its 'welfare to work' programme for young people under 25.

What is evident is that these policies are all very much directed at the *supply of* labour rather than the *demand for* it. The supposition is that attention to the deficiencies in that supply will bring a consequent increase in demand. One of the issues which will be examined in chapter 9 will be whether such social policy measures can help to cope with unemployment or whether it is primarily an economic problem. Doubts are increasingly raised about whether specific national policy interventions can influence global developments in the labour market. There is evidence that the character of demand for labour is changing. New investment is often capital-intensive and unable to absorb much labour. New work opportunities occur in forms in which flexibility is required, which means that jobs are insecure. Many new opportunities offer poor rates of pay, where work can be moved to the economies where labour is cheapest.

Education

In the period 1951–64, of all the policy areas with which this book is concerned, it was probably education that saw the most innovation. This was, however, very much localized and piecemeal within the general structure laid down by the Butler Act of 1944. That had, as was stressed, laid the foundation for the creation of a sound secondary education system. Initially the orthodox view was that such a system should be selective and tripartite, with children routed at the age of '11-plus' into grammar, technical or secondary modern schools according to their aptitudes and abilities. The concept of a separate form of technical education did not become established (Sanderson, 1991). Then, as time passed, even the notion of a bipartite system was increasingly questioned and an alternative, non-selective, comprehensive model was championed. Various local authorities began to introduce comprehensive schools in the 1950s, motivated sometimes by political and educational ideology but sometimes, particularly in rural areas, by a recognition that such schools were a more realistic response to local needs. It was not until the 1960s that battle lines began to be drawn up with Labour in favour of comprehensivization and the Conservatives against; and even then the Conservatives in central government were not hard-line opponents of this policy in the way that, by the end of the decade, Labour had become hard-line advocates. Nevertheless, Labour legislation requiring local authorities to introduce comprehensivization schemes, enacted in 1976, was repealed by the Conservatives in 1980.

In a variety of other ways, the Conservative governments of the period 1951–64 rapidly increased the resources available to state education. In many respects, this was a necessary response to the child population 'bulge' created by the 'baby boom' of the immediate post-war years. This, in itself, created a need for new schools and teachers and, therefore, provided a platform for educational innovation. Clearly, governments were ready to encourage innovatory thinking. Advisory groups were created to look at various educational issues. These produced a memorable series of reports: on early leaving (Central Advisory Council for Education, 1954), on education between fifteen and eighteen (Central Advisory Council for Education, 1959), on the education of less academic children (Central Advisory Council for Education, 1963), on higher education (Robins Committee, 1963) and on primary education (Central Advisory Council for Education, 1967). The crucial policy changes influenced by all this committee activity were the rapid expansion of higher education in the 1960s, the raising of the school-leaving age to sixteen in 1973 (after delays in implementing a change first announced in 1964), and a distinct shift away from streaming and selectivity at all stages before the teenage years. It was the change in amounts of public money spent on education, however, that was most important.

By the mid-1970s, the 'bulge' had nearly worked its way through the system, and this, together with disillusion with innovation in education, brought to an end the role of the education service as an expenditure growth-leader among the public services. Controversy grew about some of the bolder experiments in egalitarian education, and it was increasingly alleged that basic education was being neglected. Some people put some of the responsibility for the growing youth unemployment on educational inadequacies, giving sustenance to the Department of Employment's bid to control low-level post-school education. Once the Conservatives came to power in 1979, the unrest began to be translated into policy. The completion of the comprehensivization programme was arrested, and new opportunities were created for state financed places at private schools. The 1980 Education Act, which extended parental choice of schools, was seen as creating pressures for the raising of academic standards and had the effect of increasing the tendency towards social segregation.

The 1988 Education Act was much more fundamental, largely replacing the 1944 Act as the framework law for state education in England and Wales. This Act lays down a requirement that there should be a 'national curriculum' of 'core' subjects (English, Maths and Science) and 'foundation subjects'; see pages 194–5. It requires children to be tested regularly, starting at the age of seven, to assess the extent to which attainment targets have been achieved, and information about test outcomes is published. This legislation also weakens local government control over education by strengthening the autonomy of individual school managements, and by enabling schools to apply to become directly funded by central government (grant maintained schools). This legislation, supplemented by further measures, also extends central control over higher and further education, and has removed the last vestiges of local authority responsibility for these sectors.

The arrival of the Labour government in 1997 did not reverse the general thrust of the measures enacted by their Conservative predecessors. In some respect, indeed, they are even more vehement about the need for central control over a pragmatically relevant education system. Their difference lies in a greater concern with the less privileged sectors of the system.

Conservative policy on higher education went through various phases in the period 1979–97. The government's general objectives were to tighten control and keep costs down while recognizing the high demand for places. The old polytechnic sector was assimilated into the university sector (or perhaps, in the light of the attack on the latter, it is more appropriate to put that the other way round). Students' grants were cut in real terms and a loan scheme introduced to make up the shortfall. Labour's 1997–8 addition to this was to require all but the poorest students to pay fees but to mitigate, in some respects, the terms under which the inevitably larger loans have to be paid back.

Health

In the 1950s, the principal government concern about the health service was with difficulties in controlling costs. No substantial changes resulted from this preoccupation. The relationship of the doctors to the government was, and remains, a sensitive area. A great deal of attention was given to their terms of service and remuneration.

The only major item of legislation in the health field between 1951 and 1970 was the Mental Health Act of 1959 which altered the procedures for the compulsory admission and retention of the mentally ill in hospital, abolishing the old 'certification' procedure. The treatment of mental illness was advancing considerably at that time, and it probably contributed more than the legislative change to reducing both the use of compulsory procedures and the incidence of long stays in hospital. A further Mental Health Act in 1983 continued the liberalization of the treatment of mentally ill people.

In the 1960s, as part of the wholesale review of the institutions of central and local government, proposals were introduced for the reorganization of the National Health Service. Two Green Papers were produced, suggesting different ways of doing this (DHSS, 1967, 1968). Eventually the change was effected by the Conservatives in 1974. This change created a new structure, with the former local authority community health services integrated with the rest of the service. Lay participation in the running of the service was reduced; in its place, community health councils were created to represent the public. The new structure – with its three tiers of regions, areas and districts – was criticized as over-elaborate almost as soon as it was created. Discontent over the operation of the new service was one of the factors that led the Labour government to set up a Royal Commission for the National Health Service in 1976. This recommended the removal of a tier (HMSO, 1979); the new Conservative government responded, by eliminating areas but enlarging some districts, in 1982.

Two important stimuli to the search for the right structure for the NHS are a concern about effective policy control in the face of professional domination, and anxiety about the extent of inequalities in health between social classes and between regions. These two concerns were brought together during the 1970s with a development of a system for the allocation of resources between regions and districts based on health indices. They, and particularly the former, also fuelled a concern to strengthen management. In the Griffith's report (1983), a hierarchy of general managers was advocated for the NHS, weakening the influence of the nominated regional and district 'authorities'. This proposal was enacted.

Despite these changes, the rising costs of the NHS, due largely to the ageing of the population and advances in medicine, led the Conservatives to explore further structural changes. Their 'right wing' urged them to privatize the system. While being unprepared to go this far, the government, in the National Health Service and Community Care Act of 1990, encouraged hospitals to become quasi-independent 'National Health Service Trusts' and general medical practices to become 'fundholders'. Both of these measures were designed to bring about increases in efficiency, accompanied by general arrangements for a managerial split between 'purchasers' and 'providers'. The overall aim was to create an 'internal market' system within the NHS in which hospitals were in competition with each other. All hospitals and community health services changed to trust status. The development of a system of GPs as fundholders was more limited. These developments made desirable another alteration in the structure of the system, eliminating 'regions' (except as administrative outposts of the centre) and amalgamating the authorities which managed the family practitioner services with the district health authorities in 1996.

The new Labour government is now changing the system yet again. The system of trusts is to remain but their relationship with those who commission heath care is to be more stable. Note the change of terminology from 'purchasing' to 'commissioning'; the largely unrealized 'internal market' ideal is to be abandoned. GPs' fund holding is to be abolished but now these providers of 'primary care' are to be linked collectively into the commissioning process, in Primary Care Groups.

Personal social services

The development of the personal social services between the 1940s and the 1970s is a story of steady consolidation and one important structural change. At the end of the 1940s, local authorities organized these services within two or three departments. Children's services were the responsibility of one department, required by statute. Children's departments built up a body of social work expertise, and gradually extended their activities, from work to deal with acute child care problems into work designed to prevent child neglect and abuse and into work with delinquent children. Two Children and Young Persons Acts, in 1963 and 1969, legitimized and encouraged these changes in emphasis.

The other local authority welfare services, or personal social services, were organized by welfare departments and by health departments (or by departments that combined these two functions). A social work career was developed in connection with this work, but not so effectively as was the case in the children's departments. A government report in 1959 made recommendations that influenced developments in the training of social work staff of this kind. However, the activities of these departments were growing in other ways, too. Their legacy from the poor-law was a stock of homes for the elderly and disabled, which were ex-workhouses. A central task, therefore, was to phase out these institutions replacing them by smaller, more welcoming civilized homes, and also to seek to develop ways of caring for people within the community. Developments in day care, the home-help service and other domiciliary services were the currency of growth in these departments. In 1970, the Chronically Sick and Disabled Persons Act placed obligations on the local authorities to identify and to help disabled people. Progress in this area of policy should not necessarily be measured by statutes, though. Earlier, permissive legislation had already enabled some authorities to innovate in services for disabled people.

The important structural change for all these local authority services was an Act passed in 1970, on the recommendations of the Seebohm Committee (HMSO, 1968), which created integrated 'social services departments' in local authorities in England and Wales. In Scotland, the Social Work (Scotland) Act of 1968 had already created integrated 'social work departments', in that case including the probation officers who remained in a separate service independent of local government in England and Wales. The structural change in England and Wales was accompanied by a change in central government organization, whereby the Home Office's responsibility for children's services was passed over to the Department of Health and Social Security, which was already responsible for other welfare services. These changes represent another example of the statutory creation of a 'platform for growth'. This duly occurred, but by the 1980s had been checked by constraints on local government spending.

With that check came renewed questioning about the balance between services provided by the social services departments and the many forms of family, neighbourhood and commercially purchased care that they supplemented. Within social work, the quest continued for the best way to organize a service that could be responsive to community need (Barclay, 1982). Outside social work, doubts were increasingly raised about the adequacies of that profession, particularly in the face of a growing number of child abuse 'scandals'. Child protection legislation was consolidated and updated in the Children Act of 1989.

A related problem, exacerbated by the ageing of the population, has concerned the balance between community and residential care. This is a complex issue, because it is not merely an issue about forms of care but also about who should bear the costs of care. The community care debate is about both care in the community and care by the community. In the 1980s, a strange piece of government carelessness brought the whole issue to a head. The social security minister relaxed the rules under which means-tested benefits could be used to subsidize private residential care. The result was an explosive growth of this sector, making demands on the social security budget that were difficult to control. The Conservative government's eventual response to this problem was to try to develop a version of the health service's purchaser/provider split in which local authorities would be purchasers and the various forms of community care would be provided by a range of organizations in which private and voluntary enterprises would be dominant. The 1990 Act, which developed similar ideas for the NHS, authorized this and was brought into full force in April 1993. That measure highlighted issues at the boundary of the health and personal social services systems. As these are given attention in the implementation of the legislation, they are generating the examination of changes to the formal arrangements for that boundary by the new Labour government.

The local government system

During the period 1964–95, the local government structure, within which many of the social services are based, came under review. In 1972, the Local Government Act made the first major change in the local government system of England and Wales, apart from restructuring in London, which took place in 1963, since the nineteenth century. This reform created a new two-tier system of local government. In the metropolitan areas, the model, like the earlier one adopted in London, was of most purpose lower-tier authorities and of top-tier counties responsible primarily for structural planning. Outside the metropolitan areas, the division of the social policy functions was more even; the counties acquired responsibility for education and social services while the districts were made responsible for housing. Similar changes followed in Scotland soon afterwards. Then, in 1986, the government abolished the metropolitan counties; their functions were either devolved to the districts or given to single purpose joint boards. Later, in the 1990s, a programme of *ad hoc* changes involved increases in the numbers of single tier authorities in the more urbanized parts of England. In Scotland and Wales, there was a wholesale restructuring to create single tier authorities everywhere.

An accompanying central government preoccupation about local government in this period was the fact that it was becoming an increasing spender (not surprisingly in the light of central government's expectations of it in areas like education, personal social services and housing). In the period up to the middle 1970s, central government steadily increased its grant contributions to local expenditure. It also struggled, rather fruitlessly, to find ways of wholly or partly replacing the system of local taxation, the rates assessed on property. In the later years of the 1974–9 Labour government, the central contribution to local expenditure began to be cut. After 1979, the Thatcher government continued this process, much more zealously, developing a formula which deliberately penalized those authorities they deemed to be over-spenders. Then, in addition, they decided they must limit local authorities' powers to go on increasing local rates. They developed a power that enabled them to 'rate cap' authorities whom they deemed to be high spenders. Finally, they decided to abolish rates and replace them by a poll tax known as the 'community charge'. This measure proved to be enormously unpopular, and contributed to Margaret Thatcher's political downfall (Butler et al., 1994). Her successor as Prime Minister, John Major, rushed legislation through Parliament to try to remove the stigma of the poll tax. He sharply increased the central subsidy to local finance and enacted a modified version of the old domestic rating system known as the 'council tax'.

What is clear from this flurry of activity concerning local government and its finance is that central control over the resources available at the local level has become very strong, and is likely to remain so. With that control has come increasing efforts to influence the content of local policies. The end of Conservative rule is contributing to some easing of central–local conflict (not least because the government and the major urban authorities are now under the control of the same party). Some central controls are being eased, or more likely taking more subtle forms – for example, the replacement of compulsory competitive tendering by a requirement to achieve 'best value' in public contracts. However, the centre shows no willingness to reduce its intervention in local affairs. The debate about the appropriate relationship between the respective levels of authority continues. Devolution of power to Scotland and Wales, and the establishment of a new overarching authority for London, is injecting a new, and unpredictable, element into that debate.

The Emergence of a Crisis for British Social Policy?

The last section has described policy developments in a period in which the Conservatives and Labour alternated in power. Thirteen years of Conservative rule was followed by nearly seven years of Labour rule. Then there was an episode of nearly four years of Conservative government. After that, Labour 'enjoyed' a period of four years in government in which their continuance in office depended on the support of the Liberals. Then, in 1979, the Conservatives won a clear majority. They won a second term of office in 1983, and a third term in 1987. Margaret Thatcher lost the leadership of the Conservatives in late 1991. In April 1992, her successor, John Major, led the Conservatives in another successful election campaign, but one in which there was a marked fall in their majority. Then, in 1997, Labour returned to power with a large majority. There were massive Conservative seat losses, both to Labour and to a newly emergent Liberal party.

In many respects, with each political change, social policy issues have become more central to the political debate. In the period between 1951 and 1975, levels of controversy over social policies were, arguably, not particularly high. Conservative ideologists had

had much to say about the case for bringing market conditions more effectively to bear on the distribution of social services, but only in the housing field had Conservative governments taken steps that represented major responses to this viewpoint. Labour disappointed many of its supporters, who closely identified the party with the advancement of the welfare state. A succession of economic crises limited the money available for new social policies. Yet both parties considerably advanced public expenditure, particularly on social policies, to the point where some economists had argued that this kind of expenditure had become an inflationary force, limiting the scope for new wealth-creating private investment. This is a view politicians have taken very seriously. The most staggering growth was in public employment and in social security transfer payments, two forms of growth that politicians find very difficult to limit.

It is tempting to attribute the change in the climate for social policy in Britain to the election of Margaret Thatcher in 1979, but changes had been gradually emerging before that date, and those changes were rooted as much in economic changes as in ideological ones. It was a Labour minister, Anthony Crosland, speaking in 1975, who warned local government that, as far as public spending increases were concerned, the 'party is over'.

In the 1950s, Keynesian economic management techniques, involving manipulation of levels of government expenditure and taxation, were employed to try to retain full employment without inflation. Critics of policies of that period such as Samuel Brittan (1971) have suggested that Chancellors of the Exchequer found it difficult to time their uses of the economic 'brake' or 'accelerator' properly, and that the 'stop–go' pattern that emerged provided a poor economic environment for investment decisions, and thus inhibited British growth. The particular motivation for some fairly panicky use of the 'brake' was a concern with Britain's tendency to run into balance of payments problems, importing more than it was exporting. However, during this period, a rate of growth was achieved that was good by later standards, full employment was maintained, and inflation, while ever present, was never so high as to cause alarm.

In the 1960s, despite an increasing commitment to economic planning, the cyclical pattern worsened. Inflation increased, balance of payments crises forced strong restraints to be applied to public expenditure and private incomes on a number of occasions, and, at the depressed point of the cycle, quite marked increases in unemployment occurred. In the mid-1970s, Britain faced a more severe crisis, in which very high inflation, a balance of payments problem and continuing high unemployment occurred all at the same time. Measures to cope with the first two by traditional means worsened the third. At a time when governments seemed to have learnt a great deal about economic management, they found it increasingly difficult to put it into practice. In fact, the rise in economic management problems can be correlated with the dramatic increase in the number of economists in the civil service!

Different schools of economists have preached different solutions to these problems. On the Right, the 'monetarist' school of thought became increasingly influential, arguing that governments must control the money supply and let economic forces bring the system under control (Friedman, 1962, 1977); for an overview of this theory, see Bosanquet (1983). This viewpoint had some influence over policies in the 1970s, but politicians were reluctant to let bankruptcies and redundancies occur on a sufficient scale to test the monetarist hypothesis properly. More influential, and more in conformity with Keynesian orthodoxy, were those economists who argued that income restraint was necessary to bring unemployment and inflation into balance, and to prevent Britain's balance of payments becoming unmanageable as rising wages led us to import goods we could ill afford, while making it more difficult to sell things. In their view, what was happening was that wage bargaining was no longer restrained by the social and political forces that hitherto limited rises to figures that would not disrupt the economy. Incomes policies were seen as crucial to solving our problems, yet over and over again governments found that political pressures made these very difficult to sustain for any length of time. The whole picture was, however, complicated by changes in the pattern of trade in the world and, particularly, by rises in prices of primary commodities, especially oil.

After 1979, the 'monetarist' theory was more boldly put into practice. The government treated the money supply, and particularly the public sector borrowing rate, as the key phenomena to keep under control. It was prepared to let unemployment rise rapidly in the cause of the war against inflation. It abandoned incomes policy in the private sector, seeking only to keep pay increases to public employees tightly under control. Initially, it found the removal of pay controls and its own taxation adjustments produced severely inflationary effects. It was subsequently successful in bringing inflation under control, but achieved that at the expense of a rapid increase in unemployment. Numbers registered as out of work rose from just over a million in 1979 to over three million in 1983.

Later in the 1980s, the government abandoned any rigorous attempt to keep the money supply under control, concentrating attention instead on the foreign exchange value of the pound. However, it continued its tight control of public borrowing. By the 1990s, with the economy depressed and the 1992 election approaching, even the latter monetarist nostrum was abandoned by the Conservatives.

The whole subject of exchange control has been influenced by the move towards a single European monetary system. Tony Blair's Labour government, while continuing the Conservative policy of refusing to join the single currency system in 1999, has shown much greater sympathy to the ultimate goal of joining. Monetary policy has been designed to shadow EU developments. The control over interest rates has been delegated to the Bank of England as a measure designed to ensure monetary stability. The acceptance of the Conservative's public expenditure targets and the adoption of strict limits on public borrowing may also be seen as measures indicating a commitment to orthodox – we may perhaps say 'post-monetarist' – economic policies approved by global business interests.

The Conservatives, particularly in the period in which Margaret Thatcher was dominant, were undoubtedly hostile to state social policy. This hostility was rooted in a commitment to privatization, the curbing of public services and a lack of concern about inequality. Paradoxically, while the Conservatives were committed to public expenditure restraint, they found social policy expenditure very difficult to curb. Public sector housing expenditure did experience severe cuts. Education expenditure remained more or less static in real terms. Health and personal social services expenditure trends are more difficult to interpret. The figures indicate growth in real terms but needs and specific health care costs have also risen so that there has been some decline in volume terms. Nevertheless, social policy expenditure as a whole grew, driven upwards by the considerable growth in its major component, the social security budget; see Glennerster and Hills (1998) for a detailed analysis of these trends.

Demographic and economic changes have had a strong impact on these trends. There have, as was shown in the last section, been many detailed changes to social policy many of which were initiated in the hope of reducing expenditure. Their long-run legacy may be, more than anything else, a new institutional map of social policy – the commissioner/provider split, a reduced role for local government, greater participation of private providers and so on. Certainly, the Labour government elected in 1997 is much more sympathetic to mixed public/private institutions to deal with social policy issues than was any earlier Labour government. Also, while 'new' Labour clearly approaches issues about social policy expenditure without a 'Thatcherite' ideological enthusiasm for cuts, they nevertheless believe that pressures, needs and demands for increased social spending must continue to take second place to what are seen as overriding economic considerations.

Suggestions for further reading

Such is the wealth of historical literature that it has been difficult to decide what to footnote in this chapter. References have been confined to some of the more significant primary sources and to secondary sources that readers may find particularly interesting or readable. Some of the major historical works on which the author has depended have not been cited.

Derek Fraser's *The Evolution of the British Welfare State* (1984) is a good general historical textbook but is stronger on the nineteenth than the twentieth century. Pat Thane's *Foundations of the Welfare State* (1996) deals with the period from 1870 onward. The inter-war period is well covered by Gilbert (1970). A number of recent books deal with the 1945–51 Labour government. Among these Morgan's *Labour in Power 1945–51* (1984) is recommended and Hennessy's *Never Again: Britain 1945–51* (1992).

Five books which deal specifically with social policy history since 1945 are the author's own *The Welfare State in Britain* (Hill, 1993), Rodney Lowe's *The Welfare State in Britain since 1945* (1999), Nicholas Deakin's *The Politics of Welfare: Continuities and Change* (1994), Howard Glennerster's *British Social Policy since 1945* (1995) and Timmins' *The Five Giants: A Biography of the Welfare State* (1996).

The impact of the Thatcher and Major governments on social policy has provoked various accounts, each rapidly dated by further developments. Norman Johnson's *Reconstructing the Welfare State* (1990) provides an account of the impact of the Thatcher governments, Pierson's *Dismantling the Welfare State* (1994) compares the impact of Thatcherism with the Reagan era in the USA, while a collection edited by Savage, Atkinson and Robins (1994) carries the story a little further forward. The impact of John Major's premiership is explored in Dorey's *The Major Premiership* (1999). Helen Jones and Susanne MacGregor's *Social Issues and Party Politics* (1998) highlights the issues facing the new Blair government. Later assessments of the new Labour regime will surely rapidly appear.

Chapter 3

THE MAKING OF
SOCIAL POLICY

Introduction

This chapter deals with the social policy-making system, introducing the key institutions involved in the process in Britain; chapter 4 looks at the implementation of social policy. The two chapters must be considered together; dividing the policy processes between 'making' and 'implementation' is, in various respects, difficult. It is difficult to identify a dividing line at which making can be said to be completed and implementation to start. There is also a considerable amount of feedback from implementation which influences further policy making, and many policies are so skeletal that their real impact depends on the way they are interpreted at the implementation stage.

The starting point in this chapter is the ideal to which the British system of government is presumed to correspond, in which policy making is seen as the responsibility of our representatives in Parliament, who answer to the people at the general election for their stewardship of the public interest. This chapter first looks at the features of the system that correspond to this model, and at the institutions that are reputedly responsible for the policy-making process. It also looks at the implications of the presence of lower-tier organs of government, at local levels, and at the way in which representative government seems to be expected to work within them.

Having done this, the discussion then turns to consider the various ways in which the model of representative government is modified, or perhaps even undermined, in practice. It considers how the people's will is translated into political action. It looks at the part played by pressure groups in the system, and examines the case that has been made for regarding democracy as significantly undermined by 'political elites'. The relationship between government and Parliament is scrutinized, together with its parallels in local government. Attention is given to the role played by the machinery of government, by the civil service and by local government officers in the policy-making process, and some general points are made about what we mean by that 'process'. These later issues lead naturally into the examination of the implementation process in the next chapter.

The Representative Government Model

When the systems of government in Britain, the USA, most of Western Europe and much of the Commonwealth are claimed to be democratic, that proposition rests on a view that a form of representation of the people prevails in their governmental systems. Clearly, these systems do not involve direct democracy since, in complex societies, large numbers of decisions are taken by small numbers of representatives. Some countries seek to involve the people more directly, from time to time, by the use of plebiscites.

There is a further sense in which representative government is indirect. A distinction is often made between representatives and delegates. Delegates are regarded as mandated by those who elect them to support specific policies and to return to explain their subsequent decisions. British politicians have persistently rejected the view that they should be regarded as delegates, arguing instead that their duty is to make judgements for themselves in terms of their understanding of their constituents' best interests, while recognizing that they may, of course, be rejected at the next election if they become seriously out of touch with the people they represent. In this sense, they claim to be concerned with the interests of all their constituents, and not just those who voted for them. This doctrine was first expounded by Edmund Burke in the late eighteenth century.

Today, of course, the importance of political parties makes it difficult for Members of Parliament to claim to represent all their constituents; but equally this makes it difficult for them to assume delegate roles. The presence in Parliament, and in the local councils, of party groups exerts an influence in favour of party programmes and away from a direct relationship between Member and constituency. The modern modification of representative democracy is therefore to see the public as being allowed to choose from time to time between two or more broad political programmes, and being able to reject a party that has failed to carry out its promises (Schumpeter, 1950).

According to the theory on which this model of democracy is based, social policies may be expected to be determined by the commitments of the political parties, and proposals for policy changes will be set out in election manifestos. The growth of the welfare state can be clearly related to the growth of democracy, with the people choosing to see their society change in this way. There are weaknesses in this view of the policy-making process, which are explored later in this chapter. First, there is a need to identify more explicitly the institutions of government to which such an analysis must relate. Those who have previously taken courses on the British constitution may wish to skip the next two sections.

The Central Government System

The curious feature of the British constitution is that Britain has democratized institutions that were created in an undemocratic age. Most countries have systems of government that are relatively modern creations, either designed after cataclysmic political events which required the setting up of entirely new institutions, or set up to meet the needs of newly created or newly independent states. The governments of France and Germany, for example, fall into the first of these categories, and those of the USA and the Commonwealth countries into the second. The British pride themselves on having developed a system of government that has been a model for the rest of the world. The truth is that, while certainly many constitutional ideas have been borrowed from Britain, the British system contains features that no one designing a system of government today would conceivably want to adopt.

The monarchy and the House of Lords are the two most significant British 'anomalies'. Formally, neither has much influence on the policy-making process. Monarchs have relinquished their rights to interfere; the House of Lords has been largely stripped of its rights by successive Acts since 1911 (and, at the time of writing, there is legislation under consideration which further emasculates it). This discussion need not go into the residual rights and responsibilities of these two.

The House of Commons is elected from over 600 constituencies (an exact number has not been quoted as regular constituency boundary changes alter it), each of which returns the candidate who gains a simple majority of votes at each election. After a general election, the monarch has the formal responsibility to ask the leader of the majority party to form a government. On most occasions, the monarch's duty is clear, but situations in which there is no party with a clear majority may complicate the task. Broadly, the expectation is that the monarch will not have to take a decision that will then prove to be a violation of the democratic process, because it will be the responsibility of whoever agrees to form a government in these circumstances to prove that he or she has adequate parliamentary support. In other words, the position of a minority government can be made untenable if all the other parties combine against it. There are, however, ambiguities in such a situation, as the lives of minority governments may be perpetuated more by a reluctance to force them to resign than by any positive commitment to their support.

The newly appointed Prime Minister will then form a government, giving a hundred or more governmental offices to his or her supporters. Again, the normal assumption is that these will be members of his or her own party, but exceptionally a coalition may be formed in which government offices go to other parties. All those given office will normally be, or will be expected to become, members of either the Commons or the Lords. Most will be members of the Commons (known as 'Members of Parliament' or 'MPs'). The choice of members of the government rests significantly on the preferences of the Prime Minister. However, he or she cannot disregard interests and factions within his or her own party, and will obviously give some attention to the competence of those appointed.

The most important Prime Ministerial appointments will be those of the members of Cabinet. The normal practice is to appoint a Cabinet of fifteen to twenty-five members. It will include the heads of the main departments of government, together with some members who do not have departmental responsibilities, who may be given political or co-ordinating roles. The Cabinet, chaired by the Prime Minister, is the key decision-making body within the government. New policy departures of any significance and new legislation will need Cabinet approval, and conflicts of interests between departments will have to fought out in the Cabinet or its committees. Each

Cabinet sets up a number of committees to do more detailed work. Some of these will draw on the help of non-Cabinet ministers.

The government departments to which attention must be given in the discussion of social policy in England (the different situation in the other component countries of the UK is outlined later) are the Treasury, the Department of Health, the Department of Social Security, the Department of the Environment, Transport and the Regions (DETR), and the Department for Education and Employment (DfEE). Two other departments, the Cabinet Office and the Home Office, also play a small part. Readers must be warned that it has been the practice of governments in recent years to alter the departmental structure from time to time, ostensibly in an effort to find the best possible framework for policy co-ordination, but – it may be suggested – with less elevated political motives in mind too. Accordingly, it may be the case that, by the time this book is in your hands, departments may have new names and policy responsibilities may have been moved from one department to another. For example, in 1995, the Departments for Education and Employment were combined, while, after the 1997 election, the Department of the Environment's responsibilities were enlarged and it acquired the unwieldy title set out above.

The Prime Minister is technically the First Lord of the Treasury. This archaic title serves to remind us that, while today we regard the Chancellor of the Exchequer as the senior Treasury minister, the Prime Minister is, above all, bound to be involved in major decisions on expenditure, taxation and the management of the economy. The importance of this aspect of policy is so great that there are often other Treasury ministers in the Cabinet, such as the Chief Secretary to the Treasury and the Paymaster General. These may be expected to play important roles in relation to decisions on public expenditure.

Each of the departments listed above has its senior minister, the secretary of state, in the Cabinet. Again, the Prime Minister may choose to have other ministers from specific departments as Cabinet members. Each department head has the support of several junior ministers, known as ministers of state or under-secretaries, who may take on particular responsibilities for specific policy areas.

The role of the minister who is also a Cabinet member involves a quite considerable conflict between a position as a member of the central policy co-ordination team within the government and responsibility for the protection and advancement of the interests of a department. In his *Diaries of a Cabinet Minister*, Richard Crossman (1975, 1976, 1977) gave considerable attention to this problem. It is personally difficult for any individual to give wholehearted attention both to departmental issues and to the main political strategy problems arising outside his or her own responsibilities. There is, likewise, a crucial problem for a rational approach to government in which strategic questions may not be best resolved by bargaining between a group of individuals all of whom have conflicting, 'tunnel vision', images dictated by departmental needs and priorities. There is a number of, still competing, ways of trying to resolve this problem. Prime Ministers have developed the Cabinet Office to help them to do this task. The Treasury's overall responsibility for public expenditure has led them, particularly under powerful and ambitious Chancellors, to try to perform a co-ordinating role (Deakin and Parry, 1998). Members of the Cabinet without departmental responsibilities may be expected to help in the resolution of this problem, but they often suffer from a sense of being outsiders without the detailed departmental briefs possessed by their colleagues (Crossman, 1976). The creation of a group of special civil servants, including individuals recruited from outside the public service for their expertise or political connections, was seen in the 1970s as a further device to strengthen strategic thinking in government. There would seem, however, to be a continuing and inevitable conflict here.

As far as departmental duties are concerned a minister's work will fall into roughly four categories:

1   He or she may be responsible for putting forward new legislation. Clearly, this is something the ambitious politician will want to do. He or she will hope to secure a job that involves the initiation of policies from the party's programme.

2   He or she will have a large amount of day-to-day administration to oversee. Much of this will involve the formulation of new policies that do not require legislation, or the determination of responses to new crises within the department. It is in this kind of work that the distinction between policy making and implementation becomes so unclear. In many respects, any issue that a department regards as requiring a ministerial decision is likely to be describable as a 'policy issue'.

3   He or she will have to deal with questions from MPs about the policies and activities of the department. While this may be seen primarily as a defensive kind of action, involving much routine work by civil servants who are required to produce the information required for parliamentary answers, it may also provide opportunities for publicizing new policy initiatives. Indeed, many questions are planted by friendly MPs, from the backbenches on the minister's own side, to enable activities to be advertised.

4 The minister has a wide public relations role beyond Parliament. This will involve a programme of speeches, meetings and visits relating the department's activities to the world outside.

Several references have already been made to the support of ministers by civil servants. It is self-evident that civil servants have an important role to play in implementing policy. What also needs to be emphasized is that civil servants are heavily involved in making policy. Each major department has, at its headquarters, a group of a hundred or so civil servants, up to the top position of 'permanent secretary', who are concerned with decisions of a 'policy' kind, many of which require ministerial approval. The theory of representative government clearly requires that they be called the servants of the minister, ostensibly providing information and evidence on policy alternatives but not taking policy decisions.

The British system of government involves more than a network of departments headed by ministers. Responsibility for various specific public services is hived off to a range of special agencies, though, in each case, ultimate responsibility for policy lies with one of the central departments. Again, these subordinate bodies might be described as being concerned with implementation and not with policy making, but, while this is broadly true, many do this within only general guidelines and have therefore an important, if subordinate, policy-making role. Students of social policy will come across a number of important examples of bodies of this kind; some with a nation-wide remit, others with local or regional responsibilities. They have grown in numbers and importance in recent years, to such an extent that a 'new public management' (Hood, 1991) system has been seen to emerge in which a formerly single civil service has been replaced by a network of different organizations with different terms of service for their employees, In central government, the 'next steps initiative', started in the 1980s, has led to the delegation of most routine governmental tasks to separate 'agencies'. While most of these remain wholly public in character, some are private organizations working under contract for the government (such as the Stationery Office Ltd., which publishes government documents). In social policy, the most significant of these agencies are those concerned with social security and unemployment, particularly the Benefits Agency, and The Employment Service; see chapter 4 for a further discussion of agencies.

The discussion in this section has moved from the consideration of the composition of Parliament, and the nature of the relationship of government to Parliament, to a more detailed account of the organizations concerned with policy making. There is a need, however, to look a little more at the role of Parliament. It has been shown that about 100 of the 600 members elected to Parliament become involved in specific government jobs. What role do the rest play in policy making?

Primary policy making involves the promulgation of Acts of Parliament. The overwhelming majority of these are promoted by government, and thus the initial 'Bills' are prepared by civil servants within the departments. Bills then go through four stages in each House (Commons and Lords):

1   A 'first reading', which simply involves the formal presentation of the Bill
2   A 'second reading', at which there is likely to be a large-scale debate on the basic principles of the Bill
3   A 'committee stage', when the legislation is examined in detail (normally by a small 'standing committee' and not by the whole House)
4   A 'report stage' and 'third reading', at which the Bill that emerges from the committee is approved, but may be re-amended to undo some of the actions of the committee

Clearly, members without ministerial office may participate in all of these stages, and opposition members will take particular care to scrutinize and attack government action. The leading opposition party organizes a 'shadow cabinet' to provide for a considered and specialized response to the activities of the government.

Backbench MPs may be able to promote new policies through 'private members' Bills'. These cannot have direct financial implications for the government, and they have little chance of becoming law without government support. Occasionally, governments assist private members with their Bills, particularly by allowing extra parliamentary time. Some significant social policy measures have become law in this way. The Abortion Act of 1967, for example, was promoted by a Liberal MP, David Steel, and became law because many key ministers were sympathetic. In this case, the Bill concerned an issue of conscience on which many felt it would be inappropriate for Parliament to divide on party lines. The abolition of capital punishment and reform of the law on homosexuality came about in a similar way. In the 1970s, the Labour government supported a private member's Bill which took over an item which would have been included in its own programme if there had been sufficient parliamentary time. This curious reversal of roles may have owed something to the agreement of the Liberals to support a government without a clear majority; the legislation was the Housing (Homeless Persons) Act of 1977 promoted by a Liberal, Stephen Ross.

In addition to Acts of Parliament, both Houses have to deal with a great deal of what is known as 'subordinate' or 'delegated' legislation. Many Acts allow governments to promote subsequent changes and new regulations. It is important to recognize that many policy changes pass through Parliament in this way. It would be an extravagant use of parliamentary time to require new legislation for all detailed changes of this kind. Controversy arises, however, over the extent of the use of delegated legislation, since some Acts convey wide scope for this kind of ministerial action. To promote subordinate legislation, the government has to publish a 'statutory instrument' which is open to scrutiny by MPs. Some of these require parliamentary approval; others may be annulled if a negative resolution is passed by either House within 40 days of their initial publication. Hence, backbenchers may intervene to prevent subordinate legislation. A joint committee of the Commons and the Lords has been set up to scrutinize statutory instruments, and therefore to facilitate parliamentary review of subordinate legislation. They have, however, a mammoth task and only give detailed attention to a limited number of the statutory instruments that are put before Parliament.

Readers will find good examples of legislation for which statutory instruments are important in most social security measures. For example, they will look in vain in the 1986 Social Security Act for detailed information on the housing benefit scheme or the 'social fund'. This is contained in subsequent regulations. In particular, actual benefit rates are not included in such legislation, but are set out in regulations which are regularly updated and amended.

Reference has already been made to parliamentary questions as providing an opportunity for backbench scrutiny of government actions. Members put down initial questions in advance. Many questions are answered in writing, but those that receive oral answers may result in supplementary questions. In addition to the powers to ask questions, various parliamentary procedures provide scope for MPs to promote short debates on topics that concern them. The main opposition party is extended more specific facilities of this kind, so there are days allocated for debates on topics of its own choice.

One peculiar characteristic of the British Parliament that distinguishes it from many legislatures in other countries, and particularly from the US Congress, is the slight use made of specialized committees. This is also a difference between the central government system and the local government system in Britain. The committees that consider Bills are in no way specialized; they consider new legislation in rotation regardless of subject and do not do any separate investigatory work.

There is also, however, a system of rather more specialized select committees. Perhaps the most important of these is the Public Accounts Committee, concerned to look at the way in which public money has been spent. Then, there are select committees on the work of the Parliamentary Commissioner for Administration (the 'Ombudsman'), on Statutory Instruments and on European legislation. In 1979, a system of fourteen committees was set up to concern themselves with the work of specific (or in some cases two specific) government departments. In the field of social policy, the social services committee has conducted a number of influential invest-igations of issues. *Ad hoc* committees may also be set up to investi-gate specific subjects. However, such is the power of the executive in our system that it is doubtful whether these committees can do other than play a rather superior pressure-group role. They investigate specific topics, with the aid of specialist advisers, and have issued some influential reports, but, as stressed on page 58, they have no role with regard to legislation.

This account of the institutions of British central government has shown that elected representatives have a wide range of parliament-ary duties. If they belong to the party that wins power they may well take on a government office of some kind. If they do not achieve office, they are still in a special relationship to government in which, while some advantages may accrue from being a member of the ruling party and having many colleagues and friends in office, there will also be disadvantages in that party allegiance implies a duty to support the government. Some of the scope for the criticism of policy that comes to opposition members is denied to government support-ers. On the other hand, opposition, in a Parliament organized strictly on party lines, implies a situation in which it is very difficult to secure majority support for your own ideas.

Devolution

During its first two years in office, Tony Blair's Labour government has initiated major changes to the arrangements for the government of Northern Ireland, Scotland and Wales.

In the case of Northern Ireland, what was involved was a complex agreement, involving Eire as well, designed to solve the long-standing conflict there. As far as social policy is concerned this will, if the constitutional change process is completed, mean that once again (as was the case from 1922, with a brief intermission in 1971–3, until the imposition of 'direct rule' from Westminster in 1974), there will be an elected Northern Ireland government responsible for the making of policy. However, even under direct rule, there is a separate administration for Northern Ireland. The government of Northern Ireland under direct rule is through a secretary of state for Northern Ireland at Westminster who heads a Northern Ireland Office. Within Northern Ireland itself, the former separate departments operate but all are technically under the jurisdiction of the Northern Ireland Office. The various junior ministers in the Northern Ireland Office share the 'ministerial' responsibilities for these departments. The Northern Ireland departments operate on the basis of legislation much of which was passed before the imposition of direct rule.

Scotland has secured a devolved government system, such as it has not enjoyed since it was united with England in 1707. A referendum vote in favour of devolution followed by legislation ensured the election of a Scottish Parliament in May 1999. That Parliament has legislative and tax varying powers and, therefore, it may be said that Scotland can make its own social policy. In practice, change may be comparatively slow, particularly as the dismantling of intertwined taxation and spending powers is a complex matter.

Scotland's affairs had been conducted from Westminster by way of a secretary of state for Scotland and a separate Scottish Office, split into several departments. Much Scottish legislation is already separate. Those social services that come under local government – housing, personal social services and education – had their control devolved to the Scottish Office and were regulated by separate legislation. The health service in Scotland has a slightly different structure and some separate legislation, but here the centralizing tendency for control from London was very strong. The social security system has been, and remains, on the other hand, a Great Britain wide one.

A similar process of devolution of power to Wales has occurred, although devolution to Wales is not so extensive. There are no separate taxation powers, but there is scope for separate Welsh legislation on health, social welfare, education and housing. There had been a separate Welsh Office for some time, but most current legislation deals jointly with England and Wales. In many respects, the Welsh Office was little more than an integrated 'regional office' bringing together, in a way not present in the English regions, the responsibilities now devolved to the Welsh assembly.

The Channel Islands and the Isle of Man have substantially more independent systems of government, and do not send MPs to Westminster. In view of their small size, however, it does not seem appropriate to say anything more about them.

The speedy establishment of the arrangements for devolution without any changes to the UK Parliament, or to the government of England, has created anomalies which, in the view of the author, will have to be addressed before long. Social legislation in Scotland and Northern Ireland, and to a lesser extent in Wales, is – or may be – in the hands of autonomous national governments. Yet, as already pointed out, there will be some interlocking financial arrangements between these governments and the UK one. It will also be the case that social policy for England will be made by a body whose members come from the whole of the UK. While conventions may be developed under which MPs from one of the other countries do not participate in the discussion of English legislation, it is far from clear what will happen if (as is quite likely) a situation arises in which a party which does not have the majority support of English MPs is in power at Westminster by virtue of its support in the other countries.

The logical way to address this issue is by the establishment of a federal system of government, with a UK Parliament for those issues not devolved to the individual countries and separate Parliaments (including an English one) for all devolved issues. That would involve a fundamental constitutional change. In that sense, the limited devolution measures open up wider matters. Arguments would also need to be considered about the extent to which England, with a population over five times that of the other countries together, might be divided into several regional units. The government has committed itself to look at regional issues. At the present time, most government departments with responsibilities for local services have systems of regional offices. These existing regional structures appear to have comparatively little significance for policy making and, of course, there is no system for the election of representatives at this level.

Local Government

Local government in England is organized into two distinctive systems. In the metropolitan areas of London, West Midlands, South Yorkshire, Greater Manchester, Merseyside and Tyne and Wear, there is a long-established one-tier system of metropolitan districts responsible for personal social services, education and housing. After 1996, a number of further one-tier authorities came into operation.

These are mostly in urbanized areas, with enlarged districts taking over powers from counties. In some cases – Avon and Cleveland, for example – county authorities disappeared altogether.

In the rest of England, there are county authorities which are responsible for education and personal social services, but also a lower tier of districts which include housing among their responsibilities. Planning responsibilities are shared between the two tiers.

There were a number of metropolitan counties, including one covering London. These were abolished in the 1980s and their powers dispersed either to districts or to *ad hoc* authorities. The Blair government has restored an overriding Greater London Authority, with a directly elected mayor and an elected assembly. This will not have specific implications for social policy, but will be concerned with certain conurbation wide issues such as transport and the environment.

There is also, in the counties, a third tier of parish councils, with minimal powers. While many of these are old parishes, others are towns that previously had significant powers of their own, some retaining mayors and calling themselves town councils. None of these third-tier authorities have significant social policy responsibilities, so they will not be examined further here.

The local government system of Scotland has been totally restructured; throughout that country since April 1996, there is a one-tier system of local government. There is a similar but slightly more complicated situation in Wales, with most powers being in single-tier authorities, known either as counties or county boroughs, except that there is also a system of community councils resembling the parish councils in England.

Local government in Northern Ireland has been stripped of almost all its significant powers. It had previously been notorious in some areas for the manipulation of electoral boundaries and for the practice of religious discrimination. Health services and personal social services come together under four appointed boards. Education is the responsibility of three separate education and libraries boards. Public housing is the concern of the Northern Ireland Housing Executive.

The health service, outside Northern Ireland, has its own separate system of single-tier authorities, originally designed with some regard to local government boundaries.

National legislation defines the powers of local authorities, and may set limits to those powers. It also imposes on local government a range of duties. The relationship between central and local government in Britain is a complex one. Local government is not autonomous, but neither is it merely local administration. Some statutes impose fairly clear tasks for local authorities, but many give powers, and indicate ways in which those powers should be used, without undermining the scope for local initiative. Other Acts of Parliament merely grant local authorities powers, which they may choose whether to use. Exceptionally, a local authority may itself promote a 'private' Act to secure powers to undertake new ventures. Local authorities are therefore able to make or elaborate policies and are not merely implementing agencies.

However, the relationship between central and local government involves both partnership and conflict. Central government seeks to impose its will not merely through legislation, but also through the communication of large amounts of guidance. This may be embodied in circulars, regularly sent from central departments to local authorities, or through less formal communications from ministers, administrators and professional advisers. Central intervention will be justified in terms of national political commitments, to ensure that central policies have an impact on all localities. There is an inherent conflict between the demands of local autonomy and the principle of 'territorial justice', requiring that citizens in different geographical areas secure comparable treatment.

The Conservative governments led by Margaret Thatcher and John Major considerably curbed the powers and autonomy of local government. They imposed increased financial controls, partly removed some services from local government (such as education), increased the regulation of others and forced authorities to consider contracting out services. One Conservative minister, Nicholas Ridley, argued that local authorities should become 'enabling authorities' planning services and then letting contracts to private and voluntary sector service providers (Ridley, 1988). The new Labour government has made it clear that, while it distances itself from some of the Conservative measures, it has some sympathy with Ridley's view. In his introduction to a White Paper *Modern Local Government in Touch with the People* (DETR, 1998, p. 2), the Secretary of State, John Prescott says:

> There is no future in the old model of councils trying to plan and run most services. It does not provide the services which people want, and cannot do so in today's world. Equally there is no future for councils which are inward looking – more concerned to maintain their structures and protect their vested interests than listening to their local people and leading their communities.
> ... our modernising agenda is seeking nothing less than a radical

refocusing of councils' traditional roles. A fundamental shift of culture throughout local government is essential . . .
So we have a demanding agenda for change, which we in central government will take forward in partnership with local government.

At the time of writing, what this actually means is only just beginning to emerge. The Conservative Compulsory Competitive Tendering legislation has been replaced by a wide requirement for councils to seek 'best value' in the design of all their services and there are signs that the central surveillance system is being strengthened. The White Paper indicates discontent with the working of local democracy and argues for the streamlining of management arrangements.

Central government often justifies its interventions in local government in terms of its own concern with national economic management. It is its financial control over local government that tends to weaken its claim that the central–local relationship is a partnership. The problem is compounded by a lack of a satisfactory way for local government to raise its own revenue.

Local authorities have three major sources of income: local taxes, payments for the provisions of services and government grants. The first of these was, until the mid 1980s, a system of rates on property, both domestic and business. Then the government replaced domestic rates by a tax on individuals, the community charge or 'poll tax', and centralized control over business rates. The poll tax was met by a popular reaction which contributed to the end of Margaret Thatcher's career as Prime Minister (Butler et al., 1994). After her fall, her successor sharply increased the central government grant to soften the impact of the poll tax, financing this out of an increase in value added tax. He then, in 1993, replaced the poll tax by the 'council tax'. The latter is a simplified form of the former domestic rates, with the number of adult occupants of the property partly taken into account.

All these changes to local taxation involved a sharp reduction in the independence of local government. Even before the poll tax, the Conservative government had given itself powers to prevent local authorities from raising local taxation over centrally prescribed limits. It continued this 'capping' practice. At the same time, the centralization of the commercial rating system had the effect of bringing three quarters of local revenue under direct central control; and the panic reaction to reduce the impact of the poll tax, after Margaret Thatcher's fall, had the effect of pushing the centrally controlled proportion up to around 80 per cent of local government revenue (Central Statistical Office, 1995b, p. 24). Given the inflexibility of property-based taxation systems, by contrast with income tax or value added tax, it is unlikely that any future government will dare to reverse this situation. Indeed, while the Blair government has indicated that it will end 'crude' council tax capping, it retains a 'reserve power to control excessive council tax increases' (DETR, 1998, para 5.7, p. 34) It is certainly not increasing the central funds going to local government. It intends to retain the proceeds of the business rate, but may allow authorities the opportunity to levy supplementary rates or to give rebates (para 10.8, p. 77).

Central government also maintains control over local authority borrowing. The trend, in recent years, has been away from a system of strict, item by item, controls to broad limitations on total borrowing. The system is currently a complex combination of these two approaches to control.

Policy making in local government is the responsibility of elected members. These represent districts, or wards, within each authority in much the same way as MPs represent constituencies. Today, a great deal of local politics is arranged along party lines, and most councillors represent the political parties that are also found at Westminster. The politicization of local government has intensified the conflict between central and local government. This was particularly sharp in the early 1980s between radical Labour authorities and the central Conservative administration.

In the traditional system, local authority members each belong to a number of committees. Most business is transacted in these committees, so that the meetings of the full councils are largely rubber-stamping affairs, affording opportunities for the making of political points. These committee structures have been primarily related to the various functional responsibilities of the authority. Many local authorities have also developed 'policy committees', which aim to co-ordinate the activities of the authority as a whole. In most authorities, the parties are represented on the committees in proportion to their distribution on the whole council. Generally the majority party will assume the chairmanship of each of the committees. It is in respect of these issues that the White Paper *Modern Local Government in Touch with the People* (DETR, 1998) indicates an interest in encouraging change – increasing co-ordination and centralization within authorities through 'cabinet', 'city manager' or 'elected mayor' systems.

The United Kingdom in Europe

There is one part of the political and administrative system which needs to be mentioned at the end of this discussion, even though its impact on social policy is slight. The UK's membership of the EU has had an impact on its constitution and on its policy making process. There are areas of the law which are now determined by the institutions of the EEC, where the role of the UK Parliament is limited to one of administering implementation.

It is mainly economic activity which is subject to this European dominance. The origins of the EEC lie in the aspiration to build a supra-national trading area. Other European legislation has followed from that aspiration for several reasons:

1   The presence of different regulatory systems in different countries to deal with production standards, consumer protection, environmental control and terms of employment will have an influence on competition. Countries with lower standards may have competitive advantages over those with higher ones, which the latter will want to be eliminated.
2   Economic co-operation between nations is enhanced if they enjoy broadly similar opportunities for employment and standards of living.
3   The concept of a single market embraces a single labour market, in which workers can move freely across boundaries in search of work. They will want to carry social rights with them if they do so.

Hence, the evolution of the EEC has led it to develop 'social policy' alongside economic and environment policy, but that policy has been principally concerned with the rights of employees and with efforts to stimulate employment through investment and training. The principal social policy interventions have been limited efforts to harmonize rules relating to employment and the provision of funds to help to create work and aid training programmes (Gold, 1993). The European Social Fund – not to be confused with the social fund in social security (see chapter 5) – which sounds like a major social policy instrument, is in fact a vehicle for the subsidization of training (and to a lesser extent work creation). Compared with agricultural support, Social Fund expenditure is low, and countries receiving this money have to add matching contributions to schemes which it supports. There is, additionally, a rather larger Regional Fund, which certainly has 'social effects' as it is used to try to stimulate economic development in regions suffering from underdevelopment or economic decline.

Social policy has figured in the arguments about the scope of the role of the EU, in which British Conservative governments have – during the 1980s and 1990s – been advocates of a limited and cautious approach. Britain secured agreement that it need not accept the 'social chapter' in the 'Maastricht Treaty' of 1992. The Labour government has reversed that decision. However, it is important to recognize that the aspirations of that 'chapter' – towards a greater harmonization of social conditions and of social protection legislation – will not be easy to realize. At whatever 'speed' the EU may be moving towards greater unification, social policy is likely to be a weak element. The areas where change has occurred, and will continue to occur, concern the elimination of discrimination in the labour market.

However, there are two ways in which the progress of European social policy may be accelerated. One is the presence in Brussels of a Directorate which aspires to advance European social policy – which sets out goals for policy, which encourages social policy experiments (the European poverty programmes) and which publishes data on social conditions and social security systems – provides a source of pressure on national governments and helps to keep social policy issues on the agenda (Commission of the European Communities, 1993). The other is the shift towards the political Left in Europe as a whole – particularly the formation of a Social Democrat / Green coalition government in Germany – which is tending to put issues about the harmonization of tax and social security on the European agenda in the context of arguments for a European strategy to combat unemployment.

The Voice of the People?

It has already been noted that, in the British system of government, MPs and councillors are elected in individual constituencies on the basis of a procedure in which the candidate with a simple majority is the winner. It is generally the case that the voter has to choose between two to four candidates, each of whom is the representative of a specific political party. In this way, electoral choice is peculiarly structured. Voters have to make their decision on the basis of assessments of particular people, with their own special policy commitments, in relation to the more general political biases and policy commitments of their parties. The parties' intentions are of more importance than individuals' commitments. However, what the parties offer are broad packages of policies, within which voters may like some items while disliking others.

Hence the individual voter's starting point in trying to influence policy through the electoral process is a situation of limited choice in which it is general policy biases, or even more general considerations, often described as 'party images', that must govern his or her selection of an MP. Moreover, his or her vote will be taken together with large numbers of other votes, perhaps motivated by very different policy preferences. Hence, one person's voting choice might be influenced by a party's commitment to raise pensions, which leads him or her to support it despite its commitment to other policies – say increasing educational expenditure – with which he or she disagrees. Others who vote for the same party might be motivated by directly opposite considerations – a strong commitment to education, say, but no concern about pensions.

The above example was chosen to illustrate the basic underlying problem about the use of choices between representatives as a means of settling policy priorities. The reality is that party platforms are considerably more complex, with choices between desirable ends deliberately obscured. No party presents the electorate with explicit choices between widely desired ends; they generally seek to convince it that they can bring a little more of everything that is wanted, probably at less cost. Voters are forced to discriminate between the parties in terms of their general ideologies, value biases and images.

Furthermore, most voters do not really make electoral *choices*. Many vote for the same party every time they vote, and probably give little attention to the personalities or policies of specific candidates. Voters behave in ways that, as far as the collective pattern of choices is concerned, political scientists are to a large extent able to predict from their occupations, social origins and personalities. Only a minority of the electorate changes sides between elections. Indeed, many of the changes that alter the balance in power in Parliament are no more than changes between voting and non-voting, or vice versa. Research findings suggest, moreover, that the people most likely to change their votes – the floating voters – are generally the least informed within the electorate, and are thus not people who can be said to be making careful choices between policies. It is suggested, instead, that political *images* are particularly significant – the personalities of the leaders, their projections of competence and of their capacities to deal with the nation's problems. An important consideration at a general election is the success or failure of the government in power in coping with the economic situation. In this sense, a verdict may be given on its policies, but only in a very general way.

Clearly, therefore, electors are not normally provided with opportunities to make clear choices about social policies, or between social policy options. There are certainly general characteristics of the parties' approaches to social policies that may help people to decide between them; and, at particular elections, ones for or against social policy may be particularly clear. At other times, it may be very difficult to single out policy issues that divide the parties. In 1970, the Child Poverty Action Group attacked the Labour Government's failure to deal effectively with family poverty and secured a pledge from the Conservatives that family allowances would be increased. The Conservatives did not increase these allowances, but it is doubtful whether many voters were influenced to change their allegiances on this issue. Those who studied the parties' platforms carefully would have had to relate the Labour Party's generally stronger commitment to universal social security policies to the Conservative's specific pledge. It may be suggested that what the Child Poverty Action Group expected, and wanted, was a new Labour government returned to power, chastened by criticism of their family policies, and not a Conservative government (McCarthy, 1986).

Another characteristic of social policies is that, while some involve broad responses to popular needs and wishes, many are specific measures to assist quite small disadvantaged groups in the population. Policies to assist disabled people, for example, may be viewed as generally desirable and, in that sense, may have electoral appeal; but the number of people they benefit directly or indirectly is a minority in the population. Disabled people may be a relatively 'popular' minority group; but what about policies to help the long-term unemployed, rehabilitate criminals or provide facilities for vagrant alcoholics, for example? If there were a direct relationship between the pursuit of electoral popularity and the determination of social policies, surely minority causes would receive much less attention than they do now, and unpopular minority causes would receive no attention at all (or even more punitive responses). Opinion polls suggest that a variety of social reforms carried out in Britain – the abolition of capital punishment and the liberalization of the law relating to homosexuality, for example – were enacted in the face of popular opposition.

Other survey evidence suggests, moreover, that, while there are strong public commitments to pensions and the health service, other social policies which favour those most in need of help from the welfare state, such as the unemployed and single parents, have little popular support (Taylor-Gooby, 1985; Edgell and Duke, 1991).

It is additionally important to add to this examination of the impact of 'the voice of the people' on social policy determination the observation that our 'first past the post' electoral system can convey an ambiguous message. The victors in general elections tend to have much larger majorities in Parliament than the size of their overall vote in the country would seem to justify. Often more electors have voted against the winning party than have voted for it.

A shift to some form of proportional representation is now on the agenda. Such systems have been adopted for the elections to the Scottish, Welsh and Northern Irish Parliaments and for the European Parliament elections. Similar ideas are under consideration for Westminster and for local government. However, of course, the introduction of some kind of proportional representation system does not necessarily solve the general 'political arithmetic' problem outlined above, policy priorities would then be influenced by the way negotiations between potential coalition parties developed.

Influences on Policy Making

Pressure groups

Much of the detailed analysis of the role of pressure groups in the policy-making process has been carried out in the USA. There, the political system has several characteristics that particularly facilitate the mobilization of small groups of people to influence decisions. First, power within the system is fragmented – between President and the two houses of Congress, between the federal government and the states, and between the state government and local government. Second, in that vast and diverse country, political choices are much more dictated by local interests than they are in Britain. Hence, the relationship between a congress member and his or her local electorate is much less affected by national party considerations. Third, at federal level, the parties are accordingly much less unified by political ideologies. Political actors are therefore readily influenced by small groups which can effectively threaten to have an electoral impact.

In Britain, pressure groups are probably just as much in evidence as they are in the USA. A number of studies (Finer, 1958; Roberts, 1970; Wootton, 1970; Jordan and Richardson, 1987) have dispelled the notion that they are of no importance in the British system, but there is a need to beware of the assumption that they have as direct an impact on the political system as they do in the USA. Their importance in the politics of that country has led political scientists to propound a modification of the theory of representative government in which the weakness of the individual voter, discussed in the last section, is seen as compensated by his or her membership of interest groups (Dahl, 1961). Democracy is thus seen as 'pluralist' in character with politicians engaged in continuing processes of compromise with multiple groups. Such a theory is then seen as explaining the deference of politicians to the interests of minorities; and a new and perhaps superior version of democratic theory is presented which has as its hallmark the achievement of a political consensus in which minority interests are protected.

This theory has, however, come under fire in the USA. It has been pointed out that there are biases in the system that make it much easier for some interests to be heard than others, and much easier for modifications to the *status quo* to be vetoed than to be supported (Schattschneider, 1960; Bachrach, 1969).

These general points about the plurality of pressure groups are worthy of our attention since they suggest important questions about the way the British system operates. The contrasts made above between the political systems on the two sides of the Atlantic suggest that it may be much more difficult for British pressure groups to identify points at which the political system is particularly open to influence. In individual constituencies, grievances with the established political parties have to be very deeply felt, and widely shared, to upset national electoral swings. Direct interventions in elections motivated by local issues are rare, except in the areas where nationalist parties can have an impact. Outside Scotland and Wales, politicians have often been able to be singularly insensitive to local issues, and the current three or more party system further distorts the picture. Here, too, the introduction of proportional representation could make some difference.

There are similar problems for a national pressure group in persuading political parties that disregard of its case carries electoral dangers. Furthermore, any interest group able to threaten in this way probably has a special relationship with a major political party, and is acknowledged as important in that sense. Many of the most powerful of the British pressure groups tend to have an established relationship with one or other political party. The trade unions are, of course, the clearest example of this phenomenon. They played a key role in the original establishment of the Labour Party. Although the modern party is trying to distance itself from them, they still provide a significant proportion of its funds. Correspondingly, the other side of industry is an important paymaster for the Conservative Party. In an earlier version of this book, it was suggested that it was unlikely that the major elements in either of these groups will actually change sides. In fact, at the time of writing the Conservative Party seems to be losing business support quite fast, while the Labour Party is gaining it.

It is important to look more closely at the ways in which particular groups enjoy an institutionalized relationship to the political system. In particular, it is necessary to go beyond the examples of close relationships to political parties to consider whether the positions some groups enjoy in relation to the political system owe nothing to particular party allegiances. Indeed, there are groups whose very power in Britain might be jeopardized if they were seen as identified with specific political parties.

Political elites

The power of some pressure groups can only be explained in terms of what may be called an 'insider' status within the policy-making system. This implies a further deviation from democratic theory, a system within which some individuals and groups have special status. A number of political scientists and sociologists have suggested that societies possess a political 'elite' – see Bottomore (1966) and, specifically on Britain, Urry and Wakeford (1973) and Stanworth and Giddens (1974) – that decision makers are drawn from a narrow spectrum within a society. Traditional Marxist analyses of the social structure suggest that the political system is dominated by representatives of the bourgeoisie, the capitalist class. Modern updates of this theory have pointed out the relevance of patterns of domination based on race and gender as well (Williams, 1989). Other political theories, notably those of Pareto and Mosca, suggest there is a ruling elite that is not necessarily characterized by the possession of economic resources.

Modern interpretations of elite theories seek to show either that key policy offices are held by people from a narrow spectrum of social origins, or that a limited number of people, characterized by close links with one another, dominate decision-making roles. For Britain, it has been shown that Cabinet ministers, senior civil servants, members of key advisory bodies and the heads of prestigious organizations tend to be drawn from a relatively narrow social class group, characterized by education at public schools and Oxbridge, and by having had parents in a similarly narrow range of upper-middle class occupations. The picture is, however, not simple, and there is some evidence that the backgrounds of top decision makers have changed in recent years to embrace a slightly wider range of social origins. While, certainly, it seems plausible to suggest that, if there are people from similar social or educational backgrounds in a number of key roles, the relationships between those people will facilitate the sharing of ideas and opinions, the processes involved cannot necessarily be explained as simply as this.

What is more important to explain the place of some of the pressure groups in Britain in relation to the structure of power is to examine the sense in which the policy-making process is perceived as involving assumptions that some interests should be consulted. Such assumptions rest on several foundations. One of them is that expertise conveys the ability to help with public decision making. This is the technocratic view: that experts' opinions carry a greater weight than other people's. It is the basis on which academics sometimes secure a measure of influence in government. Similarly, some pressure groups secure attention because of their expert knowledge. In the educational and medical fields, such 'heavyweight' pressure groups abound. It has been suggested that there are a number of 'policy networks' or 'policy communities' in the various specialized policy areas, in which regular consultations occur between policy makers and representatives of pressure groups (including groups representing employees, particularly professional ones) who have been granted partial insider roles (Smith, 1993).

Another foundation on which pressure groups may secure influence is their association with traditional elite groups. Voluntary organizations believe they benefit by royal sponsorship and by the acquisition of prestigious figures as vice-presidents and supporters. Such sponsorship is not always easily earned. It is clearly helpful to have a cause that readily attracts the sympathy of influential people. It may also be important to behave in ways that are deemed respectable. This is a curious feature of this kind of pressure group activity; to some extent, the power of groups depends on their ability to forswear the more direct weapons in the pressure group armoury, to avoid mounting vociferous opinion-forming campaigns or threatening forms of direct action. The supposition, here, is based on a belief that there is an underlying elitist approach to government in Britain. A fairly narrow range of people are responsible for key decisions; some of these attain such positions through democratic representational procedures, but they co-opt others to their ranks. These other people may be individuals of shared social backgrounds, but the process of co-optation may be more haphazard. Individuals from pressure groups, or at least representing specific interests, secure entry into the ranks of those who exercise power by virtue not only of expertise but also of personal qualities, such as persistence and charm, which enable them to persuade others that they have something to contribute to public decision making. They also generally have to establish that they understand some of the unspoken rules relating to public participation: that they don't embarrass their sponsors by the use of direct tactics or indiscreet communications with the press or unseemly behaviour in committee situations. In so doing, they join that list of people who have been called on over and over again to sit on public committees and advisory bodies.

This argument, then, is that political influence may be secured in Britain without the aid of independent power. The system co-opts others to join its ranks, and pays attention to some citizens much more readily than others. In this day and age, people are rightly cynical about propositions about the power of ideas; they look around for other explanations and ulterior motives. Yet, in the study of social policy, the importance of individuals should not be wholly underestimated. There are examples of people who, through the strength of their commitments and the power of their attention to detail, have secured a place in the policy-making process. In the first half of this century, William Beveridge (Harris, 1977) was such an individual. In the 1980s, experienced businessmen were turned to as advisers, and one (Sir Roy Griffiths) had an important influence on the organization of the health service and on community care policy. There are many lesser examples around, of people whose influence on policy making owes nothing either to any notion of representative government or to the cruder theories about pressure group activity.

A great deal of pressure group activity is, of course, concerned with 'good causes'. Again, a theory of the policy-making process needs to find room for 'good causes' as well as for 'good people'. There are important questions that should not be brushed aside about the place of altruism in policy making. It is not naive to argue that politicians, or if you prefer some politicians, have commitments to ideals. It is certainly important to recognize that many politicians want to be seen as supporters of 'good causes'. Hence, pressure groups for disabled or elderly people, neglected children and so on will exert influence out of proportion to their naked power. For them, the skilful use of mass media may be important, and key contacts in positions of power will be a great help. In this sense, they aim to be co-opted into 'policy communities'.

No account of social policy making should disregard the potential influence of these 'good causes', however much there may be scope for controversy about their real power in situations where interests are in conflict. Indeed one of the frustrating phenomena many pressure groups of this kind experience is continuing assertions by politicians that they do matter, which is accompanied by minimal concrete action. It is difficult to predict the political circumstances that will favour interests of this kind; but, manifestly, many have secured benefits without the use of any perceptible political 'muscle'. It is perhaps useful here to bear in mind the distinction often made in the study of pressure groups between 'interest' groups and 'cause' groups, though in the tactical struggle for influence each may seek to co-opt the support of the other. Interests seek to be recognized as 'good causes', and causes try to enlist the backing of more powerful 'interests'.

It has been suggested earlier that pressure groups provide a crucial qualification to the notion of a simple relationship between electors and elected. Some writers have suggested that they solve the problem of the powerlessness of the individual in relation to the political machine (Dahl, 1961; Beer, 1965). While there are many circumstances in which that is true, it seems important to acknowledge that the political system contains biases that make it much easier for some groups to secure influence than others. In addition, in Britain, there is the peculiar phenomenon of the exercise of influence by groups that, according to the crude calculations of political arithmetic, do not seem to have a power base at all. This must lead us to look at the shortcomings of the 'how many divisions has the Pope' approach to the estimation of political influence. It implies, however, a recognition that the minority who occupy powerful positions in British society are able to make choices, based neither on notions of democracy nor on calculations about who has power, but about whom they will listen to or consult.

Ministerial Power: The Role of Officials and the Influence of Outside Groups and Policy Communities

The author (Hill, 1972, 1997 a, b) has developed a typology of government styles to try to elucidate different characteristics of politician/official relationships in different political situations. Three types of political system are identified: 'ideological politics', 'administrative politics' and 'bargaining politics'.

A system of 'ideological politics' relates most clearly to the model of 'representative government'. It is one in which the traditional distinction between politics and administration is most easily made.

Political parties compete to win elections by submitting distinct programmes from which the electorate can choose. Politicians instruct administrators to frame policies compatible with their mandates and commitments. The Thatcher governments stood out as examples of this phenomenon.

'Administrative politics' describes a contrasting system in which full-time officials are much more clearly dominant. The 'politics' are organizational rather than public, and many of the key conflicts are between departments. Ministers in central government, while formally possessing the key decision-making powers, in fact find themselves involved primarily in expounding views and defending policies generated within their departments. Politicians of the majority party without ministerial office find themselves frustratingly shut out from a decision-making process into which they are given few insights. In British local government, the committee system provides scope for the wider use of elected representatives in an administrator-dominated context, though here such involvement may further undermine representative government since it will depend primarily on personal characteristics.

The concept of 'bargaining politics' was derived from examination of accounts of local politics in the USA. Partly as a result of exposure to the US literature and partly because of a desire to adopt a tough-minded approach towards power, British social and political scientists have been on the look-out for signs of a similar system in Britain. In such a system political outcomes are seen to depend on inputs of resources of power. Those who hold elected positions are not 'representatives' so much as 'brokers' bringing together coalitions of interests. Their desire for re-election forces them to adopt strategies in which they are highly sensitive to pressure groups. Some reservations about this view have already been suggested, but it was acknowledged that elements of bargaining are by no means absent from the British scene. Bargaining politics implies a clear role for politicians which may suggest that officials will occupy subordinate positions. While this is true inasmuch as political futures are at stake, it has been suggested that in Britain deals with quite explicit electoral implications are rare. Bargaining may therefore be more concerned with the maintenance of specific policies or particular organizational arrangements. If this is the case, it may be that officials have more to lose, or have more explicit commitments, than the politicians. Key conflicts concern relationships between departments and the outside world; ministers are expected to support the defence of departmental interests.

It is not suggested that the individual types fit any specific political system. British central government must be noted as a context where conflicts often appear to be of an ideological nature and where the representative model is treated as of some importance. Yet a key theme in discussions of relationships between ministers and their departments has been the extent to which politicians enter with apparent policy commitments, but become socialized into roles determined by the permanent administrators and particularly by the need for 'policy maintenance' within their department (this was cleverly satirized in the television series *Yes Minister*). Furthermore, a related theme to the ministerial discovery that cherished policy innovations are not administratively feasible is the recognition that vested interests and pressure groups carry a political 'clout' that had not been realized when policies were planned outside government. Policy-making outcomes may be determined by the interaction of three forces: political input (ideological politics), organizational considerations within departments (administrative politics), and external pressures (bargaining politics). Marsh and Rhodes' *Implementing Thatcherite Policies* (1992a) offers a good account of the way in which ideological politics was muted in practice in the 1980s. Conversely, Campbell and Wilson (1995) show civil service domination has been partly undermined by the tendency of the Thatcher and Major governments to advance civil servants who have been prepared to offer them uncritical assistance in the pursuit of ideological goals.

Beyond these generalizations, the more detailed study of the factors that influence the way that policy is made needs to take various considerations into account. First, what kinds of policies are involved? This raises the question so far evaded in this book: What is policy? Writers on policy analysis are agreed that a policy is something more than a decision. Friend and his colleagues (Friend, Power and Yewlett, 1974, p. 40) suggest that 'policy is essentially a stance which, once articulated, contributes to the context within which a succession of future decisions will be made'. Jenkins (1978) similarly stresses the notion of interrelated decisions concerned with the selection of goals and the adoption of a course of action. Smith suggests that 'the concept of policy denotes . . . deliberate choice of action or inaction, rather than the effects of interrelating forces'. He emphasizes 'inaction' and reminds us that 'attention should not focus exclusively on decisions which produce change, but must also be sensitive to those which resist change and are difficult to observe because they are not represented in the policy-making process by legislative enactment' (Smith, 1976, p. 13); see also Marsh and Rhodes (1992b).

Policies are thus not easy to define. It is doubtful whether much can be gained by trying to achieve any greater precision than that suggested in the definitions above. It is more fruitful to look, in a concrete way, at the relevance of policies for the activity of a minister and his or her department. On appointment to office, a new minister will take over responsibility for many departmental policies. The overwhelming majority of these will be just existing ways of doing things. A good many will be enshrined in Acts of Parliament, but these will be accompanied by organizational arrangements, systems of administration and working conventions which will also help to define policy. There is a distinction to be made between policy and arrangements made for its implementation. This will be explored further in chapter 4; here it must be stressed that these arrangements will, in many cases, have a quite fundamental impact on the character of the policy and may thus be deemed to be part of the policy.

It is this existence of policies that determines much everyday practice in a department, and therefore provides the most crucial group of constraints for a new minister. Existing policies keep most people occupied most of the time. Innovations depend on finding opportunities for staff to work on developing new policies. They may also depend on persuading people from within the department to work to change old policies, which have hitherto been regarded as quite satisfactory. Clearly, an innovating minister has to find ways to make a vast operational organization change its ways.

What is perhaps more significant is that a new minister will also find that his or her department is developing new policies. These are not necessarily merely the leftover business from a previous administration. Many of them will derive from weaknesses in existing policies that have been recognized within the department, and that administrators are striving to correct. Some, moreover, will have their roots in changes in the world on which existing policies operate, changes that are making those policies unsuccessful or irrelevant. This group of policies or 'would-be policies' is important. The new minister may find that his or her own, or the party's, policy aspirations mesh with the policy issues on which the department are working. In such circumstances, he or she may find it comparatively easy to become, or to be seen as, an innovator. However, he or she may have to face the fact that their own view of the department's policy needs are regarded as irrelevant to the main problem being tackled within it, or even that his or her own commitments lead in quite opposite directions to those being taken by those concerned with policy innovation in the department. Popular discussions of the success or failure of ministers are often carried out in terms of their personalities and their experience. Of course, it is often possible to distinguish 'strong' and 'weak' ministers; but it must not be forgotten that the comparatively temporary incumbent of the top position of a large organization may be just lucky or unlucky – in arriving when key advisers are likely to agree that exciting innovations are necessary or, conversely, in finding that the consolidation of existing policies, or the confronting of unpleasant realities, is more important than the policy changes he or she cherishes.

There are various kinds of policy initiatives. Some policies may be enacted by the passing of a law. Reform of regulatory law, for example, may have slight administrative implications. A second category of policies, with only indirect consequences for the minister's own department, are those whose enactment and implementation depend on another agency. Legislation giving powers, and even sometimes duties, to local government comes into this category. The Chronically Sick and Disabled Persons Act of 1970 is a classic example in this category. While it seems to involve the development of a national policy for disabled people, in practice, its dependence on local government makes it a gesture in which central government involvement is comparatively slight. This measure arose as the result of an initiative by a private member, Alf Morris. A later piece of legislation on this issue, the Disabled Persons Act 1986, seems to have similar characteristics. Individuals and voluntary organizations are likely to have to work hard to make local government implement it. Clearly, it is easier for a minister to accept this kind of legislation than to develop a policy that effectively changes the direction of a great deal of work going on *within* the department. In the above case, the policy making may be more 'symbolic' than real; ministers may hope to derive kudos without really enacting innovations.

On the other hand, once a minister seeks to enact policies that require the expenditure of 'new money', he or she becomes engaged in what is inevitably a more difficult political exercise. Formally, the approval of the Treasury is required, probably together with the support of the Cabinet in one of its priority-setting exercises, where the minister is involved in competition with colleagues who have alternative expenditure aspirations. What this implies for the minister's relationship with civil servants is altogether more complex. The specific expenditure commitment will be, by no means, the only one the department might undertake. Hence, there will be an intraorganizational battle about the case for that particular innovation. What the outside world sees as a minister promoting a particular project is probably the end of a long process in which different groups of civil servants within the department have argued about the case for that venture as opposed to other ventures. A minister who says 'I want to do X' will have to face civil servants who argue 'but we need money for Y, Z' and so on. The political negotiations between a minister and the Treasury ministers will be matched by much more elaborate negotiations between civil servants. A case that is comparatively weak when argued within the department will be faced with further problems in this tough forum, and a minister who successfully overrides objections within his or her own department may well lose in this wider battle. Students of government have, moreover, raised questions about the extent to which civil servants will fight effectively for their minister against the Treasury, in view of the prestige and power of the latter within the civil service as a whole (Heclo and Wildavsky, 1981).

In differentiating different kinds of policies, and in interpreting their implications for ministerial power, it must be recognized that some policies have implications for more than one department. A new approach to assistance with housing costs, for example, may have to be considered both by the Department of Social Security, with concern for social security policy, and the Department of the Environment, Transport and the Regions (DETR) with its responsibility for housing policy. In addition, local government is likely to be involved. This adds a form of complexity that greatly enhances the significance of negotiations between civil servants, and the related tendency for the maintenance of the *status quo*. Such policies place strains on the unity of the political group involved. Two key aspects of government emphasized in the Crossman diaries are the difficulties facing a minister with departmental responsibilities who tries to take an overall view of government policies as a whole, and the related tendency for ministers to take narrowly departmental views which sabotage interdepartmental co-operation.

This discussion has distinguished between policies that ministers can enact with relatively slight implications for their own departments and those that require elaborate departmental involvement. It has implied that, where ideological commitments are involved, a distinction may be made between relatively easy gestures and difficult administrative battles. Yet it may also be the case that some difficult aspects of 'bargaining politics' are involved where policy success depends on the responses of other organizations.

The Thatcher government found some of its ideas for tax and social security reform affected by the reservations of small business about new tasks for government. The power of the doctors in health policy provides related examples. In this case, the problem comes, if not exactly within the Secretary of State's own department, at least from within public agencies. Also important for the analysis of social policy is the interplay between central government and those other organs of government, particularly local government, who have a crucial role to play in the implementation of policy, but are also themselves in certain respects policy makers.

A new minister with an overall responsibility for the health and personal social services within the Department of Health, or for education, or for housing policy will find an 'established' relationship between the department and local government or the health service with certain key characteristics. There will be a body of enacted legislation, a pattern of grants from central government, a range of procedures relating to the sanctioning of new initiatives including the taking up of loans for new capital expenditure, perhaps a pattern of inspection or policy review, and a variety of policy expectations enshrined in circulars and related messages from the centre. In a few cases, the obligations of the local authorities will be quite clear. In a rather larger number of situations, the authorities will have quite explicit duties but will not have been given detailed guidance on how to carry them out. In yet other important cases, the local authorities will regard themselves as the key policy makers; the central requirements will have been specified in such general terms that the decisions that really dictate the quality of the service given to the public are made locally. Then there will be some situations in which central government has made it very clear that the policy initiative rests with local agencies, by *permitting* activities if they so wish. Finally, there will be a few situations in which local authorities have been almost entirely the innovators, in which they have sought to promote local acts through Parliament or in which they have interpreted general powers given to them in quite novel ways.

The new minister who wants to introduce changes into this pattern has a variety of options open, but each may involve complications wherever there is resistance to new ideas. New policies are expressed as much in ministerial statements, White Papers and circulars to the local authorities as in new statutes. In each case, the minister may be able to bolster a recommendation with indirect weapons: by control over loans and other powers to permit or limit activities, by co-operation or lack of it in situations in which joint central–local action is necessary. In the National Health Service (NHS), the control over funding also facilitates policy change from the centre.

The local authorities often fight hard to try to protect their independence. They may be unresponsive to ministerial suggestions, and they may make this opposition very clear through the local authority associations. The threat of non-co-operation from the local authorities may make the minister think again. The most publicized cases of such non-co-operation have occurred where some authorities have stood out against the minister on a highly political issue. The 1970s and 1980s saw some very public conflicts between central and local government. Now the centre has established such a dominance that these are less likely. Many issues are quietly negotiated in private discussions between the minister, or civil servants, and the local authority associations.

Although the local authorities are themselves, as has been suggested, policy makers, the force of influence for policy change is, however, not just one-way. Just as the new minister encounters groups of civil servants within the departments with policy concerns that conflict with his or her own, so too does he or she encounter local authorities keen to take new initiatives. They will be eager to protect their own autonomy, but may also seek to convince the minister that their local initiatives should be enshrined in national policy.

Hence, as sources of local initiatives, local government may be as important as central government. The example of comprehensive education is interesting. Before the 1964–70 Labour Government made it a central policy, a number of local authorities had already set up comprehensive schools. It is significant that, while in some areas, such as London, this development was motivated by a political commitment, in other places, for example rural Devon, it was educational administrators who had convinced councils, of a broadly Conservative persuasion, that the development of such schools was the most appropriate policy. It is equally interesting to note that the trend towards comprehensivization continued after the Thatcher government repealed the legislation which had been forcing the pace in the late 1970s.

In this section, the discussion has ranged over many of the influences on policy. Using the notion that is particularly associated with representative government, of a new minister with explicit policy commitments, attention has been given to the pressures that frustrate such commitments, or replace them by commitments derived from other sources. It has been stressed that there are strong forces in favour of the maintenance of existing policy, and that many new initiatives are, in fact, derived from concerns not so much to innovate as to correct the imperfections of existing policies.

Braybrooke and Lindblom (1963) drew attention to the extent to which the policy process is 'incremental'. That is, they were particularly concerned to attack that portrayal of the policy process which perceived it as, or able to become, a rational appraisal of all the alternative consequences of alternative policies followed by the choice of the best available. If incrementalism is perceived in these terms, there is little difficulty in understanding its applicability to social policy. As the historical chapter showed, the development of social policy has been very much a process of piling new initiatives on top of older policies, without ever clearing the ground to facilitate a fresh start. Then, as this piling-up process has proceeded, it has created new interests which future developments have to take into account. Since political values have often been at stake in conflicts over social policy, the very character of the ideological issues has precluded a cool appraisal of all the policy options.

Policy making is not a pure exercise in rational decision making. Nor is it simply the putting into practice of ideologies, or a quite incoherent process of bargaining and muddling through. Rather it is a mixture of all three, with perhaps the first least apparent and the third most in evidence.

Suggestions for further reading

Like chapter 2, this one has drawn on a vast literature, this time largely from the discipline of political science. Reference notes have largely been chosen to include some of the classic works that expounded particular theoretical viewpoints together with textbooks that most clearly interpret theories and issues for British audiences. These suggestions for further reading will be primarily in the latter category.

For those who need a basic account of political institutions, Jones et al. (1998) is recommended. Dunleavy (1997) offers a review of contemporary political issues. For more advanced accounts, written from a strong political science perspectives books by Dearlove and Saunders (1991) and Jordan and Richardson (1987) are worth consulting, the former offering a comparatively radical account of events, and the latter, a more conservative one. Smith (1993) and Marsh and Rhodes (1992b) explore the issues about 'policy networks' and 'policy communities'.

An account of the local government system is provided by Tony Byrne (1994). While it is not appropriate to recommend wide reading on the EU here, Gold's edited book, *The Social Dimension* (1993) is a good source on social policy.

Reference has been made in the text to Marsh and Rhodes' *Implementing Thatcherite Policies* (1992a); while its title suggests that it is an appropriate reading for chapter 4, its focus on the issues about the translation of ideology into polices make it relevant for the policy-making process as a whole. My book, *The Policy Process in the Modern State* (Hill, 1997a), explores many of the theoretical issues about the study of policy making.

Chapter 4

IMPLEMENTATION

Introduction

Why devote a chapter in a book on social policy to the study of policy implementation? What is the significance of this issue for our subject? There are several reasons why it is important. First, the discussion of policy making in the later part of chapter 3 suggested that many new initiatives stem from the recognition that older policies are failing to meet desired goals. This may be because these goals have changed, but it may equally be because the social world for which the original policies were designed has changed. This is an implementation problem. It may also be because there were weaknesses in the older policies, many of which became apparent once policies were implemented. In this sense, it is important to scrutinize the implementation process with some care.

Second, concern with the ineffectiveness of policies is now recognized as requiring the asking not only of questions about the character of policy but also about what is wrong with the implementation process and the organizations responsible for implementation. It may be that the policies are at fault, or it may be that corrective action is most appropriately applied to the implementing agencies. This is the central concern for what we may call the 'top-down' approach to the study of implementation, which asks: Why don't those who are expected to carry out policies do what is required of them?

Third, and finally, while it is true that the impact of all policies must be subjected to careful scrutiny, it is particularly important to give attention to what it feels like to be on the receiving end of social policy. This may be described as a concern with 'impact' rather than with 'implementation'. However, it is this concern that has led students of social policy to give increasing attention in recent years to the activities of that group of public servants who may be called 'street-level bureaucrats' (Lipsky, 1980), to ask questions about what actually happens in the exchanges between these people and the public.

Structures for Policy Implementation

This section provides a brief account of the main groups of people responsible for social policy implementation in the UK. An examination of the wide range of people involved, of the many different roles they play and of their varying involvement in or distance from the policy-making process will help to stress the importance of giving attention to implementation and to introduce the more theoretical discussion that is to follow. Since the organizational arrangements vary within the constituent countries of the UK, the comments in this section should be taken to apply only to England unless there is an observation to the contrary. However, in the cases of social security and employment there is a single system for Britain, and the system in Northern Ireland is in most respects a copy of that.

Social security benefits are calculated and paid to the public by a large number of civil servants based in regional and local offices throughout the country. These people now come under one of a number of public 'agencies', carrying out functions delegated to them by the Department of Social Security to whom they are ultimately answerable.

The Benefits Agency deals with payments of both contributory and means-tested benefits. The former are determined by a largely computerized central system. The calculation of means-tested benefits is also increasingly concentrated in a small number of offices, leaving the local offices in touch with the public to take in applications and to deal with queries. A minority of Benefits Agency staff, social fund officers, are concerned with the highly discretionary 'social fund', where the determinations are still made at the local level. There has been a separate agency which collects national insurance (NI) contributions but, at the time of writing, it is being integrated with the main tax collection body, the Inland Revenue.

A social security agency which has been the subject of considerable controversy is the Child Support Agency, set up to administer legislation enacted in 1991 to strengthen the system for securing contributions to child support from absent parents (mainly fathers). The Child Support Agency was set targets for sums to be collected which were not achievable with its resources in the face of widespread public resistance. Its first chief executive resigned in 1994, after considerable criticism, much of which might more properly have been directed, as a policy matter, to the secretary of state who appointed her.

There is only one other large group of people defined in Britain as civil servants that is concerned with the implementation of the social policies discussed in this book, and that is those involved in the employment services. These come under the Department for Education and Employment (DfEE), and are again organized into an agency (The Employment Service). This also services local Training and Enterprise Councils (TECs) whose membership is drawn from employers.

Otherwise field-level social policy implementation is the responsibility of National Health Service (NHS) and local authority officials, who, since they are not employees of the central government departments, are not regarded as civil servants. However, to relate to local implementation systems, a number of central government departments have regional offices. Examples relevant to social policy implementation are the Department of the Environment, Transport and the Regions (DETR) system of regional offices which handle many aspects of relationships with the local authorities, and the Department of Health's regional social services inspectors who advise and supervise the local authority social services departments.

The implementation of health policy in England and Wales is devolved in a complex way. At national level, there is a National Health Service Executive. This is staffed by civil servants from the Department of Health and may, in many respects, be regarded as an extension of that department with direct accountability to the Secretary of State. That Executive has a regional 'arm', which has replaced the former Regional Health Authorities. At the local level, there are Health Authorities combining responsibilities for the provision of all services at the local level including family practitioner services. Health Authorities are quasi-autonomous organizations with directors (executive and non-executive) appointed by the Secretary of State, but with their own employees.

The Health Authorities in England and Wales (their equivalents
are Health Boards in Scotland, answerable to the Secretary of State
for Scotland) commission most services from other organizations. As
far as primary health care services (general practice, dentistry, oph-
thalmic services) are concerned, there are contractual arrangements
between Health Authorities and relatively autonomous professional
providers.

As far as hospital services and most community health services are
concerned, the 'providers' are trusts set up under the terms of the
National Health Service and Community Care Act of 1990. These
trusts are not as autonomous as their names suggest. They have been
set up with Secretary of State approval and with directors appointed
by that minister. There are also some purchasing contracts between
Health Authorities and private providers, but these are of limited
importance for the system as a whole.

While recent developments in health administration have made
the managerial links in the chain, peopled largely by lay managers,
of increasing importance, health remains an area of social policy in
which professionals – particularly doctors – have extensive degrees
of autonomy. It is often difficult to make the distinction between
policy making and implementation with reference to a service operated by professionals. Day-to-day service provision decisions may
actually determine, or pre-empt, priorities. In this sense, they can be
described as policy decisions. The split between commissioning and
provision is seen as limiting the scope for this to happen. Observers
of health services are divided about the extent to which professional
power has really been curbed by this development.

Responsibility for the implementation of education policy is
divided between local authorities and a series of arrangements for
direct links between the central ministries (Education and Employment in England) and the schools and colleges.

As suggested in chapter 3, there has been a considerable amount
of conflict in recent years about the autonomy of local authorities as
'policy makers'. To some extent, the implementation issues in the
local authority education service concern the relationship between
the authorities and the schools. While the chain image is not entirely
appropriate, since varying responsibilities and degrees of autonomy
are involved, and individuals in the chain may be bypassed, it is
important to acknowledge that implementation may depend on a
series of links: local authority education committee, chief education
officer and his or her administrative staff, local authority inspectors
and advisers, school governing bodies, head teachers, departmental
heads within the schools, and class teachers. The examination of

policy implementation in the education service raises a number of interesting questions about local authority autonomy, the role of school management and the place of professional discretion. The 1986 Education Act has strengthened the powers of the governing bodies of local authority schools, laying down rules to determine their budgets and giving them autonomous responsibilities. It also enables schools to apply to the Secretary of State to become 'grant maintained schools', directly accountable to him or her rather than under local authority control. There is a special Funding Council for these schools. While the government has seen this as a form of decentralization, increasing the feasibility of parent power, the weakening of local political control through the provision of a centralized administrative framework can equally be seen as increasing centralization (Glennerster et al., 1991). The latter impression is further reinforced by the development of the national curriculum and by the power given to an independent inspectorate (Ofsted) accountable to central government.

Higher education in Britain has required special forms of organization designed to take into account the fact that many colleges serve more than the local authority area in which they are based. For the university sector, a special intermediary body has long existed. However, the 1986 Education Act replaced the comparatively independent University Grants Committee by more directly government controlled University Funding Councils. At the same time, it took the polytechnics out of local authority control, setting up a special funding council for them. Subsequently, the Further and Higher Education Act 1992 renamed the polytechnics universities and brought them under the same Funding Council as the older universities, and brought the remaining local authority colleges of higher and further education under ministerial control through another Funding Council.

The personal social services in Britain are usually the responsibility, inasmuch as they are under public rather than voluntary control, of social services departments (social work departments in Scotland) within local authorities. However, some local authorities have developed alternative ways of organizing these services, linking their management to that for other community services or housing. The increasing recognition of a need to co-ordinate social services with health services at the local level is also leading to innovations which link health services staff into care management arrangements. It may be the case that there will eventually be radical organizational changes that will move some or all personal social services into the health service (or it is conceivable but unlikely that the shift would be in the other direction). We will return to this theme in chapter 7.

Since 1993, local authorities are required to operate, in respect of their community care services but not their child care services, a purchaser/ provider system in which they seek the best value service. Providers may be sections within the local authority department required to operate with some degree of managerial and, particularly, accounting autonomy. They may also be voluntary or profit-making organizations; they may also be health service trusts. The government has been concerned that providers from outside the local authority shall have a good chance of competing for personal social services contracts. In the area of the provision of residential care, which was already heavily privatized, local authority direct provision is rapidly disappearing. Some authorities also contract out some parts of their child care services.

Many directors and senior staff in social services departments are professionally qualified social workers, but a relatively small proportion of the staff is engaged in social work. Other key workers include home helps, residential care staff and occupational therapists. Policy implementation is often influenced by the character of co-operation between these different occupational groups.

While for education there is a major department of state, the Department for Education and Employment (DfEE), which is responsible for national policy and the relationship between the centre and the local authorities, the personal social services is very much a small proportion of the policy concerns of the Department of Health. One implementation problem here is that the central department responsible for local government is the Department of the Environment, Transport and the Regions (DETR). This department, together with the Treasury, deals with the main financial and legal links with local government, but has no responsibility for education or social services policy. This exacerbates a tension, at the local level, between the demands of an integrated and corporate approach to local government and the separable service interests of these two large, heavy-spending, activities providing education and social services. The statement in the last paragraph only applies to England. Arrangements in Scotland and Wales may be better co-ordinated.

Local authority housing in Britain is the responsibility of the unitary or lower-tier local authorities. In Northern Ireland, protests about discrimination by local authorities led to the creation of a province-wide Housing Executive; and, in Scotland, there is an important nationwide 'public' housing association to supplement the work of the local authorities. There is also, in England and Wales, a Housing Corporation, responsible for the provision of funds for housing associations. A feature of recent government policy has been a quest for new ways of managing and financing housing. This is increasing the importance of bodies like the housing associations, financed by public money or by a combination of public and private money.

The implementation of housing policy is fragmented not only because of the mixture of kinds of housing authorities but also because this is an area of social policy in which many significant decisions are made by private agencies. Since there are three main types of housing tenure – renting from a local authority or housing association ('social housing'), owner-occupation, and renting from a private landlord – and the government intervenes, or has intervened, to try to influence the quality and cost of each type, policy implementation is often a very complex matter. In studying it, attention has to be given not only to the relationship between government and the local authorities, but also to government attempts to influence the behaviour of building societies, landlords and private house builders. There are also some other public–private interactions of some significance for housing policy. For example, there have been government efforts to influence the price of land and to curb land speculation, government interventions in the money market, and government manipulation of the costs and benefits of various statuses in the housing market by means of taxation and social security policy.

Support for the housing costs of low-income tenants comes from housing benefit. In Britain, policy responsibility for this lies with the Department of Social Security but local authorities administer the scheme. They receive direct reimbursement of most of their costs, except in respect of a few rather difficult issues (such as the treatment of some high rents) where they are given discretion at their own expense.

Finally, it is misleading to suggest that the relationships between government and the various private sectors are of no concern to the local housing authorities. The latter increasingly seek to influence housing opportunities of all kinds in their areas, and to give advice to those they do not house themselves. Moreover the housing authorities, of course, have a significant interest in land prices, and have planning responsibilities to relate housing activities to other kinds of developments in their areas. Housing policy implementation thus has many dimensions.

The Relationship between Policy and
its Implementation

In chapter 3, it was suggested that policies are complex phenomena which are difficult to define with any precision. This obviously makes for difficulties in distinguishing policy making and implementation, and for identifying implementation issues and problems. The distinction between policy making and implementation seems to need to rest on the identification of decision points at which a policy is deemed to be made and ready for implementation, like a commodity that is manufactured and ready for selling. The difficulty, however, with this analogy is that policy making and implementation merge. The policy-making process is like the design of a building for a specific occupant by an architect; the implementation process affects policy design quite early on and will continue to influence some details of it even after implementation has begun, just as modifications are made to buildings after occupancy. Or, to use another analogy, Glennerster has compared an implementation process he studied, the introduction of general practitioner (GP) fundholding, with a geographical exploration process filling in details of unknown territory from a known starting point like the head of a river (Glennerster et al., 1994, p. 30).

Policies have characteristics that must affect the nature of the implementation process. Many policies will be complex, setting out to achieve objectives x, x_1, x_2, ... under conditions y, y_1, y_2, ... These complexities may well influence the implementation process. Some policies will involve vague and ambiguous specifications of objectives and conditions. These will tend to become more specific during the implementation process.

Constraints are not merely contained within new policies themselves. While it is possible, in the abstract, to treat policies in isolation from other policies, in practice, any new policy will be adopted in a context in which there are already many other policies. Some of these other policies will supply precedents for the new policy, others will supply conditions, and some may be in conflict with it. The process of inaugurating new policies will continue after the adoption of the policy and will then further affect implementation.

A further general constraint that must not be overlooked is, of course, the fact that the scarcity and control of public finance frequently sets limits to policy development. In some cases, these limits are quite explicitly set by central government. Perhaps they arise because the government does not recognize the true costs of their new policies, or perhaps because of a resistance to making a particular policy effective which comes from within the central government machine. In other cases, the split between central government as a policy initiator and local government in the role of implementer produces a situation in which central intentions appear to be thwarted by local scarcities. In the area of community care, local authorities in the mid 1990s received some additional funds to enable them to meets costs which were previously met by central government from the social security budget. At the same time, they were subjected to centrally imposed limits on their capacity to raise local revenues. Many considered that their resources fell far short of their responsibilities under the new legislation. There is a certain political duplicity in legislation which expects local agencies to provide benefits that the centre makes them unlikely to be able to afford.

Policy goals are often specified, as has been pointed out, in general, or unclear, terms. We may identify a number of different reasons for this lack of clarity. First, it may be simply that policy makers are far from clear about what they really want. The lack of clarity may be so total that it is comparatively meaningless to seek to identify a policy or to study its implementation. Some of the 'policies' of this kind derive from political aspirations to demonstrate a popularly desirable commitment. It was suggested in chapter 3 that some so-called 'policies' may be merely symbolic. This is true of some aspects of the legislation which appears to give rights to disabled people.

Second, it is important to take account of the extent to which a lack of clarity about policy stems from a lack of potential consensus. Policies emerge that are not merely compromises, but also remain obscure on key points of implementation. Where this occurs, it is likely that there will be a lack of consensus among the implementers, too. Hence, wide variations in practice may emerge, together with a range of conflicts surrounding the implementation process. The 1977 Housing (Homeless Persons) Act provided examples of implementation problems – concerning the definition of priority groups, the extent of the duty to provide help and advice and the identification of the responsible authority – that would seem to have emerged from the conflict during the legislation process.

This source of implementation problems is closely related to another of some importance. Sometimes, the political ambivalence about a policy is reflected not so much in the policy itself as in the constraints that are set for the implementation process. The simplest form of constraint here is, of course, the failure to provide the means, in money and staff, to enable a policy to be implemented properly.

Another example of a quite deliberately imposed implementation problem is the adoption of administrative procedures that are explicitly designed to affect the impact of a policy. Thus Deacon has shown how 'the genuinely seeking work test' was manipulated in the 1920s to make it difficult for unemployed people to establish their claim to benefit (Deacon, 1976). He describes it as imposed as a quite explicit deterrent, without reference to the actual availability of work. The modern parallel with this is the conditions under which the 'job seekers allowance' is paid.

While acknowledging that many policies are made complex and ambiguous by the conflicts within the policy-making process, it is important to recognize that it is intrinsically difficult to specify some policy goals in terms that will render the implementation process quite clear and unambiguous. This is one important source of discretion for implementers. Jowell (1973) has drawn attention to examples where the concern of policy is with 'standards' that are not susceptible to precise factual definition. He argues that standards may be rendered more precise by 'criteria', facts that are to be taken into account, but that 'the feature of standards that distinguishes them from rules is their flexibility and susceptibility to change over time'. Questions about adequate levels of safety on the roads or in factories, or about purity in food, are of this kind. So are many of the issues about need in social policy; see the discussion on pages 174–6. Discretionary judgement is likely to be required by policy, alongside the more precise rules that it is possible to promulgate.

If a policy is a complex and ambiguous phenomenon, with aspects that go 'too far' for some people and 'not far enough' for others, it is important to acknowledge that the dissension that attends its 'birth' will continue to affect its implementation. It may therefore provide opportunities for some implementing agencies to develop new initiatives that were perhaps not originally envisaged. However, policies also often contain 'footholds' for those who are opposed to their general thrust, or who wish to divert them to serve their own ends. Bardach (1977) has developed an extensive analysis of the various 'implementation games' that may be played by those who perceive ways in which policies may be delayed, altered or deflected. While some policies contain few features that their opponents can interfere with – laying down, for example, a clear duty to provide a particular service or benefit – others, such as the Department of Health's commitment to the development of community care for mentally ill people, depend heavily on the commitments of implementers, and are relatively easily diverted in other directions or even rendered ineffective.

It is important to raise questions about the ways in which policies are expressed, and the evidence required to establish the extent of implementation. Policies may be conveyed to local implementers in a range of ways from, at one extreme, the explicit imposition of duties and responsibilities to, at the other end of the continuum, the loose granting of powers which may or may not be used. We can contrast, for example, the comparatively strict ways in which regulations under the 1986 Social Security Act instruct local authorities in the administration of housing benefit, with powers given (originally in the 1963 Children and Young Persons Act, now in the 1989 Children Act) to local authorities to make money payments, in exceptional circumstances to prevent children being taken into care, where no attempt has been made to prescribe how this should be done.

In this discussion, it has been difficult to draw the line between issues that are essentially *characteristics of policy* that affect implementation, and points that are really observations about the characteristics of either the relationships between central policy makers and local implementers or of the organization of the implementing agencies. While it is helpful to make a distinction between policies on the one hand and the implementation process on the other, this must raise problems at the margin. Policies are formulated with the implementation process in mind, and often it is more realistic to see policies as *products* of implementation rather than as 'top-down' inputs into the process.

The 'Centre–periphery' Relationship

It is possible, to some degree, to distinguish between those implementation issues that arise essentially from the 'distance' between what we may describe as 'centre' and 'periphery' and those that are facets of other aspects of relationships within complex organizations. The latter, which will be discussed in the section after this, are of course considerably complicated by the problem of 'distance', particularly when two or more separate organizations are involved.

In British public administration, the 'centre' will generally have been involved in the policy-making process, but where implementation is delegated to other organizations, the 'centre' generally maintains an interest in the implementation process. Equally, the 'periphery' has an interest in policy making and can be expected to contribute to a feedback process from implementation into policy elaboration. However, there are several different kinds of centre-periphery relationships that significantly influence the implementation process. The simplest model is clearly that in which the centre and the periphery belong to the same organization. The most complex occurs where policy implementation depends on co-operation between separate autonomous organizations and, particularly, where responsibility at the periphery is (a) delegated to several organizations with separate territories and (b) dependent on co-ordinated action between two or more local organizations. Health and personal social services collaboration tends to fall into this category.

Recognition that there may be issues to consider about 'levels' emphasizes the importance of this dimension for the study of implementation where separate organizations are involved. It is clearly important to identify not merely the issue of the relationship between different levels of elected government but also the existence of a variety of organizations whose relationships to either central or local government, or both, is often ambiguous: the health authorities, the funding councils for universities, the various quasi-autonomous inspectorates and so on.

The new 'agencies' set up to administer central services – like the Benefits Agency – seem, prima facie, to have clearer mandates. They are governed by framework agreements which seem to make their implementation responsibilities explicit. Yet the intrinsic difficulties in drawing a clear distinction between policy making and implementation mean that anything they may do to alter the service they provide to the public may raise political concerns (Ling, 1994). Furthermore, as the case of the Child Support Agency, discussed on page 87, has indicated, when something goes wrong, there will be argument about whether an agency has failed to fulfil its mandate or whether that mandate was flawed. In fact, as was the case in this example, their apparent separation enables their executive staff to be offered as sacrifices for ministerial mistakes.

In some situations, it is important to bear in mind the wide range of inter-agency linkages that may be necessary. Pressman and Wildavsky (1973) have made a tentative attempt to draw attention to what may loosely be described as the mathematics of implementation, the way in which the mere quantity of agreements necessary may, even when all parties are committed to a policy, undermine or delay effective action. Hence, it is necessary to give attention to these issues about centre–periphery relations:

1   A relationship will be likely to involve two or more organizations at either the 'centre' or the 'periphery' or both. Effective implementation may depend on co-operation, not merely between the

two 'levels' but also between different organizations at the same level.

2   A centre–periphery relationship may be mediated through one or more intermediaries or regional bodies.

3   Relationships between agencies will, in practice, involve a number of different issues, and the symmetry that it is possible to draw in an abstract model will not be the same for each issue.

In reality, any organization will be involved in a web of relationships, which vary in character and intensity according to the issue. Hence, local authorities have to deal with a number of different central government departments, but the extent to which this is the case varies from issue to issue. Equally, some activities require considerable co-operation between 'peripheral' agencies while others require very little. However, it may be misleading to lose sight of the overall pattern since the outcome of one relationship will affect responses to another. Relationships are ongoing; each will have a history that conditions reactions to any new issues. Equally, each organization will have developed its own sense of its task, mission and role in relation to others. These will affect its response to anything new.

One issue deserving of attention is the 'special' agency set up to concern itself with policy making and implementation in a specifically limited policy field. Three motives can perhaps be identified for the creation of special agencies in Britain, although there are, of course, dangers in taking ostensible motives as real ones: to create an effective separate and accountable 'management system', to reduce political 'interference', and to provide for the direct representation of special interests. In Britain today, the last of these is clearly the dominant motive, where organizations like the Training and Education Councils (TECs) have been designed to try to ensure that employers control the local implementation of training policy.

The removal of some aspects of the elaboration of policy from direct political influence, particularly when there are powerful special interests within the quasi-autonomous body, introduce complications that make it particularly difficult to distinguish policy making from implementation. These agencies may be seen alternatively as implementers that affect the character of policy or as independent creators of policy forever in a relationship of tension with the 'centre'. It is this tension that can then sometimes be seen as leading to central efforts to curb the independence of agencies whose initial freedom was provided by government.

The Organizational Characteristics of Implementing Agencies

In the study of agencies concerned with policy implementation, there are two significant bodies of literature that can be drawn on:

1   Studies by organizational sociologists that suggest the limitations for the formal control of subordinates by means of rules; see, for example, Crozier (1964) and Argyris (1960)
2   Behavioural studies of law enforcement, which have emphasized the significance of bargaining and discretion in the activities of the police and other rule enforcers (Hawkins, 1992; Baldwin, 1995)

Both suggest that there are finite limits for the prescription of subordinate behaviour. Detailed rule making is a difficult and time-consuming activity. If it requires close supervision and control, a point may be reached where such activities are self-defeating. If the subordinate has to be so elaborately controlled, the supervisor might just as well undertake the task. Conformity to rules relies primarily on compliance, on a willingness to work within a regulated framework which Etzioni (1961) has suggested rests either on acceptance of a 'utilitarian' financial bargain or on a 'normative' commitment. A key point about the former is that it also invokes in practice some measure of 'tolerance' on both sides; some concept of 'trust' (Fox, 1974). This applies limits to the things the supervisor can require the subordinate to do, and involves acceptance by the superior of limited deviations by the subordinate from the activities that are expected.

It is interesting to note how much manufacturing industry has moved away from what has been described as the 'Fordist' model of routine mass production work. Managerial gurus like Peters and Waterman (1982) extol the virtues of flexible forms of organization, engaging the commitments of employees and enabling them to innovate and cope with organizational change. This approach has been seen as relevant to government too (Pollitt, 1990; Butcher, 1995). Such thinking seems to have influenced such innovations as the creation of agencies and the split between commissioners (or purchasers) and provider. Yet public administration is likely to demand the performance of tasks, particularly the more mechanical ones, in a consistent way, in the interest of equity. There is a conflict here which has tended to limit the autonomy of agencies and to undermine efforts to establish quasi-markets.

The Citizens Charter movement in Britain, which John Major saw as his big contribution to the country, leads the public to expect speedy and consistent services from public bodies. The administration of means-tested benefits in Britain has evolved from one permeated by discretionary powers to (with the exception of the social fund) a largely formula-driven system. Yet its own internal auditing system has found massive error rates in many areas of benefit decision making. This may be largely because of staffing levels, so that pressure to process quickly large numbers of claims leads to mistakes. However, there must be concerns about the extent to which a group of officials – entering the job with increasingly high educational qualifications – are required to work in a traditional 'Fordist' manner.

In many other areas of social policy, there will be a strong element of discretion in many tasks. Earlier in this chapter three sources of discretion were identified:

1 Deliberate recognition of local autonomy
2 'Political' difficulties in resolving key policy dilemmas
3 'Logical' problems in prescribing 'standards'

This discussion has added two more:

4 The inherent limits to the regulation of tasks
5 The human motivation problems which follow from trying to regulate them

In practice, prescriptions for policy implementation convey discretionary powers to field-level staff for reasons that are combinations of these 'sources' of discretion.

An alternative way of looking at the phenomenon of discretion is to see the field official (including the teacher or social worker) as a 'street-level bureaucrat' (Lipsky, 1980). His or her job is characterized by inadequate resources for the task, by variable and often low public support for the role, and by ambiguous and often unrealizable expectations of performance. The official's concerns are with the actual impact of specific policies on their relationships with specific individuals; these may lead to a disregard of, or failure to understand, the wider policy issues that concern those 'higher-up' in the agency. The 'street-level' role is necessarily uncertain. A modicum of professional (or semi-professional, see pages 100–101) training defines the role as putting into practice a set of ideals inculcated in that training. Yet the 'street-level' bureaucrat is also the representative of a government agency, one that is itself subject to conflicting pressures. In day-to-day contact with clients and with the community at large, he or she becomes, to some degree, locked into the support of individuals and groups that may be antipathetic to the employing agency. In such a situation of role confusion and role strain, a person at the end of the line is not disposed to react to new policy initiatives from above as if he or she were a mere functionary. New policies are but factors in a whole web of demands that have to be managed; see Hudson (1997) for some British social policy examples of this.

There are 'two faces' to street level bureaucracy. It may be seen as the effective adaptation of policy to the needs of the public, or it may be seen as the manipulation of positions of power to distort policy towards stigmatization, discrimination and petty tyranny. Which it does will vary according to the policy at stake, and the values and commitments of the field workers, but this will also depend on the scope accorded by the organizational control system, for this phenomenon is not necessarily independent of 'biases' built into the policy delivery system. Workers may more easily manipulate their 'system' in favour of, or against, some clients in situations where their agency grants them licence to deploy such commitments.

Consideration of discretion and of the roles of 'street-level' bureaucrats' must also involve looking at the implications of professionalism for implementation. For Etzioni (1961), the compliance of professionals to their organizations rests on 'normative' commitments. Policy makers may be said to have to 'pay for' a lessening of day-to-day control problems with concessions in the implementation process; professionalism tends to involve participation in the determination of policy outcomes. In the NHS, for example, doctors have been able to secure a full involvement in policy making within the service as one of the prices for participation. Three interrelated points may be made about professionalism:

1 It may entail a level of expertise that makes lay scrutiny difficult.
2 Professionals may be, for whatever reason, accorded a legitimate autonomy.
3 Professionals may acquire amounts of power and influence that enable them to determine their own activities.

These sources of professional freedom clearly have a differential impact depending on (a) the profession involved, (b) the organizational setting in which professionals work, and (c) the policies that they are required to implement. The importance of the level of expertise for professional power has led some writers to make a distinction between professions and semi-professions (Etzioni, 1969) with doctors and lawyers in the former category but social workers and teachers in the latter.

The issues about expertise are, however, complex. They interact significantly with the phenomenon of 'determinacy' – the extent to which the professional response can be pre-programmed. The more complex professional tasks are a mixture of activities which can be routinized together with situations in which they must have the capacity to respond to the unexpected. For example, much doctoring is routine – either patients present clear symptoms for which there is a predictable response or there are logical testing procedures to go through to reach a diagnosis – but a good doctor has to be able to spot the exceptional condition and react to the unexpected response to treatment. Should health care systems therefore lay down 'protocols' and monitor to ensure that standard procedures are followed? Or should they allow doctors to exercise their discretion, so that they feel they are able to respond flexibly to the unexpected rather than 'Fordist' workers practising 'cookbook' medicine? This is, of course, not an either/or matter; the problem is how to find the ideal path between the extreme positions. It is one which is a very live one for the management of the NHS; at the time of writing, it is manifest in efforts to develop a system of 'clinical governance' to fuse professional freedom with public accountability.

The second point above, about autonomy, has been the subject of controversy about the impact on professional activities of organizational, and particularly public, employment. The conclusion would seem to be dictated by some of the considerations in the last paragraph. That is, in short, that 'it depends on the profession and on the organization'. On the third point, once again, a good deal depends on the nature of the policy involved.

In a large number of situations, it is expected that professional judgement will have a considerable influence on the implementation process. Clearly explicit in many policies is an expectation of this. This applies to many decisions made in face-to-face relationships between professionals and their clients. Many of the issues involved are increasingly the subject of controversy, involving arguments about 'rights' versus 'discretion'. Within these arguments, disputes occur about the significance of expertise and about the scope for effective limitation of discretionary power. The effective resolution would also impose many difficult policy questions – about moral rights to choose (for example, with reference to abortion) and the best way to allocate scarce resources (for example, with regard to kidney machines) – which are, at present, partly masked by professional discretion.

There are also some important questions here, which are difficult to resolve, about the way to link together professional autonomy in dealing with an individual relationship with a client, and a policy-based concern (or 'public concern') about the way in which professionals allocate their services as a whole. Professionals have been found to be reluctant to confront priority questions; they often prefer to deal with each patient or client as an individual in need without any reference to a collective ethic which requires some degree of priority ranking. A consequence of this may be lengthening waiting lists. The political response to these has been to treat waiting lists as crucial indices of services to the public (enshrined in charters and published). Yet doing this does not solve the problems of competing priorities. It either forces a watering down of the service offered to all or, more likely, forces attention to be given to certain issues (like the rapidity with which patients secure a certain routine operation) at the expense of others where the quantitative indices are not available or cannot be so easily interpreted. There are also problems about the extent to which indices of this kind can be manipulated by altering procedures and recording practices rather than by improving the overall service.

A further important complication for the study of implementation introduced by the involvement of professionals is that some activities depend on the co-operation of two or more professional groups. Studies of attempts to co-ordinate the efforts of various professions concerned to protect children from injury by their parents have suggested that particular professional practices, activities and terminology may intensify communication problems. There are also, clearly, some key problems about the boundaries between the various professional 'territories'.

It is important to recognize the extent to which professional involvement with policies implies not merely scope to influence implementation but also an impact on policy itself. Within the NHS, the direct influence of the doctors has been subjected to considerable attention by policy analysts (Harrison et al., 1990; Klein, 1995; Ham, 1999). What has perhaps been accorded less attention has been the ways in which policy and implementation have involved a feedback from implementation, as policies have been found inadequate to meet the demands of 'good professional practice'. Packman (1975) has examined the way in which social workers in children's departments gradually found that good child care practice required not merely the control and care powers possessed under the 1948 Children's Act but also preventive work to keep children out of 'care'. They innovated as far as possible under the 1948 Act but eventually secured a further Act, in 1963, which legitimated 'preventive' work. A similar concern to extend social work practice, to enable integrated work with whole families, led, as Hall (1976) has shown, to further legislation in 1970 integrating all local authority social work. The process Packman described is still going on. While the Children Act of 1989 was influenced by ideological concerns about the role of the state in relation to the rights and duties of parents, it must also be seen as a product of a continuing concern within social work about how to carry out 'preventive' child care work, fed by a succession of enquiries into child abuse scandals (involving under-reaction in some cases, and over-reaction in others).

The discussion in this section has developed the key points about inter-organizational practice by means of consideration of the rules–discretion dichotomy. To end it, three issues must be raised, which have been implicit rather than explicit within the argument so far:

1   The relevance of the lack of clarity within much policy
2   The significance of value conflict
3   The importance of rewards

The first of these points does not require much further emphasis at this stage. A lack of clarity in policy has already been identified as one explanation for discretion. Equally when the relationship, within a system of rules, between means and ends is far from evident, then implementers may be more disposed to break, and their supervisors may be disinclined to enforce, rules.

A lack of clarity about policy goals and conflict about values, as already suggested, often go hand in hand. Clark (1956) has written of 'precarious values'. Policies may have, among their goals, objectives that lack support in the community. Implementers will be aware of the controversial character of the policies and may not themselves subscribe to the goals entailed. The official required to secure the delivery of benefits or services to single-parent families, but also expected to prevent abuse, may well take the latter consideration more seriously than the former, letting his or her conception of morality and stereotypes about the social behaviour of the claimants influence behaviour.

However, the implications of Clark's analysis go further than this. Precarious values affect not merely day-to-day behaviour but also the way in which a whole organization may conceive its tasks. In particular, an organization that is given a task that is controversial and unpopular in many quarters, such as one charged to promote racial equality or to provide help to a stigmatized group such as vagrant alcoholics, may find that it is given an unclear mandate and is placed in a position in which it finds it difficult to acquire 'legitimacy' for its activities. This may lead to the adoption of 'safe' and uncontroversial activities, organizational security being put before any movement towards potentially disruptive goals.

The problem of 'precarious values' may also be related to the problem of rewards. We return here to Etzioni's (1961) analysis of the distinction between 'utilitarian' and 'normative' rewards. Clearly, the official placed in a position of 'role-strain' between the demands of superiors and the expectations of the public, or of 'value conflict' between his or her own ideals and those embodied in policy, will be influenced by rewards of both kinds. Benefits now and hopes of advancement may curb an inclination to deviate from the requirements of superiors; a feeling that some parts of the job are 'worth doing' may be even more influential. However, the substitution of 'unofficial' or 'official' goals may be a product of recognition that more 'worthwhile' activities may thereby be undertaken. The motivation of field-level staff is an important issue even within the most integrated organization. Where, however, 'control' is attenuated by a gap between those concerned with policy and the implementing agency, it may assume crucial significance.

It is appropriate to return here to the issue raised before about output statistics and performance indicators. In British social policy in the 1990s, the form that political hostility to traditional bureaucratic modes of delivery has taken is the creation of apparently separate organizations controlled either by means of output targets (perhaps specified in a contract as in health or by budgetary sanctions as in higher education or by performance-based employee reward systems as in social security and increasingly in education) or an expectation that the public will draw their own conclusions and withdraw support (as in schools) (Butcher, 1995). Some have spoken of these as quasi-market systems (Le Grand, 1990), but they are very far from real markets and are susceptible to political manipulation. The connection here with the points above about 'precarious values' and 'normative rewards' is that these controls encourage a utilitarian short-termism on the part of public officials.

The Social, Political and Economic Environment

Policies are evolved in a wider environment in which problems emerge that are deemed to require political solutions, and pressures occur for new political responses. Implementing agencies continuously interact with their environments. Much has already been said that has a bearing on the underlying significance of the environment.

Whatever the relationship between state and society, policies may be interpreted as responses to perceived social needs. Government is concerned with 'doing things to', 'taking things from' or 'providing things for' groups of people. Putting policies into practice involves interactions between the agencies of government and their environment. Those who do that are, of course, themselves a part of the social environment in which they operate.

However, in looking at social policy, we must also question whether the distinction between the policy system and its environment can be easily made. In chapter 1, it was established that it is misleading to see any simple equation between the activities of the social policy system and the enhancement of social welfare. Yet, just as the policy determinants of welfare are multiple, and sometimes unexpected, so individuals' welfare is influenced by phenomena that have nothing to do with the activity of the state. As pointed out, the determinants of an individual's welfare can be broadly classified as depending on their own capacity to care for themselves combined with (a) market activities and relationships, (b) the behaviour of 'significant others' as providers of 'informal care' among whom family members are likely to be the most important, and (c) the role played by the state. To study welfare requires attention to all 'determinants'. Changes in the way in which welfare is provided are particularly likely to involve shifts in the roles played by these 'determinants' and shifts in the relationships between them. In other words, the process of interaction between policy system and environment is a very active one, and those interactions occur across an ambiguous, shifting boundary. To give a concrete example, personal social services care is only one element in individual care systems in which family, neighbour and purchased care are likely also to play a part. A shift in the availability of, or character of, any one of these care ingredients is likely to have an impact on the others. Day-to-day policy implementation in the state provided sector involves the management, or indeed mismanagement, of its relationships to the other elements.

Accordingly analysts of social policy have conceived of the system as a 'mixed economy of welfare' (Webb, 1985). Furthermore, 'social divisions of welfare' have been identified, recognizing not merely that there are different sources of welfare for individuals, but also that individuals differ in the access they have to different welfare systems. Titmuss (1958), who originated the notion of 'social divisions of

welfare', identified, alongside mainstream 'public welfare' two forms
of welfare system:

1 'Fiscal welfare': the system of relief from taxation, of which the
   relief for pension contributions and for mortgage interest payments have been among the most important examples, though
   the latter is now being phased out
2 'Occupational welfare': the range of private fringe benefits available to some employees

Titmuss, together with others who developed his work, such as
Sinfield (1978) and Townsend (1979), argued that these other welfare
systems may provide large benefits additional to, or quite separate
from, the benefits provided by the more central institutions of the
welfare state. They may operate in a direction quite contrary to any
egalitarian tendencies in the mainstream policies. The 'social divisions' theme has been taken up in another way by some recent
feminist writers who have been concerned to show not merely that
many welfare provisions discriminate against women, but also that
services by females within the family and neighbourhood form crucial
separate welfare systems, enhanced in importance when other systems fail or are withdrawn (Rose, 1981; Land and Rose, 1985).
Bryson (1992) suggests that we may speak of 'men's welfare states'
and 'women's welfare states' as being very differently, and unequally,
constituted because of differences in access to benefits dependent on
economic status and dominant expectations of family roles.

These points have been emphasized in this chapter because the
implementation of many contemporary policy initiatives – privatization, the limitation of social expenditure, the extension of community
care – involve changing the balance between the various ingredients
in the 'mixed economy of welfare'. Where government withdraws or
reduces its direct contribution to welfare, it may still make an indirect
contribution if the social security system subsidizes private provision;
or it may have to acquire a new range of regulatory concerns about
the quality of private services; or it may face increased problems in
the other areas of concern, because of the new pressures placed on
individuals and families.

Relationships between the public and the organizations delivering
public policies may be studied with a view to ascertaining whether
implementation proceeds in terms of the even-handed justice that
Max Weber (1947) suggested is, or should be, characteristic of
bureaucratic administration. Clearly, questions about bias in the
behaviour of public officials, the mechanisms by which scarce benefits

or services are rationed, the roles played by 'gatekeepers' and the problems of securing effective 'take-up' of some benefits are issues of concern for the implementation of policies (Foster, 1983). In the study of these matters, many of the issues about the motivation of implementers – about 'role-strain', 'precarious values' and the exercise of discretion – concern the interaction between the nature of policy, the implementation system and the characteristics of the public. Policy delivery is not easily made an 'even-handed' process; class, gender and race differences influence access to professional services; some social security applicants are less well-informed and more easily deterred than others; and 'street-level bureaucrats' who may be regarded as highly responsive to local needs in a white neighbourhood may be seen very differently in a black one. Here the 'environment' affects the way the policy is received.

Conclusions

This chapter has portrayed the implementation process as a complex one, in many respects inextricably entwined with the policy-making process. It has suggested that, in the study of social policy, it is important to give attention to implementation problems that arise directly from the characteristics of policy, but to recognize also that there is a complicated interrelationship between these and a range of inter- and intra-organizational factors. Finally, all these complications interact with a complex environment.

An approach to the examination of social policy has been introduced here that has not been given much explicit attention in relation to the study of specific policies. One justification for this lengthy examination of policy implementation is that, while we all experience the effects of the implementation process, and many of us participate in various ways in it, very few of us are involved in policy making. Yet, it is this policy making, often particularly that which occurs at the highest level, that receives much more attention. It is hoped that, in considering the detailed discussions of particular areas of policy, contained in the next section of this book, readers will bear in mind the importance of the implementation process for the actual impact of social policies on the public.

| Suggestions for further reading |

Tony Butcher's *Delivering Welfare: The Governance of the Social Services in the 1990s* (1995) offers an excellent overview of the organizational arrangements for social policy delivery in Britain, with a strong emphasis on contemporary developments. I have contributed to further discussions of the theoretical issues raised in this chapter in chapters 6 to 9 of my book *The Policy Process in the Modern State* (Hill, 1997a), contributions to parts IV and V of my edited collection, *The Policy Process: A Reader* (1997b) are also relevant.

A large literature is emerging on the new approaches to the management of policy delivery, and its implications for professionalism. The following are recommended in addition to Butcher's book mentioned above: Clarke, Cochrane and McLaughlin's edited collection *Managing Social Policy* (1994), Hudson's *Making Sense of Markets in Health and Social Care* (1994), Rao's *Towards Welfare Pluralism* (1996) and Cutler and Waine's *Managing the Welfare State* (1997). A rather older book on professionalism, Paul Wilding's *Professional Power and Social Welfare* (1982), still raises the issues very effectively.

Chapter 5

SOCIAL SECURITY

Introduction

The term 'social security' is used here to cover all the British state systems of 'income support'. These fall into five categories:

1 Contributory benefits
2 Benefits that the state requires employers to provide
3 Non-contributory benefits which are not means-tested but are contingent on the individual being in some specific category (a child or disabled)
4 Means-tested benefits
5 Tax credits

The Department of Social Security is responsible for the main social security benefits, using a group of agencies. The main agency for the delivery of benefits, the Benefits Agency, operates through a network of local offices. There are centralized, or concentrated, computer systems for the main benefits. There are other agencies, including the Child Support Agency which collects contributions towards the maintenance of children in families dependent on 'income support' from absent parents. There is a Contributions Agency to deal with the collection of national insurance (NI) contributions, but this is being brought under the Inland Revenue. Housing benefit is administered by the unitary, or lower-tier, local authorities, under either housing or finance departments. The Department of Social Security lays down a strong rule structure for the whole system, including housing benefit. The only part of the system for which there now remains extensive local discretion is the social fund (see pages 116/117).

Contributory Benefits

The Beveridge plan for contributory benefits (Beveridge, 1942) envisaged that these should provide the main source of protection against old age, sickness, unemployment and widowhood. The legislation of the 1940s, picking up the main pieces from earlier contributory social security schemes, attempted to provide this coverage. The main contributory benefits date from that time, but the system of contributions, the nature of the benefits and the character of the alternative benefits available to back up the contributory system have all changed a great deal since then.

All employees, together with the self-employed, are required to pay NI contributions. These are calculated as a percentage of earnings, but there is a low-income threshold below which they are not required, and an income level above which additional income is not taken into account. Normally employees' contributions are deducted by employers, who also have to pay employers' NI contributions on a similar basis for those they employ. These NI contributions should not be confused with income tax deductions.

The original NI scheme set up in the 1940s specified a clear relationship between contributions and a wide range of benefit entitlements. This is no longer the case. The link between contributions and benefit entitlements has been steadily eroded since 1979, so that it is now more appropriate to see contributions as simply a tax. The limited remaining contributory benefit entitlements are discussed in this section.

There is a flat-rate pension to which insurance contributors are entitled on reaching the age of 60 if they are women, 65 if they are men (the female qualifying age will be increased to 65 by a phasing-in process in the period 2010–20). The actual pension rate depends on the length of working life.

Since 1977, there has also been in operation a state earnings-related pension scheme (SERPS) that provides earnings-related pensions. Individual employees must contribute either to this scheme or to officially approved private schemes. Those who 'contract out' will secure only the flat-rate retirement pension from the state (though benefits from a limited interim scheme which operated between 1961 and 1975 provide small additions for some people). The government is planning to replace this with a new 'state second pension' (see page 135).

The employee who is unable to work on account of sickness is initially dependent – since the enactment of the Social Security and Housing Benefits Act of 1982 – on his or her employer for support. The latter is, with some exceptions, required to provide sick pay at least at the minimum levels prescribed by Parliament for 28 weeks. This is, of course, not a contributory benefit *per se*, but this scheme replaced the former NI one, and small (formerly all) employers obtain some rebate of their NI contributions in respect of sick employees.

Those who become sick when not in employment may receive a contributory benefit if they were insurance contributors for a period until shortly before, a benefit that is now called 'short-term incapacity benefit'.

After the first six months of sickness, anyone still unfit for work moves on to a higher rate of short-term incapacity benefit, which continues until they have been sick for a year. During this period, the individual must establish that they are unfit to return to their normal occupation.

After a year of sickness, people may move on to long-term incapacity benefit. The rate of payment is a little higher than that of the short-term benefit. However, the qualification rules for this benefit are much stricter. Claimants must prove that they are unfit to do *any* work. There is what the government has described as an 'objective' test, carried out by a doctor employed by the Benefits Agency, which individuals have to pass to obtain this benefit.

This new, strict approach to long-term incapacity benefit was introduced in 1995. One consequence of continued high levels of unemployment is that people with disabilities, particularly if they are middle-aged, have increasing difficulties in returning to the workforce. Many countries (Kohli et al., 1991) have devised premature retirement schemes for this group. In Britain the official stance until 1995 was to tolerate – and indeed to some extent to encourage (so as to keep down the numbers counted as unemployed) – claims for invalidity benefit (the predecessor of incapacity benefit) as a 'pathway' to premature retirement (Kohli et al., 1991, pp. 234–5). The introduction of incapacity benefit put a stop to that, except for a group already over 58 and receiving invalidity benefit at the time of the introduction of the scheme.

However, the Labour government elected in 1997 have not been satisfied with these limitations on access to incapacity benefit. The Welfare Reform and Pensions Bill, under consideration by Parliament at the time of writing, proposes to tighten the tests of disability further, to require that a claimant has been an insurance contributor in one of the last two years before the claim and to take into account private pension payments when calculating entitlement. The last two elements are further erosions of contributory principles.

In addition to the benefits described above, there are special, in general more generous provisions, applying to those whose incapacity for work arises from an industrial accident or a pre-scribed industrial disease. These will not be considered in detail here.

There is a system of statutory maternity pay, like statutory sick pay, payable for eighteen weeks. This must be paid by employers if their employees have been with them over two years (it is proposed that this will be reduced to one year). This is backed up by a reduced state maternity allowance for women with recent work records who do not qualify for pay from their employers.

Another contributory benefit to which entitlement has been severely eroded is that for unemployed people. This is called 'job seeker's allowance'. As the name suggests, to qualify, a person has to make a clear undertaking, signing a 'job seeker's agreement', on the steps he or she will take to try to find work. However, contributory benefits for unemployed people have always been limited by strict previous contribution conditions, rules which disqualify a person if there is evidence that the unemployment may be to some extent their own fault, and a time limit to entitlement. With the introduction of the job seeker's allowance, the latter has been reduced to six months. After six months, or if the previous contributions and other tests are not satisfied, job seeker's allowance is means-tested (its rules being broadly those applying to income support; see page 115).

At a time of high unemployment, a contributory scheme for those out of work, which has initial qualifying rules and the exhaustion of entitlement after six months, leaves many in need of means-tested benefits. In particular, young new entrants to the labour force are unprotected by the contributory benefit scheme.

Widows have a contributory benefit entitlement, based on their deceased husband's contributions to widowed mother's allowances if they have children to support and to widow's pensions if they are over 45. For widow's benefits and for retirement pensions during the first five years after reaching pensionable age (60 for women, 65 for men), there are 'earnings rules' which may reduce the income received, on the basis of sliding scales which allow some, but not large amounts of, earnings. These rules apply only to earned income; in this sense, they differ from the fuller forms of means tests. Widows lose their benefits on remarriage; there is also a 'cohabitation rule' which may be invoked to treat widows living 'as wives' in the same way as 'married wives'.

In the Welfare Reform and Pensions Bill likely to be enacted in 1999, there will be provisions for a lump-sum bereavement payment of £2,000 where a spouse dies, available to males as well as females if the deceased fulfilled specified NI contribution conditions. Similarly, the Bill extends the widows benefit provisions outlined above to widowers, where the wife had satisfied NI contribution conditions.

There are no provisions for benefits to cover the ending of marriage other than through death, or to provide for the consequences of the ending of unmarried 'partnerships' due to any cause (including death). Benefits in these cases depend on means tests.

Benefits that the State Requires the Employer to Provide

The main benefits in this category were included in the discussion on page 111, since they evolved out of the earlier insurance benefits for sickness and maternity and need to be seen as still linked to related residual benefits: these are statutory sick pay and statutory maternity pay.

However, it is appropriate also to mention private pensions inasmuch as the option for employees to stay out of SERPS is only granted for approved private schemes. Furthermore, there are regulations, backed up by special agencies, to supervise all private pensions. The Welfare Reform and Pensions Bill provides for new kinds of private pension schemes, to be under much stricter state supervision, known as stakeholder pensions. It expects stakeholder pensions to be available to all but the very low paid, but will not compel people to contribute to them.

Non-contributory, Non-means-tested, Contingent Benefits

Child benefit is paid to the parents or guardians of all children under sixteen years of age and children between sixteen and eighteen who are still at school. The only qualifying condition is a residence one.

There are some non-contributory benefits available to long-term disabled people, which must not be confused with the industrial injury disablement provision or with incapacity benefit. These are the disability living allowance and attendance allowance. These are set at various rates depending on the need for care by another person. There is a range of detailed rules concerning these benefits which cannot be discussed in the space available here. There is also, at the time of writing, a general non-contributory benefit for severely disabled people, severe disablement allowance, but the Welfare Reform and Pensions Bill will replace it by an incapacity benefit entitlement for people who claim before they are twenty years old, in other words for those never able to enter the labour force.

There is also a benefit available for carers who are not gainfully employed and have to devote a substantial amount of time to the care of someone disabled. This is invalid care allowance, and its rate of pay is low.

Means-tested Benefits

A comparative study of social assistance schemes has described the UK as having an 'integrated safety net' built around 'income support' which is seen as 'a large, national, general programme providing an extensive safety net at or below social insurance levels' (Eardley et al., 1996, p. 169). This extensive means testing is necessitated by the various restrictions on the availability of contributory benefits described above. It also arises because the levels of some of the contributory benefits (flat-rate pensions, short-term incapacity benefit and job seeker's allowance) are such that claimants will often qualify for further means-tested support as well, at least in respect of housing costs.

In addition, many people in work earn insufficient for their needs, and have to apply for means-tested family and housing benefits to supplement their incomes.

The main means-tested benefit is called 'income support'. Its means test is based on a simple personal allowance structure, enhanced in some cases by 'premiums'. The specific personal allowance rates are for a couple, a single person over 25, a person between 18 and 24, and there are three age-related rates for children. Then, there are different premiums for families, lone parents, pensioners under 80, pensioners over 80, disabled people, and seriously disabled people. The idea throughout is that the determination of the appropriate overall entitlement for a household should be a simple, predictable process. Additions for special needs have been abolished. Rules determine how any income should be taken into account. People in full-time work (defined as doing sixteen or more hours in employment per week) are disqualified from receiving income support, but part-time workers may obtain it. To deal with this, an earnings rule is used, based on net income, which involves disregarding a small amount and then deducting the rest from any entitlement. Similar 'disregards' are used for some other kinds of income, but state benefits are taken into account in full. There are special rules dealing with savings, disregarding small amounts, then applying a sliding scale, reducing benefits up to an upper limit at which they disqualify a person from benefit entirely.

The new Labour government has began to describe its means-tested support for pensioners as a 'minimum income guarantee'. It claims to be setting up a system for streamlining pension and income support administration and overcoming the stigma people associate with the latter (Department of Social Security, 1998d, para. 21). It remains to be seen what this means in practice; so far, it amounts to little more than the extension of the size of the pensioners' premiums. Certainly, the minimum income guarantee still involves means testing. However, the government also says 'we are seeking views on cost-effective ways of changing the detailed rules on the treatment of income and capital, so as to reward savings (para 22).

Alongside the income support scheme there have been, since the 1970s, means-tested benefits available to low-paid workers doing over sixteen hours a week who have child dependants. First, there was 'family income support'; in 1988, it was replaced by 'family credit'. With effect from October 1999, the latter has been replaced by 'working families tax credit' supplemented by 'childcare tax credit' covering 70 per cent of child care costs arising because of employment.

The housing benefit scheme has been designed to be compatible with income support. The income support rules are used in the calculation of benefit so that anyone with a rent to pay who is at, or below, income support income level may receive the full housing benefit entitlement. Housing benefit provides support for rent; it does not provide support for house buying. However, owner-occupiers on income support may receive some help towards mortgage interest payments.

The housing benefit scheme is, in effect, extended to local taxation. Low-income council tax payers may apply for a reduction in their payments (calculated in a similar way to housing benefit).

The housing benefit maximum is generally the full rent (though there are various rent restrictions rules – applied to single persons under 25 and to accommodation deemed to be either too large or too expensive) minus contributions from other adults (apart from the claimant's 'spouse'). There are some complicated rules dealing with all these qualifications. The maximum is payable to those whose incomes are at, or below, the income support qualifying level. Similarly, for those with incomes at, or below, income support level and no adult non-dependants, the council tax benefit will provide for the remission of the whole tax liability. Where incomes are above income support level, benefit tapers off proportionately, at the rate of 65 per cent for housing benefit and 20 per cent for council tax benefit.

Chapter 10 shows how housing benefit has become the main approach to the provision of housing subsidies to low-income tenants. As a system run by local authorities on behalf of the Department of Social Security, it is not always well co-ordinated with the rest of the benefits system. It is administratively costly. It is also rather vulnerable to fraud, particularly in the private rented sector where there can be collusion between landlord and tenant to try to maximize benefit. The government is seeking ways to simplify the system. These may well involve the introduction of formulae which extend the tendency to offer less than full support to rent payments.

Under the supplementary benefit scheme operative until 1988, there were provisions enabling single payments to be made to help people with exceptional expenditures – removal costs, furnishing, house repairs and so forth. An elaborate body of rules dealt with these entitlements. The 1986 Act swept away these single payment entitlements but, in their place, set up the social fund, administered by a specially trained group of Benefits Agency officers. Under the fund there are two kinds of grants available as of right to people on income support or family credit: a lump sum maternity needs payment and a funeral needs payment (the amount of which depends on funeral costs). There is also provision for grants to be made from the social fund to assist with the promotion of community care. These may be available when someone needs help in establishing themselves in the community after a period of institutional care, to assist with some travelling expenses to visit relatives in hospitals and other institutions, and to improve the living conditions of defined 'vulnerable groups' in the community. Elaborate guidance is provided to social fund officers to help them to determine needs of this kind. They are expected to liaise closely about such matters with social services and health services staff, and to take into account powers these other departments may have to provide assistance in cash or kind. Apart from the grants, outlined above, all other help from the social fund is by way of loans, normally repayable by weekly deductions from benefits. Again, officers have been given elaborate instructions on the circumstances in which they may provide loans. The social fund, excluding the two items of benefit as of right, is 'cash limited'. Within this budget, 30 per cent is available for community care grants and 70 per cent for loans. This means that local offices have annual budgets, and are expected to relate a set of rules about priorities to the total sum available. Claimants for help from the social fund, other than claimants for maternity and funeral payments, have no right of appeal to an independent body against decisions, though there is an elaborate provision for internal 'review'.

This description of the structure for the main means-tested benefits does not exhaust the list of benefits. There is a benefit known as 'disability working allowance' for seriously disabled people who are able to work. This has its own means test. The government proposes to replace it by a 'tax credit'.

One quite important means-tested benefit administered by local authorities, entitlement to free school meals, had its availability restricted under the 1986 social security changes. Free school meals are now available only to children whose parents are on income support.

Other means-tested benefits include grants to students in higher education, relief from payment of National Health Service charges, and legal aid. Local authority social services departments also use means tests to determine charges for residential care and domiciliary services (see chapter 7).

Tax Credits

In the discussion of mean-tested benefits, reference has been made to tax credits, which the government is in the process of introducing. In many respects, a tax credit is no more than a means-tested benefit administered through the tax system. What is involved is a maximum rate, payable to those with very low incomes which tapers off as income rises until they reach the point at which they are taxed instead.

Such benefits are thus different from tax allowances, which reduce tax liability and thus only benefit those with incomes high enough to pay tax. There is, of course, a sense in which these are social security benefits too, even though they do nothing for the incomes of the poorest. Classical essays by Titmuss (1958) and Sinfield (1978) drew attention to the 'social divisions of welfare' in which tax allowances feature among the 'welfare benefits' available to the better off. However, they do not feature in official definitions of social security.

Tax credits, on the other hand, represent a new element in the government's battery of social security measures. Their emergence – in the forms described in the last section as tax credits for working families, for child care costs of workers and for disabled workers – is particularly linked to the Blair government's emphasis on labour market participation, using them to subsidize the wages of poorly paid workers. In theory, they need not be confined to those actually participating in the labour market. In proposals for negative income tax (see page 129) tax credits feature as benefits that could be available to low-income people outside the labour force. In practice there would be difficulties in developing them in this way, without radically extending the need for tax returns and developing mechanisms for linking the tax and benefits systems. It may be that this is the way the system will now evolve. Certainly, the legislation which brings the collection of social security contributions within the remit of the tax authority, the Inland Revenue, is a move in that direction.

Statistics on the Benefit System

This section contains tables giving a general idea of the cost, size and scope of the social security system. Table 5.1 sets out expenditure on the various kinds of recipient group. These are, of course, rough classifications developed by the Department of Social Security involving a combination of kinds of people and types of benefits. For example, many sick or unemployed people also have dependent children – child benefits going to them are classified as family benefits.

Data is included for a year in the early 1980s (recalculated at the price levels applying in 1997–8) to give some idea of the way in which the cost of the system has grown. This forms an important background for the discussion to come later about policy options. The figures show a quite remarkable growth in expenditure. It is

Table 5.1 Social security expenditure in Britain by recipient group (£billions at 1997–8 prices)

	1981–2	1997–8	1997–8 as % of 1981–2
Elderly people	29.7	42.8	144
Sick and disabled people	7.7	24.0	311
Short-term	1.5	1.2	80
Long-term	6.2	22.9	369
Families	10.1	18.6	171
Headed by single parents	2.2	9.9	450
Unemployed people	7.8	6.3	80
TOTAL	57.2	93.7	164

Source: Figures calculated from table 6.22, p. 116 in Office of National Statistics (1999b)

important to bear in mind that this growth occurred despite the fact that the Conservative governments of the 1980s and 1990s adopted strenuous efforts to prevent it. It is also important to recognize that, for any Chancellor of the Exchequer who wants to cut taxes, or even avoid raising them, curbing the social security budget will be a primary concern.

There are various explanations for the growth of social security expenditure. Since these figures were calculated at 1997–98 price levels, inflation-linked benefit increases should not be among them. The ageing of the population has had an important influence on the costs of benefits for the elderly and, to some extent, on benefits for disabled people. There have also been efforts to enhance some of the benefits available to disabled people. The bill for family benefits will have been influenced by three factors – increasing numbers claiming in-work benefits because of low wages, the inclusion of most housing support as housing benefit rather than as subsidy for houses (see discussion in chapter 10 on page 230) and the increase in single-parent families. It will be noted that the bill for support for the unemployed has not increased in real terms, but high rates of unemployment (particularly among people near the end of their working lives) will have had an impact on levels of applications for sickness benefits (this issue will be explored further later).

The figures in table 5.1 make no distinctions between contributory benefits and non-contributory benefits. In practice, there are only two large contributory elements – retirement pensions and invalidity benefits. Only about 13 per cent of recipients of job seeker's allowance are receiving contribution-based benefit (Department of Social Security, 1998c, table 2.2. p. 24)

Table 5.2 Recipients of benefits for elderly people in Britain by benefit type 1996–7 (thousands)

Retirement pension only	8,445	(83%)
Retirement pension and income support	1,394	(14%)
Income support only	340	(3%)

Source: Office of National Statistics (1999b), table 8.21, p. 146.

Table 5.3 Recipients of benefits for sick and disabled people by benefit type 1996–7 (thousands)

Long term	
Incapacity benefit (contributory)*	1,996
The above supplemented by income support	366
Income Support only	498
Short term	
Incapacity benefit (contributory)	117
The above supplemented by income support	48
Income support only	174
Disability living allowance (including attendance allowance)	3020

* Will also include some recipients of the non-contributory severe disablement allowance
Source: Office of National Statistics (1999b), table 8.17, p. 144.

Tables 5.2 and 5.3 set out some of the divisions between contributory and non-contributory benefits in the support of elderly and sick or disabled people, though, in the latter case, there are complex overlaps between benefits. Moreover, as pointed out above, in both cases many recipients will be entitled to means-tested housing benefits.

The Distinctive Characteristics of the British System of Social Security

The British NI scheme today bears little resemblance to commercial insurance. There is no 'funding' and investing of contributions. Annual government income from NI contributions exceeds expenditure on contributory benefits, and the separate government contribution to the fund promised in the original legislation is no longer made. Incapacity benefit continues for as long as the claimant is deemed to be unfit for work, assuming an initial fulfilment of the contribution conditions but, as shown above, even access to that is limited (with a kind of means test being applied to applicants with private pensions after the 1999 Bill is enacted). It is impossible to relate flat-rate pensions to contributions. The rate of inflation of recent years has destroyed any correspondence between contributions and payments in terms of the face value of the money involved, and no inflation-proofing assumptions were built into the original scheme. Inflation-linked upratings of insurance benefits have occurred. The considerations which have governed these are discussed in the next section.

When SERPS was set up in 1977, some consideration was given to the future relationship between amounts to be paid out to qualifiers and amounts to be contributed by participants in the scheme while in work. Concern about the relationship between these groups in the early years of the next century, when the number of SERPS beneficiaries will increase rapidly but that of SERPS contributors seems likely to be comparatively low, was seen by the Thatcher government as a justification for reducing the benefits offered. This change, together with measures to increase the extent of contracting out of SERPS into private schemes, was included in the 1986 Social Security Act. The inefficiency of SERPS for the prevention of poverty in old age is one of the central issues for contemporary pension reform (see pages 133–5).

The job seeker's allowance scheme maintains a limited insurance principle, but, as noted above, few of the unemployed receive contribution-based job seeker's allowance. The rest only receive means-tested allowance, either because they fail to meet the initial contribution conditions, or because their entitlements under the contributory rules are inadequate or because they have been unemployed over six months.

The presence in the British system of a safety net group of means-tested benefits to back up the contributory scheme is by no means peculiar to this country. Such assistance schemes are widespread and, in many countries, they remain under local control, and more closely resemble the British scheme's predecessor, the-poor law. What is perhaps peculiar to the British scene is the complex overlap between the two systems. In Britain, the contributory scheme has to be supplemented in a large number of ways.

For those who, like myself, have deplored the erosion of national insurance, the case for a reversal of the shift towards means testing is increasingly difficult to argue. The abandonment of the limitations on the availability of contributory benefits for unemployed and incapacitated people and some relatively slight increases in contributory benefit rates would markedly reduce dependence on means-tested benefits. Yet these changes would be costly to the Exchequer. Moreover, the main effect of increasing the availability of unemployment benefit would be to shift the support of a large group of people from a means-tested to a contributory benefit with little change to their income, while a relatively small number of people with other sources of income (those with private pensions who retired early) made actual income gains. Similarly, an increase in contributory benefits relative to income support would produce income gains for a group not among the least poor (not on income support), while merely altering the source of help for the very poor (who would then accuse governments of giving with one hand and taking away with the other). A later section looks at the various options for improvement of the social security system, relating them to the Blair government's pledge to be 'the party of welfare reform'; see pages 131–6.

Levels of Benefits

Clearly, it is important in assessing a system of social security to look not merely at the structure of the system but also at the level of benefits provided by it. There are examples, for instance, within the British system that look most impressive until one scrutinizes the levels of benefit available. It would be pointless, in discussing the main social security benefits, to provide specific figures, which would be dated by the time many read this section. Instead, some of the general issues about the setting of benefit levels will be outlined.

Reference has already been made to the relationship between contributory benefit levels and income support levels. Hence, a great deal of debate about poverty in Britain is concerned not about the contributory benefits as such, but about the means-tested benefit levels and about the people and families whose incomes fall below those levels. There are three ways to try to assess the adequacy of these 'poverty levels': in relation to absolute concepts of need, in relation to other incomes, and over time in relation to the movement of prices and other incomes. In the early years of national assistance, studies which attempted to relate poverty to an absolute standard, based on the cost of providing a basic minimum of necessities, were still regarded as providing a sound basis for the fixing of benefit levels. More recently, this approach has been discredited. It has been pointed out, notably by Townsend (1979), that poverty is a meaningful concept only when individual standards of living are related to those widely taken for granted in a society. The British bare minimum could certainly equate with a good absolute standard of living for poor people in the less developed countries of the world. At the same time, British views about what is necessary for an adequate way of life change over time. These changes are related to developments in living standards within the nation as a whole. When the national assistance scales – which today, much updated for inflation, form the basis for the income support scales – were first set, in 1948, television was not even available, and few households had refrigerators, washing machines or central heating systems. If a definition of the poverty level is to take into account these considerations, the key questions are, for example: to what extent should those on the official poverty line have incomes that make it difficult for them to share the way of life of the majority of the people? Or how large should the gap be between the incomes of those on the poverty line and average incomes? Or even, what should the relationship be between the lowest incomes in our society, most of which are provided by the social security system, and the highest incomes? In other words, the crucial questions are about relationships between the official minimum level and other incomes.

These issues were examined by Peter Townsend in a large study of poverty. He persuasively made a case for regarding large numbers of British people, including both people dependent on social security and many on low wages, as living in poverty (Townsend, 1979). More recent studies (Mack and Lansley, 1985; Gordon and Pantazis, 1997) lend support to Townsend's argument. They demonstrate the extent to which low-income people lack things which, according to public opinion surveys, are regarded as necessities.

A variant on this theme of considerable importance in contemporary political debate concerns the relationship between social security incomes and average earned incomes over time. After all, the real political questions are not so much about the setting of levels in the abstract as about the need for, or the amount of, benefit increases. Pressure groups regularly draw politicians' attention to the ways in which, over a period of time, those whom they represent are losing ground. Two important alternative kinds of yardsticks are used for these judgements: indices of earnings and indices of prices. The plural form is used in both instances since there have been extensive arguments about the best ways of calculating these. In particular, it has been argued that a price index for the poor should be rather different from a more general one, since the poor spend their incomes in rather different ways.

Before 1973, there was no statutory requirement for government to take specific notice of wages or price movements in determining benefit levels. *Ad hoc* political judgements governed up-rating decisions. However, there was a tendency, over time, for the relationship between short-term benefit rates and wage rates to remain roughly the same (Barr, 1981).

In the Social Security Act of 1973, the Conservatives provided a statutory link between benefits and prices. In 1975, an amendment to the Social Security Act committed the Labour Government to uprating long-term benefits in line with prices or earnings, whichever was greater, and most short-term benefits in line with prices. Heavy price inflation in the late 1970s did produce some relative gains to social security recipients. In 1979, the Conservatives amended the statutory requirement so that long-term benefits were to be linked only to prices. Also, short-term benefits might be increased by up to 5 per cent less than the inflation rate, These rules relate only to the contributory benefits but, in most cases, means-tested benefit rates have been up-rated on a similar basis. The changes after 1979 led to a serious fall in the value of all benefits relative to average wages. The new government shows little general inclination to rectify this position, except in respect of improvements it is making to child benefit and to the application of means tests for benefits for the elderly.

The relationship between social security incomes and low wages is clearly important. Several studies of poverty have related incomes to the level provided by the main means-tested scheme. Apart from drawing attention to numbers falling below it because of a failure to claim benefits, they have shown that there is a significant group who fall below that standard because of low wages. There are alternatives way of responding to it. One is to concentrate on raising wage levels. The introduction by the Blair government of a minimum wage is a modest move in this direction. It is discussed further in chapter 9. Another is to argue not that something must be done to augment the earnings of the low-wage earner, but that means-tested benefit levels should be kept below the lowest wage levels. This view is linked with a concern to lower wage costs, expressed by those who see the only way forward for the British economy to be for enterprises to have wage costs comparable to those of very much poorer countries. However, the main response has been to develop family benefits and housing benefits, available to low-income earners, designed to tackle this problem. The universal child benefit significantly contributes to supporting low-income families, along with all other families with children. The other key policies all involve means testing in some form, with now a strong shift towards the tax credit approach to the issue.

It has been argued that few of the unemployed are in fact deterred from obtaining work by benefit payments being above the levels they can obtain as earners. However, there is undoubtedly a relatively small gap between the benefits paid to some families, particularly large families, and the wages paid for low-skilled work. The deterrent effect of this will depend first on the actual costs of going to work, second on individual views of the psychological costs and benefits of work, and third on the benefits still obtainable when in work.

It is difficult to estimate the actual extent of deterrence at a time when jobs are scarce. However, there is a widespread public belief that this deterrent effect actually contributes to our high unemployment rates. Politicians share, or are sensitive to, this belief. It accordingly influences their attitudes to increases in the short-term benefits. However, the government sees the provision of in-work benefits to parents with dependent children whose net incomes are at, or below, the income support level, as dealing with this 'unemployment trap' problem. In practice, administrative problems associated with the shift from out-of-work benefits to in-work benefits complicate the situation for those actually trying to make the transition. That has an impact on take-up, an issue to which we will return; see pages 129–31.

As well as a concern about the relationship between benefits and other incomes, there is also a concern about relativities within the benefit system. The income support scheme rules make assumptions about the extent to which a couple may live more cheaply than a single person, about the extra needs of elderly and disabled people, about the different costs of children at various ages, and about the lower needs of single adults under 25. Some of these judgements are clearly controversial. In particular, the low-income support rate for single under 25s, and the particularly harsh treatment of sixteen- to eighteen-year-olds who have left school, seem to be related to an assumption that such people can live with their parents, and not form separate households. The assumptions about the costs of children made by the rules have also been challenged as unrealistic regarding the costs of teenage children. It seems fair to suggest that considerations of the evidence on actual costs have been mixed, in the determination of some of these rules, with views about who are the most deserving among the poor.

Social Security Assumptions about Family Life and Women's Roles

The assumptions about family life incorporated in the poor-law involved a household means test whereby all a household's needs were taken into account and also its resources, so that adult children of a needy couple were expected to contribute to their maintenance. The contributory benefits developed in 1911 treated the insured claimant as the sole beneficiary, providing flat-rate payments at the same level, regardless of his or her family commitments. However, in the 1920s, the principle of additions to benefits, taking into account the needs of wives and children, was introduced. The improved contributory scheme developed in the 1940s carried forward this principle, while means-tested assistance shifted from a household means test to a family one. Broadly, then, British social security policies have been developed on the assumption that the typical claimant is a married man with a non-working wife and dependent children. That is not, of course, to say that the system cannot cope with claims from single people, but that it has had difficulty in coming to terms with both female employment and multi-person families constituted other than on the basis of legal marriage.

Until the 1970s, married women were required to pay lower contributions and to receive lower benefits than men. There was additionally an arrangement, now largely phased out, under which they could contract out of all of the contributory scheme except the industrial injuries part. While this anomaly is being eliminated, others remain. Married women cannot claim contributory benefit increases in respect of dependent husbands and children. The continuation of provisions for non-employed wives to be treated as 'dependants' for whom husbands can claim additions to benefits implies that the return which an employed woman receives on her contributions may, in some cases, be worth only the difference between the full pension or benefit and the addition for a non-working wife. In other words, there are difficulties in securing a fair balance in a scheme that tries, on the one hand, to make provision for dependent wives and children and, on the other, to enable the married woman to be a contributor and claimant in her own right.

The position with regard to means-tested benefits is even more complicated when men and women live together, and perhaps have children, but are not married. A family means test requires judgements to be made about whether a family situation exists. Generally, this is straightforward; claimants agree with official interpretations of their situations. Indeed, it is to the advantage of a male claimant living with a non-employed 'wife' and children (even if they are not his) to claim them as his family. However, difficulties arise when claimants, usually female, wish to be treated as independent, but find that the Benefits Agency regards them as the 'wives' of male friends. The Department of Social Security has tried to develop a definition of 'living together as man and wife' which distinguishes stable relationships from more casual ones, but difficulties and disagreements still occur. It is only heterosexual relationships that are treated in this way; in all other cases, claimants' needs are assessed separately. The issue here, which, as was pointed out on page 113, also applies to widow's benefits, arises from the family-based approach to benefits. While it would be possible to treat unmarried 'couples' differently from married ones, the only fair way to avoid problems of this kind is to cease to make assumptions about family patterns of support, and instead have a structure of *individual* entitlements (Dale and Foster, 1986, ch. 6).

A related issue concerns the treatment of single-parent families, most of which are, of course, headed by women. The British treatment of this group has been relatively generous, by comparison with other countries. Income support has been available. Mothers have not been required to become labour market participants until their children reach sixteen years of age. Absent fathers have been expected to make contributions, though the system has found it difficult to secure these because of the extent to which the fathers are low-income men with commitments to new families.

Charles Murray's (1984) tirade against the single-headed household in the USA was taken up in Britain. Politicians began to attribute the growth in single parenthood to the availability of benefits and housing. This has stimulated a debate, reaching beyond the ranks of the extreme Right, about (a) work opportunities for single parents and (b) contributions from absent parents. Attention to the first issue involves encouraging single parents without children under five to seek employment, and it may be that this will become compulsory. Efforts to improve the in-work benefits available to low-waged parents – see the comments on page 118 about the new tax credits – offers a more positive contribution to this strategy.

The Major government decided to tackle the issue of contributions from absent parents by means of a comprehensive, formula-driven scheme to replace both the assessments made as part of the administration of the existing means-tested benefits and the assessments made by the courts in determining maintenance on the breakdown of a relationship. It enacted the Child Support Act in 1991, setting up an agency to administer it. That legislation ran into severe implementation problems. There were four main objections to the new legislation:

1   That it was retrospective in effect – agreements, including court settlements, made in the past were overturned (a particular

problem here was the overturning of agreements in which the absent parent has relinquished an interest in a house in return for a lower maintenance expectation)

2 That where the absent parent had obligations to a second family, these were given relatively low weight in the calculations

3 That the parent with care of the child had nothing to gain from collaborating with the agency if she (it is nearly always she in this situation) was on income support, since everything collected went to reimburse the state; a special problem here was the expectation of co-operation in the supply of information unless there are strong reasons to protect a woman from further indirect dealings with the father of her child

4 That the operation of a rigid formula was unfair when there are regular contacts with the absent parent and a variety of connected expenses

The enforcement of the Act was not helped by the income targets imposed on the agency and a programme of work which meant that it started with families on 'income support' and had incentives to tackle the easier cases (that was, the more compliant absent parents).

In 1995, the government brought in amending legislation. It bowed to a vociferous male lobby. It did not change the basic principles of the Act, but it did give the agency some limited leeway to modify its application in relation to the points made in (1), (2) and (4) above. However, there are still difficulties and further amending legislation has been mooted to use a simpler formula to determine liabilities and to offer some benefit for collaborating carers (Department of Social Security, 1998b).

Problems of Means Testing

There is an extensive literature on the problems of means testing. Much that has been written on this subject comes from those who advocate, as an alternative, strengthening the contributory benefits system so that it becomes more universal in its coverage and provides better benefits. We have seen already some of the political objections to this approach. Alternative approaches to this issue are also found. One of these suggests that we could have a structure of 'basic income', whereby all would be guaranteed a minimum income, and some would secure earned incomes (necessarily more heavily taxed) to supplement this state minimum (Walter, 1988; Parker, 1989). This would be a radical departure from our current system. It finds little support close to the corridors of power.

Another alternative which has awakened a wider interest is 'negative income tax' (Minford, 1984). The British 'pay-as-you-earn' (PAYE) system for the deduction of tax would seem to be the ideal vehicle for the development of a system whereby additions, rather than deductions, could be provided in some cases. However, the basis for the assessment of tax would have to be shifted from an annual to a weekly one; arrangements would have to be made for the system to operate when people were both in and out of work; and some more precise information on need would have to be available to the tax authorities. The application of the system to the large number of low-income self-employed people would also be difficult.

When the Conservative government announced its radical review of social security in 1983, it seemed possible that the negative income tax idea would be adopted. In practice, the 1986 changes were influenced by this approach, in the adoption of a common set of rules to determine benefit rates and in the use of net rather than gross income (that is, income after tax). Yet, the income tax system itself remained 'untainted' by social security considerations. However the Blair government has returned to this issue. As suggested above, its tax credit proposals may be seen as a move in this direction. At the time of writing, it is a little too early to judge how easily tax credits will sit alongside income tax, or how effectively the implementation problems outlined at the end of the last paragraph will be solved.

The general case against means tests is that they confuse, deter and stigmatize those who need help. People prefer benefits to which they have clear-cut rights, and about which they can obtain unambiguous information. Those who have to claim help are often already in trouble, about which they are ashamed or for which their neighbours criticize them; to have to reveal intimate details to an official so as to obtain benefits deepens the sense of 'stigma'. The low take-up of some benefits is attributed both to this stigma and to the complexities surrounding the administration of means tests.

It is undoubtedly the case that take-up levels for means-tested benefits are lower than for many other benefits, but there are also marked variations between the various means-tested ones. The Department of Social Security publishes estimates on the take-up rates for some benefits. It distinguishes take-up in terms of number of additional claims that could be made (col. 2 in table 5.4) and in terms of the amount of benefit left unclaimed (col. 3). This distinction is based on the fact that many non-claimers will have relatively low

Table 5.4   Estimates of non-take-up of benefits

	Missing claims	Missing benefit
Income support	17–24%	8–12%
Family credit	31%	18%
Housing benefit	4–10%	3–7%
Council tax benefit	22–30%	21–29%

Source: Calculated from tables 4.01 to 4.04 in Department of Social Security (1997)

entitlements. Table 5.4 sets out estimates of the proportions of non-claimers of benefits calculated from figures published in 1997.

The estimates for housing benefit non-take-up seem rather low. Take-up of housing benefit is influenced by two things: whether the household is also on income support and whether they are local authority tenants. In a study done by the Department of Social Security before the introduction of the 1986 Act changes, private tenants not on supplementary benefit were shown to have only a 64 per cent take-up rate, by comparison with a near 100 per cent rate for local authority tenants on supplementary benefit. The disparity between take-up of housing benefit by public tenants and that by private tenants occurs because local authorities, as the administrators of those means tests, can much more easily publicize the former among their own tenants.

Another factor that facilitates take-up of benefits is that income support is regarded as an automatic 'passport' to other benefits. This is most evidently the case with relief from NHS charges. However, this implies a cause for concern about the needs of those just above income support levels, together with those who, in not claiming small amounts of income support, may also be shutting themselves out from ready access to other benefits.

One particular problem with the multiplicity of means tests is that, operating together, they may create a poverty trap (or poverty plateau). This is a kind of 'tax effect' whereby an individual whose earned income rises may find that tax and NI contributions increase while benefit income decreases, together diminishing any gain to a very low level. The government stated that one of the main benefits of the 1986 Act was to be that, by taking into account earned income after tax and NI deductions and having the main means tests operate with a common framework, they would eliminate the poverty trap problem for most people. However, the combination of increases in tax and NI contributions with the family credit, housing benefit and council tax tapers often limited the gain from an extra £1 of gross earnings to 3 pence. That could be expressed as the equivalent of a 97 per cent tax rate (a loss which is more than twice as large as the marginal rate of income tax on people with the highest incomes!). The taper rates for the new tax credits are set lower but, in the absence of a change in housing benefit taper rate, the gain on the shift to 'working families tax credit' is only 2 pence in the pound. Other tax credits may also further complicate the picture.

It is important to bear in mind that the poverty trap effect applies with part-time work, when either of a couple on benefits together finds work, and to temporary work. In other words, there are some complex issues about disincentives to labour market participation, which flow directly from the poverty trap effect.

The poverty trap problem must afflict any unified means-testing system, including negative income tax. If the tapering-off effect is to be reduced, benefit receipt will logically spread further up the income distribution, adding to the cost of the scheme. In the last resort, this can only be compensated by increasing tax rates, either across the board or through alterations to the higher-rate bands.

A study by Alcock and Pearson (1999) shows the problem of the poverty trap may be intensified by public services for which charges are related to income. They show that this is true of a range of local authority services – social care services, charges for extra education benefits (music lessons, for example), travel passes, entry to swimming pools, etc. The problem can only be avoided if less targeted status considerations rather than income tests are used in determining concessions (age, for example). They also indicate the way in which rules about capital holdings may impose a similar 'savings trap'.

Conclusions: Towards a reform agenda?

The British system of social security has been built up by the development of a contributory system together with a limited system of family benefits, which were conceived to minimize dependence on means-tested benefits. However, the means-tested benefits have not been reduced to the safety net role envisaged for them by Beveridge and others. Indeed, in recent years an alternative strategy has been suggested: to confine expenditure on social security by putting the emphasis on means-tested benefits. While the main issue for debate about the system seems to be the conflict between the case for a comprehensive system of non-means-tested benefits, probably founded on contributory principles, and the alternative means-testing approach, this conveys an oversimplified notion of its character. In fact, the two approaches are mixed together in the system, and the overall picture is further confused by a range of *ad hoc* responses to special issues and problems: the needs of disabled people, the compensation of industrial injury victims, the requirements of support for students and schoolchildren, and so on.

The 1986 Social Security Act simplified the means-tested part of the system. This eased administration. It has limited the opportunities for errors, differential rule interpretation and outright discretion within the main means tests. However, the staff reductions which have occurred, the increases in the numbers of claimants and the high performance targets imposed on staff have meant that error rates in the calculation of benefits have remained high.

The 1986 Act offered an approach to reform around which a broad consensus might have formed were it not for the fact that the government was determined that the new scheme should be no more costly than its predecessors, and that it should make it easier for them to contain the future growth of social security costs. Such simplification inevitably implied rough justice, gainers being counterbalanced by losers. In addition, the controversial social fund was introduced, with loans as its main form of aid and cash limits, to take the strain previously imposed on the system by the complex single payments rules.

The growth of means-tested benefits relative to contributory benefits between 1964 and 1986, caused by political reluctance to increase the expensive contributory benefits, and the use of *ad hoc* measures to cope with problems of low wages and high housing costs produced a great deal of turbulence in social security policy. Yet the 1986 Act did not bring in a period of stability. It led to further attacks on the contributory system in the pursuit of more savings.

When the Labour party indicated in its election manifesto for 1997 that it would be 'the party of welfare reform', that inevitably set up a debate about what that should mean. The approach to this which would probably find most favour with Labour Party rank and file members, is what may be described as a 'back to Castle' option. The crucial reference point here is the period when Barbara Castle was Secretary of State in the Wilson Government of 1974–6. In this period, family allowance was replaced by child benefit, SERPS was introduced and the main benefit uprating principle was made indexing to prices or earnings according to which rose faster. The Thatcher Governments then, later, seriously undermined SERPS and changed the uprating principle to a link only with prices. The 'back to Castle' option in respect of pensions policy was advocated powerfully by

Barbara Castle herself in a speech to the Labour Party conference in 1996 and in a pamphlet with the emotive title 'We CAN afford the welfare state' (Castle and Townsend, n.d.).

The 'back to Castle' option itself can be seen as a development of what has been called 'the back to Beveridge' or 'new Beveridge' approach to social security policy which sees the ideal way forward to be a combination of the restoration of those parts of the original Beveridge social insurance edifice undermined by the Conservatives, the restoration of the earnings related additions Labour put in during the 1960s (together with the restoration of SERPS to its original form) with development of new ways to put into the social insurance framework protection for those who have difficulties in building insurance entitlements (carers, part-time workers etc.). The comparative ideal here is the strong, and largely inclusive, Swedish social insurance system with its good minimum provisions for those unable to contribute.

A variant on this approach to the reform of social security is an even more radical option, the advocacy of a 'citizen's income' or 'basic income' for all; see the comment on pages 128–9. There is also a version of this perspective which involves arguing for a 'participation income' for specific contingent groups such as the elderly or the sick (Atkinson, 1994). What is important about this approach is that it sees both means tests with their deterrent effects and social insurance with its contribution tests as irrelevant and difficult to administer in a world in which much work is temporary, part-time and insecure.

These ideas would constitute a satisfactory basis for a 'radical' reform of social security. It does not take much imagination to see why they are being rejected – because of their costs. A good idea of the cost implications of these options can be gained from looking at one of the most modest proposals from the 'back to Castle' perspective. If the link between basic insurance pensions and wages were to be restored to parity with the ratio between pensions and earnings established by 1979, it would mean an increase for every pensioner of at least £20 per week (Lynes, 1997a). That would mean an addition to the social security budget of over ten billion pounds a year. That is hardly an acceptable prospect to the government, which has committed itself to public expenditure restraint, and knows that its predecessors were unable to curb the growth of social security expenditure (as was shown vividly in the statistics in table 5.1).

What other options are there for radical social security reform? One is to increase the privatized element in the social security system. Already Britain is a long way down that road. Private pension schemes have always been salient elements in the British system. By 1963, about 48 per cent of employees were enrolled in occupational pension schemes. The percentage has remained much the same ever since (Lynes, 1997b, p. 323). The privatization theme was particularly picked up by Frank Field, during his brief period as junior minister in the Department of Social Security. Field (1998) argued:

> Part of our reform strategy is to restore the link between welfare and self-improvement. This may not prove as difficult as some think: people are increasingly providing for themselves and their families. Occupational pension funds are the unsung heroes of the post-war welfare system ... We want to see a mixed economy of welfare provision, and we recognize the desire of people for more control over their own provision.

A stance on private provision could involve saying that the state will stand back and only protect those unable to protect themselves. That, in many ways, was the stance of the last Conservative Government. The Field perspective goes further than that. Field has long been a critic of means tests. Inasmuch as he is now an advocate of private provision he sees the future as involving a public/private partnership (Field, 1996). The state must be the regulator of the private sector and the guarantor of last resort. These may imply a role for some future Government, which is not anticipated by the planners of today – if capitalism falls down on its long-term promises. Yet, more importantly for the politics of today, what this partnership involves is a state role to buy into private and funded provisions on behalf of those who cannot do so for themselves.

It does seem to be an important plank in the Government's philosophy of welfare that something must be done to assist people who cannot benefit from a labour-market participation related insurance scheme. This is an important issue as far as social protection for women is concerned. It may also be a necessary adaptation to a changing labour market, where long-term full-time employment cannot be guaranteed for all.

However, this option is also bound to be viewed with suspicion because of the key role it gives to the private sector. Among the Government's most immediate commitments is the recovery of benefits for people who were misled or robbed by the over-selling of private 'money purchase' pensions in the wake of the Conservatives' attack on SERPS in 1986.

Yet there is a more pragmatic objection to the public/private partnership option which is that it does not deal with the issues about current social security policy. New pension schemes do not offer anything for current pensioners.

That leaves either a need for more general taxation to cope with that problem or a situation in which social insurance payment obligations are unchanged but new contributions are required from employees towards private pensions. In other words, the Government has to embark on the politically dangerous course of requiring the young to pay twice – for current pensioners and for themselves. Governments not surprisingly back away from schemes that impose extra costs on today's electorate to solve future problems!

Field's approach is, as suggested above, much influenced by his opposition to means testing. By contrast, the government have evidently seen this as the way forward. It has been indicated, on page 118, that the development of tax credits is occurring in respect of in-work benefits. At the same time, the so-called 'minimum income guarantee' represents the central plank in the government's approach to the current generation of pensioners. This shift towards a greater emphasis on means-tested benefits is reinforced by the cuts to the availability of insurance-based incapacity benefit described above.

The nature of the Blair government's strategy is evident in the proposals put forward in its Green Paper on pensions (Department of Social Security, 1998d):

- Maintenance of the basic flat-rate contributory pension
- Voluntary 'stakeholder pension schemes designed to offer an alternative to entirely private pensions for those on 'middle incomes (between roughly £9,000 and £18,500 a year)' (para 27) which will be low-cost, flexible and secure, apparently involving private investment under statutory surveillance
- A state second pension for those unable to join private or stakeholder schemes, essentially low earners and those in caring roles, which they claim will offer a better deal than SERPS; the Green Paper speaks of credited contributions for carers, the extent of expectation of contributions from low earners is not clear
- A minimum income guarantee for current pensioners

This mixed strategy for pensions, together with tax credits for people of working age, does not offer an approach to welfare reform which is a significant departure from the past; neither does it help to solve the peculiar muddle which is British social security. Some of its key elements could still be derailed by the strategy's heavy dependence on labour market participation to deal both with the problems of poverty among the young and to deliver ultimately prospects of satisfactory pensions.

Suggestions for further reading

An up-to-date book on social security policy has, at the time of writing, just been published: *Social Security in Britain* by Mckay and Rowlingson (1999). This fills a gap left by the dating of the author's own book on this subject. Another good overview of the issues discussed here is Alcock's *Understanding Poverty*; unfortunately, the latest edition of this (the second) came out in 1997 before the change of government.

The Child Poverty Action Group (CPAG) annual handbooks on means-tested and contributory benefits are the key sources for details, including benefit rates, which change at least annually (and have not therefore been quoted here). Other good, general, up-to-date sources are CPAG's journal *Poverty* and a journal published by the University of Nottingham called *Benefits*. CPAG pamphlets are useful critical sources of information on the system.

Deacon and Bradshaw's *Reserved for the Poor* (1983) is an excellent review of the issues regarding means testing and the various alternatives to it, but is now much dated. Parker (1989) provides a good critique of the illogicalities of both means testing and social insurance, coupled with advocacy of 'basic income'. The report of the Commission on Social Justice (1994) has much to say about social security policy, particularly in relation to benefits and work. The best discussions of poverty and social security are Townsend's important poverty survey (1979) and the later surveys by Mack and Lansley (1985) and Gordon and Pantazis (1997).

Chapter 6

THE HEALTH SERVICE

Introduction

This chapter is less concerned than chapter 5 with what the service does – people are relatively more clear about this – but more concerned with how it does it, and particularly how it is organized. The ingredients of the health service are hospitals, the family or primary care practitioners (doctors, dentists, pharmacists and opticians operating outside the hospitals), and other community-based services (community nursing, health visiting and preventive medicine).

The next three sections of this chapter all concern issues about the organizational arrangements for the delivery of these services. The exploration of these goes to the heart of contemporary controversy about the National Health Service (NHS), dealing with issues about accountability and about the financing of the service. Many of the concerns about need and rationing, and about the extent to which the service deals effectively with health inequalities, which the later parts of the chapter explore, have to be seen in the context of the organizational complications about the NHS. Conversely, much of the continuing search for the best organizational structure is motivated by a view that this is the key to solving problems of equity. Sceptics may argue that this search

> for an organizational 'fix' cannot solve a basic underlying problem
> of underfunding, but the political imperative to seek to provide a
> good health service at the lowest possible cost inevitably links
> these two issues together.

The Organization and Management of the Service

The Secretary of State for Health is responsible for the health service
in England. In Wales, Scotland and Northern Ireland, it is the
responsibility of the devolved governments. The Secretary of State is
assisted by a policy board, which he or she chairs. Then, to deal with
operational matters, there is a management executive chaired by a
chief executive. While this seems to involve a departure from the
normal top civil service control structure towards a system which
mimics that of a private company, the NHS executive is not a
separate agency like the Benefits Agency.

Below the NHS executive, the structure is now really quite simple.
Accounts of the history of health policy – see, for example, Webster
(1998) – show how there has been a succession of alternative
organizational arrangements for the NHS of varying complexity.
Now, most of the complications have been swept away. There used
to be quasi-independent regional health authorities; now there are
simply eight regional offices of the NHS executive in England. Then,
at the local level, there are health authorities responsible for the
planning of services in their areas; for further discussion of this see
page 140. At the time of writing, Scotland and Wales have no
regional management systems, merely single authorities (called
boards in Scotland). The arrangement in Northern Ireland involves
four health and social services boards with 'area' responsibilities,
each responsible for a number of units.

The organization of primary care has changed relatively little since
the foundation of the NHS. The most important primary care service
is that provided by general medical practitioners (GPs). (Comments
on the primary care provided by community medical and nursing
services and by dentists and opticians is included later; see page 141.)
GPs operate under contracts granted by the health authorities. Broadly
speaking, they are free to decide how they will organize their practices,
and are free to accept or reject patients. They are paid primarily on a
'capitation' basis, so much for each patient on their list, plus an allowance for practice expenses and special payments for various exceptional tasks undertaken. Ever since the introduction of the NHS, the

system of payments has been the subject of regular negotiations and conflict between the doctors and the government, in the course of which the scheme has been elaborated in a variety of ways to include such things as additional fees for elderly people on doctors' lists and payments for night and weekend work. While the doctors have clearly been eager to secure maximum rewards but to remain within a system that preserves their freedom, the government's objectives in these negotiations have included the encouragement of forms of group practice, the development of health centres and an increase in the number of doctors practising in some areas. In the last few years, the GP service has become much more sophisticated. Isolated independent practice has declined, and group practices, providing a wide range of medical services, have multiplied. In 1997, legislation even provided for the possibility of the direct employment of GPs.

The secondary care service (that is care primarily offered through hospitals) was reorganized by the Conservatives in the early 1990s in a way which split purchasing of services from provision thereof. The health authorities were purchasers, but only exceptionally direct providers. What this meant was that the health authorities were required to enter into specific contracts to secure the services needed for the patients in their area. The providers which were engaged in this way did not necessarily need to be in the health authority's geographical patch. The providers were organized into 'trusts'. An additional complication was that some GPs (known as GP fundholders) were allowed to be purchasers of hospital and other services.

These changes created what was often described as an 'internal market' or 'quasi-market' system of health authorities and GP fundholders as purchasers of services and trusts as providers. This arrangement generated considerable controversy. The case for the internal market was that the separation of purchasers and providers helped to undermine the tendency for those who provide services to exaggerate their value and hide their inefficient aspects. Bureaucratic allocation procedures had been replaced by a system of contracts, giving purchasers the capacity to make choices between providers and to change them if they did not deliver what was required.

The system was criticized as promoting efficiency at the expense of quality, but it was alternatively argued that the use of contracts in fact produced inefficiencies: spare capacity because contracts were fulfilled early, under-use of expensive facilities in hospitals which lost out in contracting processes, and high costs on all sides associated with the renegotiation of contracts (transaction costs).

The system that actually developed did not measure up to the aspirations of the market advocates. Political and managerial interventions sought to allay some of the anxieties expressed by the opponents of the internal market. It proved to be very much a managed market, with its potential effects on some hospitals and some services damped down (Le Grand et al., 1998).

The change to a contracting process was necessarily an incremental one. Much contracting involved continuing an existing service with only marginal adjustments. In this respect, the GP fundholders were a maverick element – able to exert purchaser pressure better than the health authorities, but, because of that, likely to produce unpredictable distortions in the service (Glennerster et al., 1994).

That system has been reorganized again in 1999. The new government declared, at the outset, that it wanted to end the 'internal market'. However, it accepts the idea of a purchaser/ provider split but wants to operate it in a way which has more stability. It also accepts the idea of GP involvement in secondary care purchase, but is unhappy about the way in which the GP fundholder system operated in parallel with the health authority purchase arrangements. Under the new arrangements, health authorities (Department of Health, 1997, para 4.3) have a number of strategic planning tasks:

- Assessing the health needs of the local population
- Drawing up a strategy for meeting those needs, in the form of a Health Improvement Programme, developed in partnership with all the local interests
- Deciding on the range and location of health care services
- Determining local targets and standards

They are then required to set up Primary Care Groups to commission services for their area, supplying them with the necessary resources and ultimately 'holding them to account' (para 4.3). Note the use of the word 'commission' rather than purchase. Reflecting this, arrangements are expected to run for longer periods of time than the 'contracts' they replace – up to five years. Primary Care Groups are expected to take responsibility for ensuring that there is an integrated system of primary care in their area as well as commissioning secondary care.

The government indicated it wanted a flexible approach, taking into account arrangements previously adopted in each area. There are requirements of the Primary Care Groups, however (para 5.15):

- To be representative of all GP practices in the Group
- To have a governing body which includes community nursing and social services as well as GPs

- To take account of social services as well as Health Authority boundaries, so as to promote integration in service planning and provision
- To have clear arrangements for public involvement

The government also set up, in April 1998, some Health Action Zones, to operate as pioneers in the development of Health Improvement Programmes.

Access of patients to the health service, except in emergencies, is by way of the primary care practitioners. These practitioners are thus the 'gate keepers' of the service, making judgements about when referral to the more specialized secondary services is appropriate. Direct self-referral is accepted in the event of accidents and emergencies. This tends to increase, therefore, when primary care services are slow to react or when waiting lists for hospital consultations impose unacceptable delays.

Once under hospital care, individuals may be treated as in-patients or out-patients. The general notion here is of a hospital-based service for problems that are beyond either the expertise or resources of GPs and the 'primary care' teams. However, the lines are sometimes blurred. Modern health centres can often provide services that are elsewhere provided by hospitals. The system of GP fundholding developed by the Conservatives further encouraged this development. Its abolition will probably not reverse that development. Community hospitals provide, in some areas, limited service of a kind once provided by 'cottage hospitals', and they may involve GPs in their work.

Dentists, opticians and pharmacists are paid on a fee-for-service basis. However, there are problems, particularly as far as dentists are concerned, about the setting of a system of remuneration that rewards most adequately the best practice, is administratively straightforward and can be supervised without detailed surveillance of day-to-day activities.

The dental, optical and pharmaceutical services are, like general medical practice, administered by the health authorities. The latter have responsibilities to see that the various services are available in their district, to help patients to obtain practitioners and to deal with complaints.

There is also a range of community health services. These include community nursing services, the running of maternity clinics, preventive services offered by doctors and health visitors and measures to prevent the spread of infectious diseases. These are sometimes run by separate trusts, sometimes organized as part of the work of hospital-based trusts and sometimes organized by GPs. There is a particular need for these services to work closely with local authorities. There are clear overlaps between their concerns and those of social services authorities. Education authorities and schools have concerns about the services they offer to children. There is also a need for liaison between local government services to deal with environmental hazards and community health services. Some issues regarding relationships between the health service and social care services run by the local authorities are examined in chapter 7.

Management and the Issue of Professional Accountability

All over the world, health services have largely been set up on terms dictated by doctors. Doctors have been closely involved in the politics of the creation of state health care systems, often securing organizational arrangements that suited them as a profession. They have acquired high financial rewards and they have secured positions of power from which to influence the day-to-day running of services. In doing all this, they have defined good health, health care needs and the responsibilities of health services in ways which put them in a central and indispensable role (Friedson, 1970; Harrison, Hunter and Pollitt, 1990; Moran and Wood, 1993; Ham, 1999). As people and politicians have begun to demand more control over social services, and as it has become increasingly recognized that it is difficult to control the costs of 'provider led' services, so efforts to curb medical power have assumed a central place on health policy reform agendas. Much of the rest of this chapter, and particularly this section, is concerned with aspects of this theme.

Until the 1980s, the managerial arrangements for the NHS could have been described as broadly 'collegial': that is, the various professionals within the service were represented in the management structure. Then, after 1983, each region, district and unit was required to appoint a general manager, on a fixed-term contract. Many of these general managers were already health service administrators, but there were appointments from outside and, in a few cases, senior professionals, particularly doctors, but occasionally nurses, received these posts. These managers were accountable to the relevant appointed authorities. Then, under the changes enacted in 1990, the health authorities were restructured to comprise up to five 'executive members', to include the chief executive and the finance director, and five non-executive members (including a non-executive chairman).

Non-executive members are appointed by the secretary of state. Trusts have similar management structures.

Hospital doctors have traditionally exercised a considerable degree of autonomy. Crucial for this is the concept of clinical freedom, which can be effectively extended from a right to determine the treatment of individual patients to a right to plan the pattern of care as a whole. The managerial arrangements adopted in the 1990s, and the significance of the contracting system for patterns of work, have been seen by some to threaten that freedom (Harrison et al., 1990). It is difficult to say how significant that threat is, since much depends on the internal management arrangements made within the trusts. There is a requirement to make a senior medical appointment, which may place one doctor in a strong position, probably working closely with the chief executive. Alternatively, he or she may be seen merely as a figurehead to represent the consultant group as a whole, without disturbing individual autonomy.

Consultants may be part-time appointees, who combine private practice with NHS work. Junior hospital doctors, below consultant status, are organized in consultant-led teams. Most of them are in short-term appointments, which are seen as building blocks of trainee experience leading to consultant status. There are problems of relatively low pay, heavy duties and insecurity for junior doctors, enhanced by difficulties in advancing to consultancies.

The last Conservative government placed, briefly, some faith in the feasibility of the internal market as a device to control doctors. The new Labour government is exploring alternative ways to increase the public accountability of doctors, and other professional staff. It sees a need to do this by involving these people in the managerial and monitoring arrangements for the service rather than by simply imposing hierarchical controls. Key aspects of its strategy are itemized in a list by the Department of Health (1998a, para 6.4):

- To involve trusts in the shaping of their local Health Improvement Programmes
- To ensure that explicit quality standards are set in local agreements
- To involve professional staff in the design of service agreements
- To develop a system of 'clinical governance'

The concept of 'clinical governance' requires that the processes that are currently used in the NHS to try to improve the quality of clinical work are integrated with quality planning for the trusts (and ultimately the NHS) as a whole. An earlier measure was a requirement that systems of 'clinical audit' should be set up in each trust to review clinical work, but this has been criticized as being a private review process within the medical profession, which individual doctors do not always take seriously and for which there is no system of external accountability. Now this is to be 'integrated with the quality program for the organization as a whole' (p. 47). There are also requirements that better use should be made of what the profession calls 'evidence-based practice', with wider dissemination of new examples of good practice. A National Institute of Clinical Excellence has been set up to promote clinical effectiveness and to produce and disseminate clinical guidelines.

Scally and Donaldson (1998) note how the new initiative requires senior managements of health care organizations to set in place structures and processes which 'integrate financial control, service performance and clinical quality at every level of their operation'. They also recognize that the new initiative will require 'an organization-wide transformation with an emphasis on local professional self regulation . . . and that its implementation will need to be rigorous in its application, organization-wide in its emphasis, accountable in its delivery, developmental in its thrust, and positive in its connotations'.

Clinical governance is another attempt by government to bring about significant shifts in the way that medical staff conceive of their work and hence bring about substantial change in relations within clinical settings. For it to be successful there will need to be major investments in information systems, and programmes to increase clinical effectiveness.

The government describe it as 'a partnership between the Government and the clinical professions. In that partnership, the Government does what only the Government can do and the professions do what only they can do' (Department of Health, 1998a, para 1.13). It goes on to argue (para 3.9):

> Clinical governance requires partnerships within health care teams, between health professionals (including academic staff) and managers, between individuals and the organizations in which they work and between the NHS, patients and the public.

Sceptics may feel that this is merely another attempt by the government to convince the public that it has clinical autonomy under control. However, it does seem to involve a much more explicit attempt to integrate professional accountability with managerial accountability in the NHS. The whole issue was given a greater degree of urgency by the emergence into the public arena in summer 1998 of a scandal at the United Bristol Healthcare Trust. At that time, the doctor's disciplinary body, the General Medical Council (GMC), found three senior hospital consultants guilty of serious professional misconduct. The three included a former Medical Director of the Trust and the Trust's medically qualified Chief Executive. There had been serious problems about the way heart operations had been carried out on children, leading to deaths that could have been prevented. The evidence on this problem had been suppressed for quite a long while (though quite widely suspected within informed medical circles). Clearly, the direct involvement of some very senior doctors, whose patronage would be important for more junior staff contributed to this. It was eventually brought to light by an anaesthetist, who was sacked for his 'whistle-blowing' activities and emigrated to Australia before being eventually vindicated. The Secretary of State reacted angrily to the disciplinary body's report, setting up an inquiry and stressing that the new accountability measures must bring to light deficiencies in medical practice.

The Financing of the Health Service

The NHS is financed out of national taxation. In 1996–7, in the UK, it cost £45 billion (this figure does not include any income offsets) (Office of National Statistics, 1999b, p. 139. Table 6.1 gives a breakdown of the expenditure for England (it will be noted that, in this and in chapter 7, most of the detailed statistics are for England – this is because the split administrative responsibility means that data is often supplied for each country rather than for the UK as a whole).

Charges to recipients of services bring some money back to the health service, about 5 per cent of the NHS's total income. Charges cover much of the cost of spectacles and dental treatment and part of the cost of the supply of drugs and medical appliances. They are not applied to hospital in-patients or to children and the elderly. There are means tests that enable low-income people to secure remission of charges. In the cases of dentistry and optical services these charges are sufficiently high now to mean that those who have to pay the full charges enjoy little benefit from the NHS. Opticians have always been largely private practitioners mixing private with NHS subsidized work, but now much dentistry is private, and dentists offering NHS services are difficult to find in some areas.

Table 6.1   Gross expenditure on the National Health Service in England by functional divisions 1996–7

	Total (£ millions)	Percentages of total
Hospital and community health service	23,877	69
Family health services	8,192	24
Capital investments	1,753	5
Other costs: central administration, etc.	906	3
Total	34,727	

Source: Calculated from Department of Health 1998b, table E2, p. 79.

Throughout its history, the growth of the cost of the health service to the Exchequer has been a matter of political concern. Demographic changes affecting need, technological changes affecting the quality of treatment, and rising staff costs mean that the cost of the NHS increases without there necessarily being any improvement in the service it provides. Attempts have been made to estimate how much expenditure has to grow each year merely to maintain a consistent level of services to the public. A conservative estimate puts it at 2 per cent, but many suggest that it is nearer 4 or 5 per cent (Robinson and Judge, 1987; see also the discussion of this difficult, controversial subject in Glennerster and Hills (1998, ch. 4). This is important in explaining why, in recent years, both the public and NHS practitioners regularly complain about falling standards, supported by concrete evidence from increasing waiting lists for operations, while governments claim they are spending more, in real terms, than ever before on the health service.

Public investment in new hospitals and other health care facilities is kept under strict control by central government, with the Treasury eager to ensure that public sector debt is kept down. The Conservatives developed a device to try to deal with the lack of investment which followed from this control. It allowed trusts to bring forward, for approval, plans for privately financed developments. What this implied was that facilities, including support services such as portering, catering and cleaning (but not professional services), would, in effect, be rented from private ventures. Such ventures would be interested in linking other money-making activities with hospital building, for example the inclusion of shops within a hospital complex. Objectors to this 'private finance initiative' were concerned that health policy priorities might be distorted by these ventures, and even that this might be the 'thin end of a wedge' that would lead to health service privatization. Perhaps a more cogent concern still was that this approach to capital underfunding merely shifted costs forward, since health service budgets would become increasingly encumbered by rent commitments. It might have been expected that a new Labour government would abandon the private finance initiative. This has been far from the case. Its commitment to continue to keep down public sector borrowing coupled with its desire to be seen as the party of health service development has led it to approve a number of new ventures under the initiative.

Need and the Rationing of the Health Service

The main medical services provided by British health service are, broadly speaking, free and universally available. The general issues raised by the absence of a price mechanism to convert needs into effective demands will be discussed in the next chapter. One of the political preoccupations ever since the founding of the NHS has been the apparently limitless character of need.

There seem to be two crucial problems that were given insufficient attention by those, in the 1940s, who forecasted a decline in need for health services once the NHS was in place. One is that everyone whose life is saved, lives on to become ill again. More precisely, increases in life expectancy bring with them the likelihood of increased work for the service in dealing with the chronic illnesses that particularly affect elderly people. The size of this group has grown rapidly over recent years. Over-65s now constitute 18 per cent of the population, and over-80s, 4 per cent (Central Statistical Office, 1996, p. 39, table 1.5). The growth in the proportion of elderly people has temporarily stopped, but will start again just after 2010, as the post-World War II baby boom population begins to reach 65.

The other problem in predicting need for health services arises from difficulties in defining need. There is a growing understanding that the relationship between having a medical need and seeking medical attention is complex and obscure. Individuals may experience considerable suffering from a condition that manifests no pathological abnormality. Conversely, they may have serious medical problems, yet experience little suffering. Perhaps more significantly in quantitative terms, minor deviations from 'good health' are tolerated by many people for long periods of time without medical attention being sought. This applies, for example, to problems like indigestion, recurrent headaches and skin complaints. It is important to recognize that 'Illness is the subjective state which is experienced by an individual, a feeling of ill-being. Disease is a pathological condition recognized by indications agreed among biomedical practitioners' (Stacey, 1988, p. 171).

The definitions of 'biomedical practitioners' are no more valid than people's subjective judgements. They are subject to variation over time and between 'experts', and are conditional on the dominant paradigms in medical knowledge. They are, however, crucial in influencing demand for health services. This is the sense in which there may be a problem for health services about 'producer'-determined demand, deriving from 'biomedical practitioners' claims to competence and, in some circumstances, their tendency – encouraged by public faith in medicine – to 'medicalize' social problems.

There is a choice between the policy conclusions to be drawn from these findings. One is that a great deal more should be spent on the health service, and, in particular, many more efforts should be made to screen for unidentified illness in the population at large. The quite opposite view is that the fact that many people manage without medical treatment for many complaints suggests that those who do 'bother' doctors with similar problems should be encouraged to become more self-reliant and to make more use of self-medication. A less extreme version of this view suggests that, since medical resources are clearly limited, it is important to control access to the services in such a way that the more serious complaints are treated, while doctors are not overburdened with the trivial. Another issue on the agenda is the exclusion of some kinds of treatments from the NHS; for example, one much-debated example is the treatment of infertility.

At the moment access to the whole NHS system depends primarily on GPs' judgements for controlling demand on the system. Are there ways of pushing the responsibility for demand back to the patients? This provides one argument for the exploration of the case for 'cost sharing' charging systems to control demands on the service. One possibility is the introduction of 'hotel charges' for hospital stays. The problem with this is that stays are becoming shorter. The administrative costs of billing and collecting charges for the many very short stays would be considerable. Further complications would be introduced if, as with prescriptions, some patients were not required to pay. A case for health service charges is also argued in terms of the desirability of choice and competition. This case has been made most cogently in the USA by Friedson (1970), who sees the power of the consumer as enhanced by a relationship with the doctor in which he or she has the capacity to 'hire or fire'. In Friedson's view, the British model of health service organization places individuals in a very weak position in dealing with doctors, and provides the community at large with an absence of weapons for bargaining with a medical profession that would not be so united were doctors in competition with each other.

The fundamental point in favour of a free service is that charges may deter people from seeking necessary help (Abel-Smith, 1976). This is particularly likely to be the case with people on low incomes. Moreover, one of the effects of ill health is naturally to reduce income and to increase other costs. The issue at stake, therefore, is not simply one of inequality in general, but specifically of inequality between the sick and the well (regardless of other determinants of income and expenditure). Clearly also, while in other areas of life people may be expected to make choices between different ways of spending money, serious illness leaves little choice. Individuals will bankrupt themselves to save their lives and those of their loved ones.

Where much of the health service is still 'in the market-place', as, for example, in the USA, the issues are rarely actually as stark as these. There are two reasons why not. One is that many people insure themselves against sickness. The other is that a 'safety net' means-tested medical system exists for the poor. Arguments in favour of a free service must therefore deal with the weaknesses of these two alternative forms of provision.

The key problems with insurance schemes are that they will not insure the 'bad risks'; they often exclude some conditions (especially preventable ones – for example, pregnancy); and they may collapse. These schemes may reduce the powers of doctors, making them dependent on the patronage of the insurance agencies; but the latter often encounter the same problems of provider-determined need as the British system has been alleged to suffer from. Moreover, they do not necessarily curb trivial demands, since subscribers may be determined to obtain their money's worth. In the 1980s, the case for an insurance-based approach to health care re-emerged on the British political agenda. Private insurance schemes had grown rapidly, facilitating the growth of private hospitals (Higgins, 1988). Debate developed, therefore, about the extension of such schemes nationwide. Those advocating such an approach argue that individuals should be required to insure themselves privately, and that the state should underwrite such schemes and make special means-tested provision for those for whom they cannot cater. This approach was given serious attention by the Conservatives in their review of policy before their 1990 changes to the system. The creation of a tier of potentially autonomous providers (the trusts) opened the way for such a development.

The problems with a means-tested health service are the requirement of a test of means before treatment, the likelihood of situations in which individuals will have to abandon resources – or wait to 'hit the bottom' – before they can ask for treatment, and the probability that (as was the case in Britain when such a system operated) two classes of health service will result. In the last resort, as implied above, the case for a free service is not that it helps to distribute resources from the rich to the poor, but that it enables the healthy to support the sick. If it is believed, on the other hand, that it is in the interests of the evolution of society that the 'weak should go to the wall', it will of course be comparatively easy to take an alternative view.

Once the Conservatives abandoned the search for new ways of rationing health services in favour of strengthened managerial controls, political attention shifted to the most obvious index of unmet need – waiting lists. Specific pledges were made to reduce waiting lists, which were inevitably echoed by the Labour opposition. Pledges in the Labour election manifesto included a commitment to remove 100,000 people from waiting lists and to end waiting for cancer surgery. Those pledges were repeated again once in power. There are, however, problems about a political emphasis on waiting list reduction. Waiting lists are, in many respects, merely a function of administrative practice. There is an easy way to shorten waiting lists, by refraining from putting people on them. Another approach is to terminate an initial wait by a consultation, that does not necessarily lead immediately on to effective treatment. Using waiting lists as a general index of unmet need will not take into account the fact that some needs are more serious than others. It may be desirable that some people are kept waiting for minor surgery in the interests of securing more rapid responses to life-threatening conditions. Simply concentrating effort on shortening waiting lists may distort the overall service provided.

Reference was made on page 141 to the standard emphasis on GP referral, and to the fact that people can go directly to hospital in emergencies. It is being alleged by some observers of the NHS that the emphasis on general waiting-list reduction is increasing the pressure on emergency departments of people in urgent need of care. That pressure particularly intensifies in the winter, when vulnerable people are affected by bad weather or by epidemics. Clearly, if there is an underlying problem of health service underfunding, efforts to restructure the way parts of the service is rationed will tend to have side-effects for other parts. The fact that the British health expenditure per head is much less than in many comparable countries may be partly attributable to the efficiency of the NHS but it may also indicate that that we have an underfunded system.

Equality of Treatment: The Impact of the Private Sector

In the atmosphere of concern about rising health service costs and advocacy of privatization by the Right, there is considerable concern in Britain on two related issues: the most appropriate relationship between the health service and the residual private medical sector, and the extent to which the health service provides equality of treatment to all the population.

These two issues are related, since the diversion of medical resources into a private sector, largely accessible only to the better off, reduces the resources available to other sectors of the population. However, the defenders of private medicine argue that the resources involved are, in a sense, extra ones, which would not necessarily be diverted into public medicine in an entirely nationalized sector. Particular bones of contention, however, have been not so much the right of the private sector to exist, as the support that sector receives from a variety of special links with the health service.

Both GPs and consultants are able to take on private patients as well as health service ones, and NHS trusts may offer private services for patients from home or abroad. The private finance initiative, discussed on page 146, may further encourage this. In these situations, health service resources are likely to be used in various ways in support of private medicine. They facilitate the undertaking of public and private work side-by-side, the use of public resources (such as expensive equipment) for private patients, and 'queue-jumping' when public beds are scarce. The way in which doctors with both public and private work distribute their time between the two may also result in subsidy to the latter, in that they may neglect NHS duties to enhance fee earning. Also, situations arise in which it is possible for doctors to say to people that, whereas health service treatment will be inadequate or long delayed, they may secure a better deal by becoming private patients. There is a substantial hidden subsidy from public to private medicine because doctors are trained in the NHS, and much medical research is publicly funded. Furthermore, private hospitals are able to turn to the public sector in emergencies.

The growth of private insurance raises the question of the overall impact on the state service of alternative ones. Is there scope here for desirable competition? Is it a valuable addition to consumer choice, enabling people who are so inclined to pay a little extra for a superior service? Or does it threaten the basic service, and reduce its capacity to meet the needs of all?

It should be added that private hospitals and private health services may be providers for the NHS. While it may be argued that this is just enabling the NHS to obtain services – at lower cost or where public providers are unavailable – such arrangements may implicitly subsidize the private sector, and may be the thin end of a wedge leading to the transformation of the free health service.

Equality of Treatment: Inequalities in Health and Medical Treatment

The health service's capacity to meet need has been subjected to extensive scrutiny. Epidemiological studies of the differential impact of mortality and morbidity have been of importance here. These show considerable differences in the experience of ill health between different regions of the country, between different social classes and between different ethnic groups (Townsend et al., 1988; Acheson, 1998). More challengingly for the NHS, as mortality rates have declined overall, these differences have not decreased, indeed, in many cases, they have increased. Particular attention has been given to what is termed 'premature' mortality. While five out of every thousand babies with parents in the Registrar General's 'social classes' I and II died in the first year of life in 1994–6, the corresponding death rates for those with parents in classes IV and V was seven out of a thousand (Acheson 1998, p. 14). Table 6.2 sets out some figures on mortality differences in mid-life, providing similar evidence of social class contrasts. It also offers, by comparing 1970–2 with 1991–3 evidence on a widening gap between the classes.

If we judge these mortality rates by giving those for class I an index of 100 then the relative mortality rate of class V was 179 in 1970–2 but 287 in 1991–3. A range of other statistics could be presented. The way official data are recorded, it is easier to derive social class indices than, for example, indices for different ethnic groups. In any case, such indices would in many respects reflect socio-economic differences between groups. That last point also applies to regional differences. Other work on this theme has looked at differences between different localities, down to quite small areas. Such work has shown (a) differences which it is possible to correlate

Table 6.2 Standardized mortality rates per 100,000 for men aged 20–64 in England and Wales

Social class		1970–72	1991–93
I	Professional	500	280
II	Managerial and technical	526	300
III(N)	Skilled (non-manual)	637	426
III(M)	Skilled (manual)	683	493
IV	Partly skilled	721	492
V	Unskilled	897	806
Whole population		624	419

Source: Acheson, 1998, table 2, p. 12.

with other indices of deprivation (including environmental factors) and (b) a tendency for these differences to widen in the last few years (Phillimore et al., 1994).

The policy questions this evidence raises obviously concern the extent to which these differentials are attributable to differences in the availability of health services; also, inasmuch as they are attributable to other factors (low income, poor housing and so on), the extent to which better health services can and should offset these disadvantages.

Differences between different places in terms of the availability of health care tend to have narrowed, as attention has been given to the distribution of doctors and medical services (see the discussion on page 154). The Acheson committee, who provide the most recent comprehensive review of these issues, tend to suggest that the key questions now relate to the extent to which sufficient services are available to those groups particularly likely to have poor health. They note (Acheson, 1998, p. 112):

Access to effective primary care is influenced by several supply factors: the geographical distribution and availability of primary care staff, the range and quality of primary care facilities, levels of training, education and recruitment of primary care staff, cultural sensitivity, timing and organization of services to the communities served, distance and the affordability of safe means of transport.

They argue that many deprived areas have difficulty in recruiting GPs and other primary care staff, and that there are many poorly equipped primary care practices in deprived areas, particularly in parts of inner London (Acheson, p. 116). They suggest (p. 112) that

'Communities most at risk of ill health tend to experience the least satisfactory access to the full range of preventative services, the so-called "inverse care law" '. They suggest that evidence on secondary services is more difficult to interpret, indicating a need for better monitoring (p. 112), but they also note continuing inequalities in the allocation of funds for hospital and community health services.

Back in 1974, the government set up a Resource Allocation Working Party (RAWP) to develop a formula to facilitate compar-isons between the resource needs of different regions. This used population estimates, weighted to take into account differential mortality, and different utilization rates based on differences in the age and the structure of the population (DHSS, 1976). Allocation of new money to the regions was based on the RAWP formula, and allocations by regions to districts were based on similar principles. This proved a difficult, controversial exercise in light of the inad-equacy of the statistics available, the difficulties in relating such data to needs, and the uncertainty about the relationship between costs and effectiveness. The 1990 changes brought the RAWP procedure to an end; some of the problems that it had had to deal with in relation to 'flows' of patients across boundaries were solved by the contracting procedure. The allocation of money to health authorities was then based on population numbers weighted to take into account some of the considerations about differential needs. The new Labour government is reviewing this. In *The New NHS* it says (Department of Health, 1997, para 9.6):

> The Government will put in place new mechanisms to distribute NHS cash more fairly. A new Advisory Committee on Resource Allocation will further improve the arrangements for distributing resources for both primary and secondary care. The healthcare needs of populations, including the impact of deprivation, will be the driving force in determining where cash goes.

While efforts to tackle some of the problems of 'territorial injust-ice' that have beset the NHS since its foundation have been widely welcomed, there are some other issues about the availability of services that require attention. As suggested in the references to the Acheson report quoted above, social class differentials in the use of health services suggest that efforts need to be made not only to ensure that adequate resources are available in underprivileged areas, but also to facilitate access to the use of those resources by all in need. This raises policy questions about the siting of surgeries and hospitals, the arrangements made by doctors to enable patients to secure appointments, the extent of the use of health service personnel – such as health visitors – who actively seek out those in need of health care, the extent of health education, and the significance of screening services.

Finally, these questions lead on to the other question raised: the extent to which there might be an expectation that health services should be better in some areas, or for some people, to help to compensate for other social disadvantages. Alternatively, to what extent should the concept of a state health service embrace a responsibility to point out how other social factors contribute to ill health?

There are a number of interrelated approaches to the prevention of ill health, many of them going beyond the simple questions about the provision of services. Healthy life styles may be regarded as a matter of personal choice. It is evident that many people have become aware of the need for exercise and the need for a healthy diet. Yet life-style options are influenced by income and environment, constraining choices. They may also be influenced by the practices of the food and drink industry, the additives they use and the things their advertisements promote. Other aspects of our living and working environments may be quite outside our control. It may be argued that governments have important regulatory responsibilities to help to protect our health. The limited list of points above about this vast subject indicates that the health of the nation depends on much more than the efforts of the NHS.

Critics of the NHS say that it is really a 'national illness service' (HMSO, 1979, p. 15). Academic studies of the health progress of the nation have suggested that changes in the environment and in behaviour have been more important than medical advances (McKeown, 1980). The Acheson report, as a product of an independent enquiry commissioned by the Secretary of State for Health, is an important step forward in indicating the wide policy agenda that has to be addressed if health inequalities are to be reduced.

The Representation and Protection of the Public

When the formation of the NHS was debated in the years before 1948, many doctors made clear their opposition to local government control. While some community services were kept within local government between 1948 and 1974, the main forms chosen for the local control of the health service were hybrid organizations in which ministerial appointees served alongside local authority nominees.

Since 1991, the arrangements for direct local government representation on health service governing bodies have disappeared. Public representation is therefore only at the national government level.

An interesting innovation in 1974 was the setting up of locally based community health councils (CHCs) to enable the public viewpoint to be expressed. However, the status of these bodies is that of officially recognized and subsidized pressure groups, with rights to make representations and to seek information. Such power as they have primarily rests on their capacity to embarrass health authorities. Even in relation to this weapon, they have an awkward choice to make, between seeking a close day-to-day working relationship, which may inhibit its use, and remaining more aloof, but thereby losing opportunities to secure information and to make informal representations. They also have difficult choices to make between concentration on individual grievances, the passing on of views of all kinds from the local groups which form their 'constituency', and the development of a carefully documented, informed critique of the service. Their low resources exacerbate these choice problems.

One point not to be forgotten about CHCs is that they are not themselves representative bodies in any of the senses in which that term is used in democratic theory. Half their members are appointed by local authorities, one-sixth by the Department of Health; the remainder are elected by relevant voluntary organizations (by means of rather haphazard election processes which do nothing to ensure that they are representative of the patients in their areas).

When in opposition, the Labour Party attacked the political influences on the selection of non-executive directors for authorities and trusts. There is now a more open approach – but a system of appointment by the minister is bound to be open to political manipulation. If a new government simply replaces 'their' people by 'our' people, no real progress will be made towards opening up the system.

The separation of commissioning and providing could facilitate the development of a new approach to the issue of democratic control. Since a commissioner is not a direct employer of clinicians, the medical objection to direct control by local politicians has little validity now. Local authorities could become commissioners. However, there is little sign that Labour is any more willing to trust local authorities than the Conservatives were. Alternatively, a system of direct election to health authorities could be developed. In chapter 3, it was suggested that devolution is opening up the debate about regional forms of government; see page 61. Perhaps issues about local control over health services will be examined in this context.

However, for many members of the public, what matters more

than representation is protection from abuse and malpractice, and the chance to be heard when dissatisfied with the service provided. Apart from the general opportunities to make representations, which apply to all the public services, there are, for the health service, a number of special procedures available. Practitioners and hospitals may be sued for tort damages, and professional malpractice may result in debarment from practice by the relevant professional organization. Patients may complain to the health authorities that primary care practitioners have acted in breach of their terms of service, and penalties may be imposed, including, at worst, 'sacking' from health service employment. Complaints against health service trusts have to be formally investigated, using a procedure that may give the complainant an opportunity to give evidence to a committee headed by a lay chairperson. Finally, a patient may complain to the Health Service Commissioner, though the powers of this official broadly preclude investigations in areas where other forms of investigation or litigation are available.

There is thus no absence of avenues for further action by individuals with grievances, but the multiplicity of procedures is confusing to patients; and all involve formal approaches which deter action. This formality is regarded as important for the protection of professionals from frivolous complaints. However, the general problem here is that evidence that things are going wrong in particular parts of the service, particularly the family practitioner parts, does not come to light easily, and thus attract corrective action, when complaints involved are insufficiently serious to activate the formal machinery.

Conclusions

Long ago, an American student of the British NHS (Lindsey, 1962), described it as 'something magnificent in scope and breathtaking in its implications'. He went on to say (p. 474):

> In the light of past accomplishments and future goals, the Health Service cannot very well be excluded from any list of notable achievements of the twentieth century. So much has it become a part of the British way of life, it is difficult for the average Englishman to imagine what it would be like without those services that have contributed so much to his physical and mental well-being.

That expresses rather well the peculiar mixture of utopian expectations and of taking the service for granted that gives a slightly exaggerated quality to British discussions of policy issues in the health service.

We have expectations of the service that often go quite beyond any capacity to deliver results. We oscillate wildly, therefore, between pride in our system and disquiet about its waiting lists and over-crowded wards. We put doctors on a pedestal as the magnificent experts who dominate the system, and we are angry about their arrogant presumptions. We demand more and more from the service, and we worry that we are perhaps becoming a nation of hypochon-driacs who can too easily make demands on it. These mixed emotions colour the reactions of both politicians and the public to the main policy dilemmas that inevitably confront the service.

Undoubtedly, a public approach to medicine involving dispropor-tionate expectations about its capacity to solve the problems of suffering and death lies at the root of some of our difficulties in putting health policies in context and coming to terms with the strengths and weaknesses of our health service. There are signs, however, that a 'demystification of medicine' is beginning to occur. This is helping us to assess, much more realistically, decisions about the allocation of resources between the hospital service and the community services, and between the health service and other public policies. Some of these issues have been considered in this chapter. Others are given attention in chapter 7.

We are beginning to ask whether we have not so far been too ready to delegate decisions involving moral questions as well as medical questions to professional practitioners. We are beginning to achieve a better understanding of the extent to which many of the determinants of the health of the nation have little to do with the quality and nature of its clinical medical services. Yet the debate about these issues is inevitably conducted in the shadow of concerns about the continuing rise of health care costs. Questions about what the NHS *cannot* and *should not* do have to be considered in a context dominated by questions about what the NHS *can afford* to do.

Suggestions for further reading

Wendy Ranade's *A Future for the NHS* (1997) offers a review of aspects of health policy in the period before the change of govern-ment in 1997. A thorough review of the internal market experiment is provided in Le Grand, Mays and Mulligan's *Learning from the NHS Internal Market* (1998). Two long-lasting textbooks which are regularly updated are Christopher Ham's *Health Policy in Britain* (1999) and Rudolph Klein's *The Politics of the NHS* (1995). The Government's new programme for the NHS is set out in its White Paper (Department of Health, 1997). Issues about finance and performance are well examined in the relevant chapter of Glennerster and Hills (1998) and in Glennerster's *Paying for Welfare* (1992).

The Acheson Report on *Inequalities and Health* (1998) is a vital source on the issues about health inequalities. It supersedes the earlier Black Report (Townsend, Davidson and Whitehead, 1988), but that remains a good source on these issues. Stacey (1988) explores the wider sociological issues which need to be taken into account in any evaluation of health policy.

Chapter 7

THE PERSONAL
SOCIAL SERVICES

Introduction

Policy for the personal social services is, at the central government level, the responsibility of the Department of Health in England, and the respective devolved authorities in Wales, Scotland and Northern Ireland. Except in Northern Ireland, where they are integrated with health services under Health and Social Services Boards, the provision of social services is the responsibility of local government. Local authorities are experiencing increasing regulation of their social services work by central government. There is an Inspectorate within the Department of Health which advises and inspects local authority social services work. In 1999, the government has set up a system of performance tables and specified targets for some services.

In earlier versions of this book, the personal social services were defined as the responsibility of the social services *departments* in England and Wales (social work departments in Scotland). While that is still true, in most cases, there are now local authorities which are organizing their services rather differently, so these services are not now always within a department with exclusive social services' responsibilities; they may be linked with other local government functions or, exceptionally, split between departments.

One way of classifying the personal social services is in terms of their contributions to the needs of specific groups in the population: elderly people, physically handicapped people, mentally ill people, people with learning difficulties (a group which used to be called 'mentally handicapped'), and children. An alternative classification is in terms of kinds of services: residential care, day care, domiciliary services and field-work. These two modes of classification can, of course, be related to each other. A two-dimensional table can be drawn up, relating kinds of clients to kinds of services. The data on personal social services expenditure is set out in this way in table 7.1, which gives figures for England in 1996–7. It highlights how much residential care is for elderly people, how much child care is outside residential settings and how much of the relatively low-cost social work effort is concentrated on the care of children.

Alternatively, services may be seen in two distinct groups: those for children (broadly governed by the Children Act of 1989) and those for adults (broadly governed by the National Health Service and Community Care Act 1990). This legislation, particularly the latter, has largely undermined the aspirations towards an integrated service with general commitments to families embodied in the legislation which set up the social services authorities in England and Wales and the social work departments in Scotland. In recognition of the fundamental importance of this new divide in the services, the first part of this chapter looks separately at these two groups of services. It should be noted that the group of services for adults is often called 'community care', and that this title is used regardless of whether the care is residential or domiciliary; see the discussion on pages 165–71.

Children's Services

The Children Act of 1989 (and a Scottish Act enacted in 1995) consolidated previous legislation on the protection of children. The complex legal framework in this Act tries to ensure that children are protected while at the same time recognizing that public interventions into family life should be kept as low as possible. It carries forward a long-standing concern to minimize the likelihood of the removal of children from their family of origin. The Act identifies a wide range

Table 7.1 Personal social services expenditure in England, 1996–7, by client group, £millions with percentages of the total spent for each client group in brackets

	Elderly people	Children	Learning disability	Adults	Mental health
Residential care	2685 (61%)	657 (15%)	665 (15%)	181 (4%)	185 (4%)
Non-residential care	1466 (44%)	907 (27%)	451 (14%)	357 (11%)	153 (6%)
Field social work	44 (21%)	113 (55%)	14 (7%)	16 (8%)	19 (9%)
Care management/ assessment	284 (35%)	321 (39%)	58 (7%)	74 (9%)	86 (10%)
Other costs*				96 (44%)	
Totals	**4575 (49%)**	**2142 (23%)**	**1208 (13%)**	**748 (8%)**	**468 (5%)**

* Note: there is an item of £123 million (1 per cent) other costs that is not included in this table because it is headquarters costs that cannot be alocated to a particular client group.

Source: Figures calculated from Department of Health 1998b, table E5, p. 82.

of ways in which authorities may spend money to try to avoid taking children into direct care.

Social workers in the social services authorities have a crucial role to play in situations in which evidence comes to light that children may be at risk of ill-treatment, abuse or neglect. Their authorities are required to maintain 'child protection registers' of children 'at risk' and offer appropriate supportive services to these children and their families. There were about 31,600 children on these registers in England in March 1998 (Department of Health, 1998b, table C2, p. 61). Only a small proportion of children at risk are taken away from their families.

The most draconian powers available to child care workers are those which enable them to activate procedures under which children may be taken into the 'legal' care of a local authority because parents are unable to care for them or are deemed to be unfit to care for them. Care decisions are the responsibility of the courts, but most action to take children into care will have been initiated by social workers in the social services authorities. Once a child has been taken into care, the local authority will seek to ensure a settled future for him or her. In some cases, this will mean return to parental care under supervision. Where this is not possible, foster care is widely used. Hence, institutional care is likely to be regarded as a temporary expedient in many cases, while the situation is assessed and longer-term plans are made.

A large proportion of the children who are in legal terms 'in the care of the local authorities' are not in fact in any kind of institution; indeed, a significant proportion of them are living in their parents' homes. There were about 53,700 children 'in care' in England in March 1998. Of these, 66 per cent were boarded out with foster parents and 5 per cent were placed for adoption. About 11 per cent were 'placed' with their parents, and there were 8 per cent 'other placements' (generally with a friend or relative). The remainder, only about 11 per cent, were in some kind of institutionalized care (Department of Health, 1998b, table C1, p. 60).

Among the children who may be deemed in need of statutory care is a group of generally older children who are considered to be out of parental control. Under the 1969 Children and Young Persons Act, local authorities acquired increased responsibilities for the care of children brought before the courts for delinquent acts. The object of this legislation was to move away from labelling young offenders as criminals, and to make the issue for decision by the juvenile courts one about responsibility for care rather than punishment for crime. Social services authorities may now have to undertake the 'supervision' of such children, or they may be given legal custody of them under a 'care order'. They may fulfil the parental responsibilities entailed in a care order in a variety of ways, including the supervision of a child within a residential institution. The former remand homes and approved schools became specially staffed 'community homes' under this legislation. Since many local authorities do not possess the residential resources to fulfil responsibilities of this kind on their own and, in particular, lack the necessary range of resources, which must include (exceptionally) a 'secure' institution, regional planning committees have been set up to facilitate the use of homes by authorities other than those responsible for their management.

Where the care responsibilities of local authorities are discharged through the use of foster parents, payment will be made, and the arrangements will be supervised by social workers. Some children in the various forms of care may eventually be legally adopted into another family. Social services authorities have responsibilities to organize and supervise adoption procedures, but these may sometimes be sub-contracted to private agencies. It is, however, important to bear in mind how low the level of adoptions is in Britain today; there were just 6,000 in England in 1996 (Department of Health, 1998b, table C3, p. 62).

There is a need to be sceptical about suggestions, made for example by popular newspapers on the basis of the fact that over 50,000 children are in care in England, that there are large numbers of unwanted young children that could be adopted. As was shown above, many children are in care in ordinary homes. Many are away from the care of their parents for relatively short periods. Over 60 per cent of the children in care are over ten years of age, and only 3 per cent are under one year of age (Department of Health, 1998b, table C1, p. 60).

In many cases, prevention of child abuse or neglect requires activities other than the formal institution of legal procedures to transfer formal responsibility for the care of children. Social workers have a number of ways in which they may try to do this. They may themselves try to offer support to families – visiting regularly, making suggestions about how to deal with stresses in the household, listening and counselling, and generally responding to cries for help from families under pressure. In doing this, they may be able to mobilize resources: domestic help, day care for children, grants or loans (see pages 180–1), help in kind. They may also try to secure help for the family from other statutory organizations: for example, better housing or attention to educational or health problems. There may also be voluntary organizations which they can mobilize to help: providing charitable help in cash or kind.

In recent years, there has been a succession of very disturbing incidents. Children have been seriously ill-treated and even killed by parents or step-parents. Typically these cases do not come 'out of the blue'. The families have been known to social services authorities beforehand and the case for the removal of the children has been considered. Social services authorities have been criticized for a lack of decisive action, but there has also been criticism of authorities for over-reacting. Furthermore, there has been a sequence of worrying cases which have come to light in which children have been abused while 'in care'. In sum, while various public inquiries and central government have, from time to time, been very critical of social services authorities, there are no easy formulae to guide authorities on when to act and when not to act (it is not appropriate to cite the various reports and inquiries here – a general discussion of these issues can be found in Department of Health, 1998c).

Local authorities may provide day care for children, and have responsibilities to supervise that provided by others (including play groups and child minding). Local authority day nurseries were largely developed during World War II, but this service has not grown since then to a really effective level. Places are few, and are generally given only to children from very deprived backgrounds. This is essentially a resource for efforts to prevent child abuse and neglect. In recent years, there has been a considerable growth of private provision for day care for young children – daily minding, day nurseries and playgroups. In 1990, there were 830,000 maintained or registered day care places for children under five (not to be confused with nursery school places) in England. Only about 22,000 (4 per cent) of these were in local authority-maintained day nurseries or playgroups. Of the remainder, 531,000 (67 per cent) were in registered day nurseries and playgroups, and 357,000 (29 per cent) were with registered child-minders (Department of Health, 1995, p. 76 table 5.51). There are also undoubtedly large numbers of unregistered child-minders!

Adult Services: 'Community Care'

In the recent past, the expression 'community care' has become used in England to describe almost all social care for adults. The White Paper which preceded the 1990 *National Health Service and Community Care Act* started by saying 'Community care means providing the services and support which people who are affected by problems of ageing, mental illness, mental handicap or physical or sensory disability need to be able to live in their own homes, or in "homely" settings in the community' (HMSO, 1989, para 1.1). The fact that the last part of that definition includes ' "homely" settings in the community' and that it has long been the aspiration that all social care institutions should be "homely" means that this definition embraces all care except that provided by hospitals.

It is reasonable also to ask what is implied by 'services and support' in that definition. There are two points about this. One is that a distinction is generally drawn between social care and health care, in which case the latter (even if given 'in the community') will not be included in definitions of community care. Nevertheless at the margins health and social care services tasks may be difficult to distinguish, and it certainly widely recognized that effective community care depends on close liaison between the providers of health care and the providers of social care. These issues are taken up later in this chapter; see pages 171–4.

The second problem embedded in the reference to 'services and support' is that it is not clear who is to provide or pay for this. An outsider reading that definition may jump to the incorrect conclusion that it is the state which is the sole provider and carrier of the costs of community care. That is very definitely not the case. In reality, anyone who seeks any form of community care has to go through rigorous tests of need and means before help is available from the public sector. Many who are clearly 'affected by problems of ageing, mental illness etc.' (as in the above definition) fail those tests and have either to go without services and support, or pay for them or receive them from their family and neighbours.

Social services authorities (and social work departments in Scotland) have a wide range of responsibilities for the social care of adults. Their predecessor departments (local authority welfare or health and welfare departments) inherited residential care responsibilities from the poor-law in 1948. To these were added a range of domiciliary services, as it became recognized that care concerns might be better met in this way rather than by admission to an institution. The restructuring of both social services and health services in the early 1970s brought further developments: the evolution of services outside health service institutions for mentally ill people and adults with learning difficulties, and the aspiration to use skilled social work services effectively in the care of adults.

In the early 1980s, while the public residential care sector was continuing to contract and hospitals were increasingly reluctant to become involved in long-term care, the number of private, voluntary residential care facilities began to increase rapidly. This growth in independent (that is, both private and voluntary) care was stimulated by an increase in availability of social security benefits to enable people (in particular, elderly people) to pay independent home charges. This came about during the early 1980s as a result of the relaxing of some of the rules relating to the means-testing of applicants from private residential homes by the Department of Social Security. To keep the story short, this can only in retrospect be described as a 'mistake', the government seemed to have thought it a good idea to subsidize private care without accurately forecasting the implications for the social security budget.

The growth of private residential care was uneven. In some areas, it dramatically reduced the demand for local authority care; in others, its impact was quite slight. An Audit Commission report on this issue in 1986 described this growth as a 'perverse effect of social security policies', distorting efforts to create the right balance between residential and community care. People might be given social security subsidies for residential care in circumstances in which social services authorities would not regard them as in need of such care. The social security authorities were not concerned with this issue; they merely carried out a test of means. This development increased regional inequalities. The greatest growth of independent care was in the south and west of England, particularly in seaside areas (Audit Commission, 1986).

An odd situation had thus developed by the end of the 1980s, to which it was necessary for the government to give attention. Local authorities had been seeking to extend forms of care within the community. The local authority burden had been reduced, relatively, in the 1980s, but not particularly through the evolution of community care. Rather, an independent sector had grown up, as a substantial charge on the social security budget, unconstrained by public authorities' concerns regarding the importance of maintaining people in their own homes and confining the use of residential places to the most needy. The government's response to this was contained in its White Paper, entitled *Caring for People* (HMSO, 1989), and legislation was enacted in 1990 to try to deal with the situation. What was decided was that local authorities should be responsible for assessing need for care (for all who sought publicly supported care), and should then purchase that care. Hence, they would be responsible for determining whether residential care was necessary or, alternatively, whether some form of domiciliary care should be provided (or, of course, nothing), and also for determining who should be the provider.

This transferring of responsibility was a complicated process. It involved mechanisms to shift resources from the social security budget to local authority social services budgets over a period of time, leaving arrangements for people already in independent care undisturbed. The new system came into full force in April 1993.

This account of events has laid a strong emphasis on the anomaly that developed because of the social security subsidy of the independent care system. I believe that the government's concern to reform the system of care stemmed particularly from the problem it had in controlling the growth of social security expenditure on independent care for elderly people. However, the case for reform was expressed in wider terms, which suggested that there was a need for the rationalization of social care as a whole. It was proposed that there were problems about the boundaries between health and social care to be resolved. It was argued that there was a need for better planning, to maximize care in the community and participant involvement in decision making. It was even suggested, though there is little evidence that what was enacted achieves this, that there was a need for the system to be more responsive to the wishes of the consumer. Hence, it was possible for practitioners to try to seize on the 'community care reforms' as an opportunity to give those in need of care and their carers a better deal.

All this occurred against a background of a growth in the numbers of those in need of social care (particularly among elderly people), a search for economies in the health service which contributed to reducing that system's contribution to care, and a central attack on local government expenditure. The specific proposals for change were laced with new pro-market language. Social services authorities were to become 'purchasers', making contracts for the supply of services with 'providers' ideally (from the government's point of view) from the private and voluntary sectors but, if not, then from separate units in their own authority. The government's aim was to increase the role of the independent sector. Not surprisingly, therefore, the process of change has been a complex one, about which claims are made as to greater efficiency and greater responsiveness to the needs of the consumer, while critics see only a deterioration of services and a pushing of social care problems back on to individuals and their families.

In England, in 1997, there were about 236,000 people in local authority supported residential places for elderly people and other adults in need of care (Department of Health, 1998b, table C6, p. 59). 'Support' in that statement will, in practice, mean 'partly supported', because all these places were means-tested. Residents are required to contribute to their care costs from their income and capital. About 25 per cent of these places were in local authority homes. The rest were in independent care and nursing homes. These independent institutions have contracts with local authorities to take people who are judged by a social services authority to be in need of care.

The social services authorities are also, at the time of writing, responsible for the registration and regular inspection of all private and voluntary care homes. They have powers to cancel a registration. Home-owners have a right to an appeal to a tribunal against refusal of registration or de-registration. However, the White Paper *Modernising Social Services* (Department of Health, 1998c) published in November 1998 proposes the setting up of independent 'Commissions for Care Standards' at regional level (in England) to take over this inspection task and to regulate all homes (including those for children) and domiciliary care providers. Legislation is expected in 1999–2000 to enact this proposal.

A distinction can be made between 'care' homes and 'nursing' homes, but there may be institutions which are both. In the old public sector, before the community care legislation, there had been a problem about maintaining a distinction between the population of local authority homes and the patients of the overburdened geriatric wards of hospitals. While (until the establishment of Commissions for Care Standards) supervision of 'nursing' homes comes under the health authorities, people in those institutions have to have their needs and means assessed by the local authorities. Of the 236,000 places mentioned above, 28 per cent are for nursing care in independent nursing homes or homes that are registered as both care and nursing homes. Long-stay hospitals are rapidly disappearing, being replaced by independent sector nursing homes as far as the elderly people are concerned and by a variety of forms of community care as far as those who are mentally ill, physically handicapped or with serious learning difficulties are concerned.

A Royal Commission on Long Term Care was set up in 1998 to examine options for a sustainable system of funding of long-term care. It was asked to report within a year and did so in March 1999. The setting up of the Royal Commission was a response to the considerable disquiet about the implications of the decline in hospital care, the impact of the 1990 Act and the operation of the means test used to assess care charges (particularly the rules to take into account capital assets). It responded with a central recommendation (Royal Commission on Long Term care, 1999, p. xvii):

> The costs of long-term care should be split between living costs, housing costs and personal care. Personal care should be available after assessment, according to need: the rest should be subject to a co-payment according to means.

The Royal Commission justify this three way split in terms of the fact that people being cared for in their homes expect to meet living and housing costs. They were obviously forced by this logic to argue that the more intensive forms of domiciliary care should be free too.

In support of this recommendation, the Royal Commission is critical of some of the exaggerations of the future burden of care. They argue that the risk of long-term care is appropriately covered by some kind of 'risk pooling' but that private insurance cannot deliver at an acceptable cost and that (p. xvii):

> A hypothecated *unfunded* social insurance fund would not be appropriate for the UK system. A *prefunded* scheme would constitute a significant lifetime burden for young people and could create an uncertain and inappropriate call on future consumption.

That last comment seems justifiable in the British context where, as the last two chapters have shown, the NHS is tax funded and the NI system has virtually collapsed. Hence the Royal Commission offers a classic justification for an universalist approach (p. xvii):

The most efficient way of pooling risk, giving the best value to the nation as a whole, is through services underwritten by general taxation, based on need rather than wealth.

Unfortunately the Royal Commission were not unanimous. Two members appended a note of dissent, arguing against the central proposal. More ominously, the government did not respond positively, the report secured minimal press coverage and rumours suggest that the key recommendation is not welcome. The Royal Commission partly anticipated this outcome with some more limited suggestions on ways to reduce the impact of the means-testing system.

After this diversion to mention the Royal Commission report, there is a need, before leaving this section, to say more about other care services. Social services authorities organize, or purchase from independent providers, a variety of day care services. For elderly people, there may be day centres where people can go for company, social activities, occupational therapy, perhaps cheap midday meals, and perhaps some aid or advice. Similar facilities are often provided for handicapped people. For the younger handicapped people, and particularly for people with learning difficulties, there are centres where company and therapy may be accompanied by productive activities. In some cases, these are more or less sheltered workshops, doing commercially sponsored work and paying pocket money to handicapped people. There are some difficult distinctions to be drawn here between sheltered work, therapy and provision for some day-time life outside the home. Under the community care legislation, the government's expectation is that local authorities will become more flexible about the range of help they provide *in the community* and, of course, that they will make use of an increasingly wide range of non-statutory providers.

The primary form of domiciliary care supported or provided by social services authorities is home-help services. These have developed remarkably from a service conceived primarily to help in maternity cases to large enterprises serving predominantly elderly people, and thus playing an important part in helping old people manage in their own homes. Local authorities in England provide, directly or through independent agencies, nearly half a million households with home help (Department of Health, 1998b, table C4, p. 63). Of course, people may purchase their own domestic help unaided by a local authority, and where services are inadequate, the gap is likely to be filled by large amounts of unpaid work by relatives and neighbours. Local authorities may charge for home-help services, and may use means tests to determine the level of the charge. In the aftermath of the community care changes, there is a serious need to rationalize charging and means-testing practices.

Local authorities may also support the provision of meals, taken to people in their own homes. These 'meals on wheels' services are often provided through a voluntary organization. Again, the extent of coverage varies widely from area to area, from, at one extreme, a 'token' meal a week to, at the other, the provision of a comprehensive, seven days a week service. Local authorities may set charges for this service, and the extent to which they subsidize it is variable.

Local authorities provide a range of other 'benefits in kind' to assist with the care of people within the community. The Chronically Sick and Disabled Persons Act of 1970 suggests a wide range of services that local authorities may offer to handicapped people. Despite the emphasis in that Act on local authority duties, the word 'may' in the last sentence is appropriate. There are wide variations in the adequacy of the help provided. Authorities may provide, and pay the rental costs of, telephones; they may adapt houses to meet the needs of disabled people; and they are able to provide a variety of aids to daily living. They tend, however, to impose budgetary limits that ration quite severely the money available for such benefits. However, a further piece of legislation, the Disabled Persons (Services, Consultation and Representation) Act of 1986, increases the rights of disabled people to be informed about provisions and consulted about their needs. This should have the effect of increasing the flow of services to the disabled people, but it has not been brought fully into operation.

The administration of these diverse mixes of services requires social services authorities to have a large work-force. The new purchaser–provider split means that the purchaser role in social services authorities has to be undertaken by 'care managers', who assess needs and commission services from the available providers.

The Relationship between Personal Social Services and the Health Service

In many respects, the concerns of the health service and those of the social services authorities overlap. People are likely to need mixtures of health care and social care. Increasingly, the NHS is trying to limit its care to what may be described as 'treatment'. Where possible, also, in-patient treatment is being replaced by out-patient treatment. Hospital stays are becoming shorter, the aim being to send patients 'home' as soon as high inputs of specialized treatment are no longer necessary. Mentally ill people are hospitalized as little as possible. It is broadly accepted that there is only very exceptionally a case for hospital care for those with severe learning difficulties. In general, there is a concern to maximize care 'within the community' rather than in hospitals.

Many people are in receipt of a combination of health treatment from GPs and community-based nursing staff, on the one hand, and social care, on the other. Deficiencies on either side may have to be made up by extra services on the other.

The discharge of patients from hospital in itself has substantial implications for personal social services provision. It is important that social support services are readily available at this stage. Hence day-to-day co-ordination between the two services is crucial.

In this context, there is a special problem when residential, including nursing home, care may be necessary. Hospital care is still free, whereas residential care deemed necessary by social services authorities is not. Charges are determined by means tests. The changes described earlier, in the arrangements made for residential care together with the increasing unwillingness of the health service to keep people in hospital, is creating situations in which people are discovering that they have to pay substantial amounts for social care in situations in which, in the past, they might have expected free hospital care. Obviously, this was one of the issues that contributed to the need for the Royal Commission's investigation reported above.

Another, very different example of the need for inter-service co-ordination and co-operation is supplied by the problem of child abuse. Doctors and health visitors frequently discover non-accidental injury to children; yet it is the social services authorities that have the responsibility for preventative and legal action in these circumstances. Conversely, where social workers suspect child abuse, they may need medical confirmation of their suspicions. Once child abuse is suspected, continued vigilance is necessary. Sometimes it is a health service worker who is best placed to maintain a watching brief; sometimes it is a social worker. In many cases, both authorities accumulate evidence on the problem; it is important that they share that evidence both formally through case conferences and informally (Hallett and Stevenson, 1979).

The importance of the overlap between health and social services has led the Department of Health to encourage, and the local agencies to adopt, a variety of means of developing links. At the service planning level, the Department of Health has led the way by emphasizing the need to look at the health service and personal social services together. Within individual localities, they have encouraged the development of formal joint planning activities. A particular stimulus to this has been provided by 'joint financing'. Money from the health service budget is made available to help to finance projects within the social services authorities that can be considered to meet needs that might otherwise have to be met by the health service. In the long run, social services authorities are expected to take over the full cost of these ventures. However, where positive progress can be made in the shift of people from institutional to community care, a more direct transfer of resources from health to personal social services may occur (but only to cover the costs of those transferred).

The restructuring of arrangements for the delivery of both health services and local authority social services at the end of the 1980s brought issues about collaboration into sharper focus. The 1989 White Paper on community care (HMSO, 1989), which preceded the 1990 legislation, devoted a chapter to 'collaborative working'. In that chapter, it was argued (p. 49):

For the past 15 years policies designed to promote effective collaboration between health and local authorities have focused mainly on the mechanics of joint planning and joint finance. Significant progress has been made but this approach no longer fits well with the Government's aims for the NHS. . . . nor with its proposals for community care'.

The document went on to stress the government's concerns to have 'strengthened incentives and clearer responsibilities' .

However, there were aspects of those parts of the 1990 Act that were particularly concerned with health service organization which may have made collaboration more difficult. Overall, the Act may be seen as imposing tighter forms of budgetary control over the health service as a whole. One of the main implications of these is that they have increased the propensity of health authorities, at the margin, to try to pass on responsibilities to other agencies. The commissioner/provider split also complicates the relationship between service planning and service delivery. In addition, one other aspect of the reforms which may work against collaboration is that it ended local authority representation on health authorities of all kinds.

Despite all this, in the ferment after the 1990 Act, collaboration between the health service and the local authority social services was given a new impetus. That impetus has continued and, as was noted in chapter 6, is picked up again in various ways in the Labour Government's White Paper *The New NHS* (Department of Health, 1997). That document speaks of a requirement for NHS Executive

Regional Offices to 'take a stronger role in ensuring local partnerships are developed between the NHS and Local Authorities' (p. 23) and it claims that 'patients with continuing health and social care needs will get access to more integrated services through the joint investment plans for continuing and community care services which all Health Authorities are being asked to produce with partner agencies' (p. 27). The local authorities are expected to be involved in the Health Improvement Programmes and in Primary Care Groups so that local policy making is co-ordinated and they are involved in health care commissioning. Arrangements are expected to emerge in which collaboration is facilitated by the pooling of resources for some community care services.

Needs and Priorities

The new community care policies require local authorities to engage in planning exercises. At the same time, the increased central control over local authority finance (discussed on pages 64–5) involves the centre in making clear what it considers social services should be at the local level. There is an inevitable conflict, given that the grant to local authorities is largely non-specific, between this and local government autonomy. An increasing range of specific grants are changing this situation, adding to the capacity of the centre to prescribe local responses.

The increased recognition in the 1980s of the limited funds available for public services and the relationship between this and the growing need for social care (as a result, for example, of the growth of the numbers of very elderly people) have sharpened concern to find ways of balancing the respective contributions to what is called the 'mixed economy of welfare'. While this is sometimes presented as a new issue, social care has always involved some combination of care within the family and the community, care which is bought, care which is provided by voluntary and charitable agencies, and care which is provided by public agencies. What is perhaps new is acceptance that the contribution from the last source is inherently limited – hence the development of a lively debate about the roles of the other forms of care.

An important part of that debate concerns the search for ways of defining need, and identifying how public agencies should respond to it. Economists have a distinctive approach to this issue. Instead of attempting to tackle the concept of 'need', they emphasize the concept of demand, which they define as a willingness to buy at a given price. This approach emphasizes the price mechanism as a means of adjusting services to demands. If there is a high demand for a particular thing, then this will be reflected in a willingness to pay higher prices. Higher rewards will attract more suppliers, and may ultimately bring down the price. Always, however, an equilibrium is maintained in which supply and demand are balanced by the price mechanism. To what extent does this offer a solution to the problem of needs in the social services? Clearly, it does not if the local authority is the only supplier of a particular service or the controller of access to that service. Equally it does not if that authority is the funder of the service for low-income people without the resources to purchase it themselves. Conditions of monopoly or near monopoly then exist, in which, in theory, the supplier can determine the price, and those unable to pay must go without. The attempt to identify real needs regardless of ability to pay is the hallmark of the public service here. Rationing according to the capacity to pay is quite widely regarded as an inferior way of distributing many such services. The price mechanism solution is also inappropriate where it is arguable that people who need particular services are either unlikely to recognize the need or to translate it into an effective, money-backed demand. Social work services designed primarily to protect children from their parents fall into this category. There remain, however, services like the home-help service that are provided both by the statutory authorities and by the private market. In some sense, the need for these services can be regarded as fairly limitless – most of us would like our domestic chores to be done by someone else. The price mechanism seems to offer a basis for distinguishing absolute need from effective demand, and of allowing for the existence, side by side, of a public and a private sector.

The use of the price mechanism may be fair enough in theory, but what happens to those with high needs, in some absolute sense, but a low capacity to pay? There are two possible answers to this objection to the use of the price mechanism. One is that social affairs should be arranged in such a way that what are really income maintenance problems do not have to be solved by the provision of subsidized services. This is an attractive argument, but one that matches poorly the real world. The other is that means tests should be devised to enable cheaper services to be given in some cases. The trouble with this latter solution is that it can cope with situations in which only a minority has to be helped outside the market-place, but it quite destroys the market concept when it has to be widespread. The reality is that for many of the personal social services (including the home-help service) some more fundamental way of defining need is required: a minority can buy the services on the open market; but there remains a large group who appear to need them free or at a reduced price, only some of whom actually receive them. The problem remains of determining how much the service should expand to meet the unmet needs (Judge, 1987); for a strong pro-pricing line see Harris and Seldon (1976).

This digression into the market approach to need was necessary, first because it has significant advocates, and second because it offers a challenge to the definition of need. The alternative is the ascertainment of some more absolute way of determining need. In some cases this does not seem too problematic; in relation to some diseases, for example, there may be a finite group whom it is generally agreed are in need of treatment. In other cases, however, the problem is one of making a distinction between 'absolute need' and some more limited concept. While I may contend that I need my house cleaned to free me to write books, you may argue that I am still physically capable of doing this work while others are not. They, you will say, are the ones really in need. So, would this be a disagreement about needs or about priorities?

For the personal social services, then, the determination of needs is complicated first by the fact that the authorities do not have the sole responsibility to meet certain kinds of needs, and second because their views of needs must be determined by their views of priorities.

Theoretically, the purchaser–provider split in community care requires the care managers to take decisions about need, based on some of the ideal considerations set out above. They must then commission the services they regard as appropriate. At that stage, means testing is likely to occur. However, it is doubtful whether this split system operates in this way in reality. The author's own experience, when seeking care for elderly relatives, is that once social services staff gather that people are unlikely to qualify for subsidized care they leave them to find their own way around the 'market'.

Social Work in Social Services Authorities

The social work aspect of local authority field-work is often emphasized; in Scotland the authorities are called 'social work departments', while in England and Wales social workers occupy many senior management roles. However, it is important to recognize two things: first, that the support of people in their own homes is carried out by a variety of workers, not all of whom are, or should be regarded as, social workers; and second, that the coming of the care management task has led to a challenge to social workers as front-line case-workers. The practical tasks of identifying what are often straight-forward, readily identifiable needs and securing the services needed to meet those needs may be performed by workers without the specific training given to social workers. Local authorities may find it more practical, and cheaper, to use other staff in these roles.

In general, the distinction here between the social work task and other tasks is a difficult one to make. The public often makes no distinction between social work and many other caring activities. This has implications not only for social workers' 'professional' aspirations, but also for the costs of various services, since trained social workers are relatively expensive.

The roots of contemporary British social work are diverse. In the nineteenth century, charities employed case-workers to enhance their capacity to discriminate between the deserving and undeserving poor, and to ensure that the alms that were provided were used efficiently. Charitable hospitals particularly needed staff to assess the extent to which people could pay for their services. Early in the twentieth century, the development of psychiatry and psychotherapy stimulated the development of some forms of case-work for people who were mentally ill, but social work in its modern form did not really take off until the setting up of Children Departments in local authorities in the 1940s (Packman, 1975). Even after that, there was still very little conception of a specific social work task in relation to other clients until the 1970s, when a notion that there could be a generic social work skill applicable to a wide range of problems was an important influence on the legislation which created the local author-ity social services function as we understand it today (Hall, 1976).

During the 1970s, the numbers of trained social workers in local authority employment increased rapidly. The advocates of genericism made some progress, and trained social workers became involved in activities in which they had hitherto been rare – such as the care of elderly people. Then there were setbacks for the profession: in particular, the concepts of care management and care assessment embodied in the 1990 Health Services and Community Care Act do not presuppose that the key workers will be formally trained social workers.

There are some forms of field-work which are seen as needing social work skills. Attention has already been drawn, in the section on children's services, to the special skills needed to determine whether children are at risk and to engage in preventative work in these circumstances. There has been a general tendency for workers in this field – other than residential workers – to have social work qualifications. Social workers have statutory duties under the 1983 Mental Health Act to assess and take appropriate action when mentally ill people appear to require compulsory hospitalization. It is perhaps anomalous that this is the only area of social services activity for which a specific qualification is mandatory. In its 1998 White Paper (Department of Health, 1998c), the government promises future legislation which will replace the existing training body for social work (the Central Council for Education and Training in Social Work) with a 'General Social Care Council which will . . . set conduct and practice standards for all social services staff; and register those in the most sensitive areas' (para 5.6). While this may in the long run imply specific training and other requirements for many areas of social care work the White Paper makes it clear that early attention will be given to issues about the staffing of homes (para 5.27) and about the operation of services for children (para 5.28).

What is clear, however, is that while there is consensus about the need for more training, there is still going to be extensive controversy about what that training should be. The model of training espoused by social work academics, based in universities and colleges, is not altogether shared by many of the decision makers in central and local government. There has been an extensive debate about what social work is, and a related one about whether it can be practised within local authority social services authorities. That debate is clearly unhelpful to those who would seek to establish unambiguous roles for social workers. Significantly, in a recent compendium, *The Blackwell Companion to Social Work* (Davies, 1997) which contains extensive discussions of many controversial issues about social work, the reader will not find a concise account of *what social work is*.

Many of the needs for social work help are seldom expressed – at least not in any straightforward sense. The pressures that lead to calls for more social work come from the anxieties of the public and politicians about child abuse, the deterioration of old people who live alone, or the disturbance caused by aggressive, mentally ill people, for example. These are issues of social control as much as of service. Pressure also results from the many requests that come to social services authorities that are not so much for specific services as for help with a wide range of problems of poverty and deprivation. Social work is seen as having a contribution to make to the problems of underprivileged communities in many different ways; indeed, these expectations often go way beyond the profession's capacities, particularly when political and economic problems are perceived as social or individual ones.

The Relationship between the Personal Social Services and Income Maintenance

Some of the functions that, today, fall to social services authorities have, at earlier times, been within local authority health, education or even housing departments. However, further back in time, before 1948, there was a strong association between the personal social services and income maintenance within the poor-law. It is worth looking a little more at the separation of these two services that exists today, and at some of the factors that partially undermine that separation, particularly because they have important implications for some of the dilemmas about the social work role.

The political commitment, in the 1940s, to separating income maintenance from the personal social services was influenced by a hatred of the poor-law. It was seen as possible to develop services for all freed from the stigma of the means test and the workhouse when the National Assistance Act of 1948 gave all income maintenance responsibilities to a national body and the duty to provide residential and domiciliary care to the local authorities. The services for children were given a quite distinct identity by the Children Act of 1948, and developed their own special approach to care within the children's departments of the local authorities. A concept of social work was able to develop that was very different from that within US welfare departments, where income maintenance and social work are closely linked. Social workers, regardless of their political persuasion, came to see it as very important that they are able to give aid, advice and support to their clients without at the same time having responsibility for their incomes. What this implies is that, whereas personal social services under the poor-law were essentially for the poor, and were very involved in the control of the lives of the poor, today in the British system it is possible to conceive of the benefits of the services as available to all without discrimination.

That, then, is the ideal; the reality is a little different (Becker and Macpherson, 1988). It is clearly the case that a very high proportion of the users of the personal social services are low-income people. It is difficult to envisage a situation in which it could be otherwise. The peculiarity of the personal social services is that they are concerned with a range of benefits that is also provided in other very different ways, by both commercial enterprises and voluntary activities. The very existence of a statutory group of services of this kind poses some delicate questions about the nature of the balance between this and individual, family and community provisions. The assumption is that the statutory provisions are necessary when the others fail. Politicians worry about the possibility that private responsibilities will be abandoned in favour of public ones or that public service 'dependencies' will be engendered. This is possible; it is in the nature of statutory intervention in areas generally the realm of private action that it may alter behaviour. However, typically, those who seek help from the personal social services do so only when other possibilities no longer exist. An absence of other ways of meeting such needs is particularly associated with poverty.

Several connections between income maintenance and the personal social services therefore exist. Most services are rationed by means of charges. Indeed, as noted above, the new community care legislation, together with financial pressures on local government, have increased the importance of charges. If charges are not to deter the poor, however, they must be abated through means tests. These need to be related to the other means tests within the social security system.

That is one connection. The other is more complicated, and more clearly explains the social work concern about the separation of their services from income maintenance. There is a correlation between the forms of pathology that come to the attention of social workers – delinquency, child abuse, even publicly threatening mental illness – and poverty (Jones, 1997). It is difficult to summarize here a very complex, and deeply value-laden, debate. Strands within it include arguments about the extent to which the rich can hide their pathology, or seek help from sources other than social services authorities; about the extent to which poverty causes social pathology, and vice versa; and about the extent to which this 'deviance' simply involves labelling the non-conformity of the poor. The fact is, however, that it is primarily low-income people who become the clients of publicly employed social workers.

It is this fact that leads many who have written about social work to stress the importance of a relationship with the poor that does not include responsibility for their incomes (Jordan, 1974). Yet, at the same time, many social workers recognize a need to help clients with their income maintenance problems. There is a power under the 1989 Children Act (carried forward and enlarged from earlier legislation dating in the first place from 1963), and under a related but rather more all-embracing provision in Scotland, enabling money payments to be made to help social services clients where these might assist in keeping children out of care. Here, then, is a statutory recognition of a connection between lack of money and social pathology. Yet this power is used comparatively little. In general, an alternative approach is preferred, in which social workers and other social services staff assist clients in claiming benefits from other agencies. Such work is generally described as 'welfare rights work' (Fimister, 1986). In some authorities, specialist workers who are often not social workers have been taken on to do this work. There has also been a considerable growth of aid and advice work on welfare benefit problems in voluntary agencies and advice bureaus. However, social workers are bound to have to take on some of this work; some do so with great commitment, while others feel that it distorts their activities and pulls them away from 'real' social work.

The character of welfare rights work has changed as the social security system has changed. Before 1980, the concern was to make supplementary benefits officers exercise their extensive discretionary powers. After 1980, the complex structure of apparent 'rights' required that poor people secured help in finding their way through the regulations, identifying things to which they were entitled, and making the increasingly hard-pressed social security administration grind into action. The social security changes brought in by the 1986 Act threw social workers and welfare rights specialists into turmoil. Rights to single payments more or less disappeared. The social fund scheme seemed to require social services personnel to replace the pursuit of rights to benefits for their clients by collaboration with social security officers to determine need for community care grants. The loans provisions for other forms of help, administered by officers with high levels of discretion, similarly suggested a need for a very different approach to allocating resources to clients. The position is further complicated by the fact that social services authorities retain their power to make grants described above. In practice, most authorities' budgets for this item are very limited. If this were to change, or if social workers were to be co-opted into helping to determine needs for social fund grants and loans, then social workers could be back into money rationing responsibilities in a big way. This development was feared when the social fund was introduced; but in practice, social workers seem to have coped with the conflict, very often by turning a deaf ear to material needs; see Becker and Silburn (1990) for a discussion of these issues.

The complicated system of benefits for disabled people, which may interact with provisions for institutional care and the provision of caring services, also poses a number of problems for social services clients where welfare rights advice can be invaluable (Fimister, 1995). In many respects, as engaging with the mainstream system of means-tested benefits has become more difficult, local authority welfare rights activity has increased its concentration on these issues, together with work like debt counselling.

The Role of the Voluntary Sector

Reference has already been made to the mixed economy of welfare. In this economy, voluntary agencies are, alongside family, community and private enterprise, an element of considerable importance. Voluntary organizations carry out many functions on behalf of social services authorities. Under the new community care provisions, they may be providers, entering into contracts with social services authorities. These entail large grants and, in some cases, the truly voluntary component of the work is small. Increasingly, services for elderly people and for specific groups of handicapped people are provided by voluntary organizations, some of which have a nationwide remit. Similarly, voluntary organizations are substantial providers of residential care.

There is a variety of ways in which individual volunteers are used in the personal social services. They may be deployed under the auspices of voluntary agencies. They may be organized under schemes requiring community service of convicted offenders, or schemes to provide work for the unemployed in return for special allowances (should those in these two categories properly be called volunteers?); or they may be individuals who undertake, by direct arrangements with the authorities, to help with particular tasks. A wide range of tasks may be involved: supportive visiting of clients, taking people from residential homes out in cars, helping social services clients with decorating or gardening, helping to run clubs and day centres, and so on.

All this voluntary input into the personal social services may be seen as helping to multiply the amount and range of services available for a given amount of public expenditure. It may also be seen as adding a community dimension to a service that is in danger of becoming too bureaucratized and professionalized. Some of it is a logical extension of the way in which the personal social services are called in to replace or buttress independent caring in the community. In this way, it may be seen as helping to put back a community support system that, in the best of all worlds, should have been there all along.

However, there are problems with this balance between statutory effort and voluntary effort. The latter may be seen as a way of achieving personal social services 'on the cheap'. People often support voluntary organizations because they want to add something extra to the statutory service, perhaps something that it cannot or will not do. They may feel that their efforts and their donations are being used simply to meet needs that the state should meet.

While it was suggested above that volunteer services may be better than bureaucratic or professional ones, they may also be worse. Social workers who are reluctant to make use of volunteers suggest that they may be unreliable; they may be indiscreet; they may give gratuitous advice where none is desired; and they may give inappropriate advice and interfere in problems they do not understand (Holme and Maizels, 1978). Voluntary help often comes from people who are very unlike the people who need help, the middle-class and the middle-aged being prominent among the ranks of volunteers.

It may be argued that what is needed in many situations is the development of community-based self-help activities, not the importation of volunteers from outside. On the other hand, it would be rash to suggest that this form of voluntary activity is without its problems. Some of the points about unreliability and indiscretion certainly also apply to this form of voluntary activity. Equally, encouraging situations in which communities help themselves may also be seen as providing social services on the cheap. If it is not to be seen like this, then another problem must be confronted: namely, that community self-help may also entail the making of demands for new services from the authorities. This form of voluntary activity may therefore entail situations in which authorities subsidize their own pressure groups. Some social services authorities have been able to accept relationships with the voluntary sector that involve this. Others have been unwilling to see volunteers in other than traditional, supplementary service-giving roles.

Conclusions

The responsibilities of the social services authorities in England and Wales, and the social work departments in Scotland, involve a wide range of activities. These extend from the provision or commissioning of relatively precise benefits and services, through a variety of residential and day care facilities, to a number of very personal, individualized services. They include a high proportion of the social work practised in these countries.

This mixture of activities has grown rapidly. The growth is perceived with quite considerable anxiety by the public, since most of the activities were hitherto undertaken outside the statutory sector, within the family and the community. One interpretation of this growth is that public services can now be provided to help to strengthen family and community life. If this view is taken, then residential care replaces the neglect of the isolated old, and social work helps families to cope with crises that would hitherto have destroyed them, and so on. However, there is an alternative view, that the growth in these services is itself an index of social pathology, that people are not coping so well with aspects of life that in the past were of little concern to public services. This ambivalence is compounded by widespread uncertainty about what social services authorities do (indeed, they are often confused with social security departments), a vague conception of the social worker's role, and a deep uncertainty about the circumstances under which help may be sought from the various specific services.

The implementation of the new community care policies complicates the position. In some respects, hidden behind the rhetoric of 'care' is a concern to push responsibility back on to the 'community', the latter meaning, in practice, often hard-pressed relatives.

Social services in Britain are going through an intense period of change, which it is difficult to portray accurately. Different authorities are changing at different rates. Two new fissures are occurring in the authorities which many tried to integrate in the late 1970s and early 1980s: between children's services and adult services, and between those given purchaser roles and those given provider roles. Government surveillance over social services is increasing. The 1998 White Paper contains indications of future policy directions which may erode local autonomy and transform the pattern of service provision: the encouragement of joint working with health authorities, new grants for specific innovations, more rigorous inspection and even the threat that inefficient service providers will be replaced.

Suggestions for further reading

There is a lack of up-to-date books on the personal social services. A volume edited by this author *Local Authority Social Services* will be published in 2000. The Department of Health's White Paper (1998c) offers both an account of some of the contemporary issues in the personal social services and ideas for the future. There are a number of accounts of the new community care policies. Means and Smith's *Community Care: Policy and Practice* (1994) is particularly recommended. The issue of the 'mixed economy of welfare' is explored in an article by Judge (1982).

The Blackwell Companion to Social Work edited by Davies (1997) offers commentaries on many of the issues about social work, but little on the organizational context. Unfortunately, much of the work on social work and social security predates the social fund, though the collection edited by Becker and Macpherson (1988) is a partial exception to this. As far as community care and social security is concerned, however, Fimister (1995) is a valuable up-to-date source.

Chapter 8

EDUCATION

Introduction

The state's role in education is a dual one; it is the major provider of education, and has also assumed a responsibility to supervise it in the sector for which it is not directly responsible. About 6 per cent of the UK's schoolchildren are in private schools.

Historically, the public sector has been seen as involving a partnership between central and local government, yet recent years have seen a shift towards much greater dominance by the centre. The introduction of the National Curriculum by the Conservative Government in the late 1980s marked a significant shift towards centralization. However, the fall of the Conservatives has brought in an even more interventionalist central administration. The next four sections of this chapter both describe the structure of the central–local relationship in respect of the control of education and explore many of its manifestations. As in chapter 6, on the health service, a full exploration of these issues is essential before moving on, in the later sections, to some of the key issues about policy context, in which concerns about educational disadvantage loom large.

The Main Features of the Education System

In Scotland, Wales and Northern Ireland, education is the responsibility of the devolved governments. In England, the relevant central government department is the Department for Education and Employment (DfEE).

The majority of schools are, as has long been the case, the responsibility of local government in Britain. They come under the counties, the metropolitan and other single-tier districts, and the London boroughs. In Northern Ireland, they come under appointed education and libraries boards. However, legislation forces local authorities to fund schools on the basis of a centrally determined formula and to delegate significant management responsibilities to their own governing bodies.

Under the 1988 Education Act, the Conservative government opened up the possibility for schools to be directly funded by central government, through funding agencies. They might apply (with the agreement of a majority of parents) to apply to become 'grant-maintained'. Their everyday management then became the responsibility of their own governing bodies. If 75 per cent achieve that status, the funding agency takes over full responsibility for provision for the area. The number of schools that secured grant-maintained status was in practice comparatively small. By 1997, there were 514 primary schools (2 per cent of the total) and 680 secondary schools (15 per cent) (DfEE, 1998a, p. 19). They were nearly all in England.

The Conservatives also set up fifteen City Technology Colleges in England and Wales, on an experimental basis, to provide some privately managed, centrally funded secondary education.

In the School Standards and Framework Act of 1998 the new Labour government abolished this grant maintained status for schools. Instead these schools have been allowed to apply to become 'foundation' schools under the overall supervision of their relevant local authority but with a status which enables them to retain special arrangements for their government and a substantial measure of autonomous control over their land and property. However they have lost the special funding position, which had derived from Conservative efforts to promote them, and some therefore find that they have less income. This has been highlighted by publicised appeals for extra support from parents for the school to which the Prime Minister sends his sons. The School Standards and Framework Act made it clear that the government accepts diverse managements for schools, particularly if the local authority's record as a manager

Table 8.1   Numbers (thousands) in further and higher education 1995–96

	Part-time	Full-time
In further education	1,839	768
Undergraduates (higher education)	531	1,048
Post-graduates	187	136

Source: Figures calculated from table 3.8 in Central Statistical Office, 1998, p. 61.

has not been good. Under the Act it has assumed powers to intervene where it considers that a local education authority has failed to carry out its duties adequately. This may involve making alternative arrangements for the management of specific parts of a local authority's service including, therefore, the management of particular schools. An example of the use of this power arose early in 1999 when the DfEE sought tenders to run a comprehensive school in Surrey that had been severely criticized by inspectors. The contract was won by the managers of a City Technology College in the West Midlands. At the time this chapter is going to press a whole local authority education system, that of the London Borough of Hackney, is threatened with replacement.

Higher education and further education are outside local authority control. In England and Wales, two government-appointed funding councils deal with the financing of these two sectors, and thus, in various respects, control them. There are separate, but broadly similar, funding councils in Scotland and Northern Ireland. The concepts of further and higher education embrace a number of different activities: vocational education, further academic education (both of a kind provided generally in schools and at higher levels) and non-vocational adult education. Education for degrees and for post-graduate qualifications is provided in universities and in colleges of higher education. Table 8.1 provides some statistics on numbers in higher and further education (overseas students are included in these numbers, but there are few of them below post-graduate level). Since people go into further and higher education at various ages, it is difficult to calculate a participation rate for a generation as a whole, but it is estimated that about a third of the young adult population experience higher education (Office of National Statistics, 1999b, table 3.13, p. 61).

The school system can be identified as involving three sectors: a small pre-primary sector, primary education and secondary education. In most cases, these sectors can be identified respectively with the education of children under five, between five and eleven, and between eleven and the school-leaving age of sixteen (with many pupils continuing at school until eighteen). However, some authorities have developed systems that deviate from the strict break between primary and secondary education at 11-plus. These have generally introduced an intermediate, middle-school system, for children in two or three of the year bands between nine and thirteen years old. A few have developed separate schools to split the secondary age group.

One innovation of the latter kind has been the introduction of 'sixth form colleges' for the over-sixteens. The educational arrangements for those over the minimal school-leaving age is further complicated by the fact that further education colleges offer both practical and academic courses for people in the sixteen to eighteen age bracket. Of all sixteen- to eighteen-year-olds, 74 per cent are in education and training. These are divided between about 21 per cent in schools, 36 per cent in further education colleges, 10 per cent on government training schemes and 7 per cent already in higher education (DfEE, 1998a).

The arrangement for the starting of compulsory education at the age of five differentiates Britain from many other countries, which do not make it compulsory until six or seven. However, the concomitant was that public pre-school education was, until recently, ill-developed. This began to change in the 1990s. By 1996–7, 58 per cent of three- and four-year-olds were in nursery schools (Central Statistical Office, 1998, p. 60). The Conservative government had, shortly before their fall in 1997, introduced a voucher system, to enable parents of four-year-old children to buy private provision or use their vouchers for any available public provision. The new Labour government repealed this scheme, committing itself instead to a dramatic increase in public provision. It provided a significant injection of cash and promised to provide places for all four-year-olds and two-thirds of all three-year-olds.

The main point of note about policies for primary education has been the ferment of experimentation through the last forty years. Initially, change took the form of diverse, often locally inspired, innovation. Primary schools were transformed from formal institutions in which uniformed children sat in straight rows in classes streamed on the basis of tests of educational ability to very informal places where pupils moved about freely to work together in little clusters drawn from mixed-ability classes. The gradual elimination of selection at 11-plus clearly contributed to this 'liberation' of primary schools. It was an interesting example of a change that developed from the bottom, and never required any formal recognition in legislation, which may nevertheless be regarded as a major policy development. However, in the late 1970s and early 1980s, its implications began to receive attention. Voices began to be raised questioning whether this largely professionally driven innovation has gone too far. There was a growing concern about levels of literacy and numeracy, with responsibility for their alleged inadequacy some-times attributed to this educational revolution. Increased controls, involving a national curriculum, testing and more rigorous inspection under the 1988 Education Act, were a response to this concern. These developments are discussed further on pages 194–7. Diversity ceased to be celebrated and there were pressures against the more extreme examples of informality. Under the new Labour government, this reversal has been continued, with quite explicit central prescrip-tions about the amounts of time to be devoted to formal teaching designed to increase literacy and numeracy (the so-called 'literacy' and 'numeracy' hours) and even recommendations about amounts of homework to be done by children.

In chapter 2 (page 38), it was shown how the idea of the compre-hensive secondary school gradually replaced the bipartite or tripartite system envisaged at the time of the passing of the 1944 Education Act. By 1979, the development of comprehensive education was nearing completion. The Labour government had, in the 1976 Edu-cation Act, required local authorities to develop plans for comprehen-sivization. A minority of authorities were holding out on this. On coming to power, the Conservatives repealed this law; this had the effect of stemming the tide, but not reversing it. In 1996–7, about 85 per cent of secondary school children in the public sector in the UK were in comprehensive schools (Central Statistical Office, 1998, p. 60, table 3.2). In the mid-1990s, the Conservative government had encouraged a partial return to selectivity, mainly by enabling schools to reserve a small proportion of their places for pupils with identified higher abilities in general or in specific subjects such as music. Labour, on return to power, in 1997, decided not to revert to its 1970s' stance of pushing through to total comprehensivization, without reference to local opinion. On the other hand, in a move characteristic of its stance on the powers of local government (see also pages 63–5 and 187–8), it did not simply leave the veto power in the hands of elected local authorities but decided instead that pro-comprehensive campaigners should be able (if they could secure the signatures of 20 per cent of eligible parents) to secure local ballots of parents on the issue, in the areas where selection was still in use.

Paradoxically, the change to the education system for those over eleven years of age, in most areas, did not have as dramatic an effect on teaching over children over eleven as it did on that for children under eleven. The continued importance of examinations at the ages of sixteen and eighteen meant that, in many respects, the comprehensive schools had to have ability divisions and different programmes of instruction within them.

Paying for the Education System

Table 8.2 provides a brief picture of the pattern of public expenditure on education in the UK. Much of the expenditure on schools will be the responsibility of local authorities, but these are (as was shown in chapter 3) heavily supported by central government grants. Public education in state schools in Britain is free. Even from the Right, there has been little challenge to the principle that education in state schools should be free. There have been some attempts on the Right to make a case for education vouchers, which could be cashed at both state and private schools. Only in the area of nursery schooling did this movement have some temporary success, until the fall of the Conservative government in 1997.

On the other hand, there has been a much more effective challenge to the maintenance of free higher education. There is a system of tuition fees for higher education, with all British students having to pay a fixed fee (at the time of writing £1000) unless their parents or they (if they are 'mature students') have very low incomes. Postgraduate education is subsidized for some through grants from research councils. There is considerable competition for these; consequently, many students (or their parents) are paying for postgraduate education. Some further, non-vocational education has to be paid for by students, but generally the fees are subsidized.

In this area of education, there is not merely an issue about fees

Table 8.2 Education expenditure in the United Kingdom

	Expenditure £ millions	Percentage of the total
Nursery and primary schools	10,191	31%
Secondary schools	9,841	30%
Special schools	1,619	5%
Higher and further education	9,820	30%
Other items	1,169	4%
Total	32,640	

Source: Calculated from Office of National Statistics, 1999b, table 3.25. p. 68.

but also about grants for maintenance costs. The former system of means-tested grants has been replaced by a loan system (which applies to all except young students whose parents have very low incomes and mature students with low incomes). Loans have to be repaid once students are in work and have incomes of over £10,000 (that is the correct figure at the time of writing but it may, of course, be raised later).

It is argued in justification of this system that students receive public funds while delaying starting to make a contribution to national income. Nevertheless, by studying, they enhance their own future earning potential. It is therefore argued to be reasonable to expect students to repay all or some of the benefit bestowed on them in this way. Critics of loan schemes point to the benefit the nation gains from its educated people, and warn that loan schemes may deter some people, particularly people from low-income families, from entering higher education.

There is an even less satisfactory situation with regard to the financial support of students outside universities, particularly with regard to those between sixteen and eighteen years of age. It is mandatory that local authorities pay grants to university students; but other further education grants are discretionary. This clearly has unfair consequences from time to time. Local authorities may pay limited means-tested maintenance awards to the parents of young-sters who are over the school-leaving age. These again are discretion-ary, and are not extensive in coverage. Those who have left school cannot even claim social security benefits. Except in exceptional cases, financial help for sixteen- to eighteen-year-olds is conditional on entering training schemes.

Control over the Education System

The control of education in Britain involves what has been described as a 'partnership' between central and local government. Yet, clearly, that partnership has been largely undermined. Since central govern-ment exercises strict control over local government expenditure, the fact that education accounts for around half of this expenditure inevitably puts it in the spotlight. Furthermore, politicians at national level take a great interest in the way education is organized and conducted. The development of comprehensive education was an issue that fundamentally divided the parties. Governments have also felt it important to take stands on such matters as literacy, the core content of the curriculum, the role of nursery education and the future of higher education. We will see evidence on this from both Conservative and Labour governments (pages 194–7). In the latter case, the rhetoric about dealing with 'failing schools' has led, as was already shown above, to a willingness to replace local authority control in some cases.

The uneasy relationship between central and local government is not the only area in which there is a power struggle within the British educational system. At the local level, the running of the system involves a number of different groups which are contending for influence or protecting their prerogatives. Most local authorities appoint an education committee, consisting primarily of councillors, but including some representatives of other groups interested in education, such as teachers, churches and local universities. It is a generally accepted convention that, on contentious political matters, the non-councillor members should restrain their intervention. The committee is served by a chief education officer, who leads a team of officials who generally have teaching qualifications. There is thus a strong professionally oriented administrative group at this level.

Schools are required to have governing bodies. These are required to consist of parents, teachers, co-opted members and local education authority nominees. As pointed out above, these bodies are now responsible for delegated budgets partly guaranteed by the secretary of state. They have significant control over appointments.

An issue which has received considerable attention has been parental choice of schools for their children. While there were high pupil–teacher ratios and pressure on school numbers in many parts of the country, the scope for parental choice was fairly limited. As school rolls have fallen, though, the situation has changed. In urban areas, in particular, variations in the popularity of schools have often become very clear. In the Education Act of 1980, the government tried to provide parents with some measure of choice over schools. Local authorities are required to give information which will help parents to choose schools, and there is an appeal procedure available for those whose wishes are not granted. Parental choice seems to be operating as a curb on innovation by teachers; it may also be helping to determine where cuts will be made. Inasmuch as it is more likely to be exercised by middle-class parents, it may be enhancing the tendency for there to be a hierarchy of schools, under the influence of geographical location. Patterns of social and ethnic segregation may thereby be enhanced (Gewirtz et al., 1995).

In the schools themselves, head teachers expect a considerable measure of freedom in determining how their school is run and the way in which subjects are taught. They operate, of course, in consultation with their teachers, but vary extensively in the extent to which they allow staff participation in decision making. In the last resort, however, the class teacher clearly has some autonomy in determining his or her input, and relationship to pupils.

However, contemporary political developments have influenced these relationships. The next section will look at the ways in which central control over the curriculum has increased. That has been accompanied by the development of a system of school inspection run by a quasi-autonomous agency – the Office for Standards in Education (universally called Ofsted) – which regularly produces reports, some of which are highly critical both of the way schools are managed and of the effectiveness of individual teachers. On top of this, now, teachers have been put even more directly under the government spotlight. In a Consultation Document published in December 1998, the Secretary of State proposed a new career structure for teachers involving the operation of a rigorous appraisal and assessment system and a salary structure that would involve extra rewards for good teachers (DfEE, 1998b).

The further and higher education systems have experienced parallel developments under the supervision of their funding councils. In higher education, the expectation that staff may be researchers as well as teachers has meant the development of a 'research assessment exercise' in which research and publications are assessed by an expert panel drawn from within the profession. Part of the funding formula for universities and colleges is based on this exercise.

All of the education system has experienced the development of a control system in which the activities of teachers are increasingly under scrutiny. Under the Conservatives, there was some attempt to make the crucial control devices market-based. The success or failure of schools and colleges were to depend on their success in attracting students (and, in higher education, and research funds). The new government is less happy with the use of such devices, but we therefore see, instead, further prescriptions about how activities should be carried out and the strengthening of methods of checking that the instructions given are followed. In the next section, this theme is explored further, with reference to the national curriculum.

The Government and the Curriculum

The 1988 Act introduced a requirement that a national curriculum should be developed for use in all state financed schools. That curriculum consists of three core subjects – English, Maths and

Science (plus Welsh in Welsh-speaking areas) – and seven foundation subjects – History, Geography, Technology, Music, Art, Physical Education and another modern language (for over-11s). There is also a requirement to provide a programme of religious education, which reflects the 'dominance' of Christianity in Britain. Curriculum councils have been set up to keep these developments under review.

Linked to that curriculum is the testing of children at seven, eleven, fourteen and sixteen years of age. The testing system involves the setting of attainment targets, and is carried out under the supervision a central curriculum and assessment body.

These measures represent a marked departure from the philosophy of the 1944 Education Act, which left most education under local government control and issues about the determination of the curriculum largely in the hands of teachers, operating with an eye on the entrance requirements of higher education and the expectations of employers.

Results of the statutory tests are published, providing data on the 'achievements' of individual schools in a form which encourages their presentation by the media in 'league tables'. Since much educational attainment is determined by factors outside the control of the schools, these can be very misleading. Some schools may be securing a considerable 'value-added' element in enhancing the achievements of children. Others may be doing very little for pupils who, by virtue of their socio-economic backgrounds, are likely to score well in tests in any case. Schools in the former group may be unfairly perceived as achieving little, while those in the latter group win unwarranted esteem. These comparisons encourage schools to try to recruit pupils with a high academic potential. Middle-class children, Asian children and girls have been regarded in some places as the pupils to attract (Gewirtz et al., 1995).

Sociological studies of education have suggested that as pupils approach school-leaving age, there are many factors, often beyond the control of the schools, that contribute to divisions between school-oriented 'academic' pupils and an anti-school group who increasingly see their education as irrelevant and who drop out of participation in all school activities (Ford, 1969; Willis, 1977). A relevant concern in secondary education, therefore, is not so much the fate of the brighter pupils – the comprehensive schools have been eager to 'prove themselves' by doing justice to the needs of this group – as the difficulties entailed in providing a relevant education for those at the other end of the ability range. There are related problems here, of course, of absenteeism and delinquency. Overall, the issue concerns the relationship of the education system to the needs of underprivileged groups in our society – for example, low-skilled workers and some ethnic minorities. Since, moreover, such groups are located in specific areas, there is a geographical dimension to this problem. One of the arguments advanced in favour of the comprehensive school is that it is able to take all the children of a limited geographical community, but suppose such a 'community' is manifestly not truly 'comprehensive', and, worse still, suppose atypical residents in that community take steps to educate their children elsewhere, then new distinctions arise between schools. This is a significant problem for comprehensive secondary education in Britain. It is one which has been intensified by government efforts to ensure that parents have maximum opportunities to choose schools for their children.

The Conservatives governments of the 1980s and 1990s seemed prepared to disregard these issues in favour of an approach to education which emphasized the raising of standards through competition between schools. The rhetoric of the Labour politicians suggests a commitment to changing this. In its manifesto, Labour argued that 'far too many children are denied the opportunity to succeed', spoke of 'zero tolerance of underperformance' and said 'no matter where a school is, Labour will not tolerate under-achievement'. The new government has given a high priority to education. It headlined the education section in its 'annual report' for 1997–8 (HMSO 1998, p. 30):

> The Government's aim is to build a world-class education system by taking excellence wherever it is found and spreading it widely. We want every school to be a good school so that parents know that wherever they send their children they will get a decent education.

Several measures aim towards that goal:

- The establishment of Education Action Zones in deprived areas, where public/private partnerships have been set up to try to secure additional investment and to encourage innovation
- Setting improvement targets for schools and assuming government powers to intervene in failing schools (including the power to impose an alternative management system, as described above)
- Establishing a network of the best performing schools as 'beacon schools' which may play a role in disseminating best practice to others
- New investments to reduce class sizes

All this has not involved any move away from the interventions in relation to central oversight of the curriculum, testing (and the publication of tests) and rigorous inspection set up by the Conservatives. The underlying question here is whether a search for 'excellence' throughout the education system, with a strong emphasis on standards can be sustained without, in the process, creating winners and losers. It is in no way to decry all this effort to point out that, in the last analysis, an education system channels people toward the limited opportunities that exist in the wider society. In aiming to raise education standards for all, the government has an obvious political need to reassure parents whose children are already benefiting from the best the system has to offer that the process is one, to borrow other words from the Labour manifesto, of 'levelling up, not levelling down'. Yet any emphasis on reducing educational disadvantage must imply, in a race that all cannot win, advancing some at the expense of others. The new government is obviously struggling with this problem. A negative assessment of this is to suggest, as for example David (1988) does, that little is really changing. An alternative view is that a shift of attention away from crude competition between schools, in which those with the right social catchment areas must inevitably win, towards a more egalitarian system is occurring, under the camouflage of an 'all can win' rhetoric designed to reassure anxious middle-class parents. The author will begin to be more convinced of that possibility when school tests results are published with an emphasis on 'value added' as opposed to the crude data on proportions of children at each level, as is the case at the time of writing.

The wider issues about educational disadvantage are explored further in the next three sections.

Education and the Disadvantaged

The discussion above has highlighted the role education plays in relation to the distribution of occupational opportunities in our society. On the Left, there has traditionally been considerable concern about the extent to which education contributes to upward mobility. There are two versions of this preoccupation. One of these involves a commitment to equality of opportunity, and therefore a demand that all able children of whatever social background should have access to educational openings. The other is a concern about equality in a more absolute sense. A naïve version of this places faith in the possibility of an education system that can help to create a more equal society. A more sophisticated approach recognizes that education cannot be, by itself, an engine of social change, but stresses that it must play a part by ensuring that children are not socially segregated and that schools attempt to compensate for other sources of inequality.

These issues have been explored in relation to socio-economic status or class, ethnicity and gender. This section will look at the first of these. The next section explores some of the issues about ethnicity. As far as gender is concerned, most explicit discrimination against females has now disappeared. In fact, there is now a female majority in higher education (52 per cent of full-time undergraduates are female, Office of National Statistics, 1999b, table 3.11, p. 60). There have been concerns about the extent to which there is within the education system a 'hidden curriculum' which socializes males and females differently – inculcating separate gender roles and influencing the subjects chosen in the later years in schools and in universities. Male underachievement has began to secure attention, with suggestions that the culture of primary schools is largely feminine. This is a complex subject which will not be explored further here. It is perhaps symptomatically of continued male dominance in society that, as soon as most discrimination against females has been eliminated, concern about male underachievement is leading to calls for explicit interventions!

As far as the issues about socio-economic class are concerned, 'equality of opportunity' is a slogan that finds quite wide political support. Differential educational opportunity and achievement have been extensively studied by sociologists and psychologists. The evidence accumulated by research in the 1950s and early 1960s (Floud et al., 1956; Jackson and Marsden, 1962; Douglas, 1964) was used in making the case for comprehensive education and for the abandonment of streaming. Later, attention shifted to those problems of underachievement in the education system that cannot be directly attributed to the way that system is structured. Two particular themes were emphasized: the significance of home background for educational success and the extent to which the 'culture' of the school system is alien to some children.

It has been shown that poverty and poor housing conditions militate against educational success (Douglas, 1964; Central Advisory Council for Education, 1967). There is little the education system can do about these problems, but it can try to compensate for them with extra efforts to help deprived children. Home backgrounds are relevant in another sense, too. There are wide variations in the extent to which parents help with the education of their children.

Such help takes many forms, involving not only the more obvious forms of encouragement and the provision of books and study facilities, but also a great deal of implicit 'teaching' through interaction with children. The latter starts when babies are very tiny, and one of its most significant ingredients is the learning of language. The children who are most deprived in these respects are often those who are also most deprived in a material sense. However, parental educational levels and abilities are also relevant. There is a variety of practical ways in which the education system may help to compensate for these less straightforwardly material disadvantages, both before and after children reach compulsory school age (Halsey, 1972).

The issue with regard to the culture of the schools is a more difficult one. In part, the problem is one of identification of the needs and special interests of children whose backgrounds differ from that of the white educated middle-class whose needs have dominated the values of the system. There is a variety of ways in which stories, educational situations and examples can be devised that seem relevant to these children. Hence there is ample scope for change here.

However, as far as social class disadvantages are concerned, there are limits to the extent to which this issue can be fully met, if only because of the extent to which it implies a conflict with the objective of facilitating social mobility through education. If a key concern of education is to prepare children to operate in a middle-class world, even perhaps to join that world, then it may not be particularly functional for it to be concerned to relate to working-class culture. There is a great dilemma here, which is relevant to the alienation of some children from an education system in which they are becoming the 'failures'. You cannot eliminate the concept of failure as long as you have the objective of enabling some to 'succeed' through the education system. It may be desirable to eliminate the more invidious aspects of competition within the system – to recognize, for example, that progress relative to ability may be as important as the easy success of the advantaged and talented – but notions of achievement, and consequently non-achievement, are fundamental to the role of education in our kind of society.

The idea of attempting to compensate for disadvantage by providing special resources for the schools in some areas was suggested in a report of the Plowden committee (Central Advisory Council for Education, 1967). Many of the measures adopted did no more than attempt to redress the imbalance of educational resources between run-down inner-city areas, where the schools were old and facilities were limited, and newer suburban areas. Additional money was made available for capital projects and current expenditure in areas where there were high levels of deprivation. In addition, the government provided for extra teachers, above the normal quotas, and special additional allowances for teachers in those areas. Areas were designated on the basis of statistics on the socio-economic status of parents, the extent of absence of housing amenities, proportions of children receiving free school meals, and proportion of school-children with serious linguistic difficulties.

The Education Action Zones established in 1997 involve a return to interventions of this kind. They are expected to involve a range of innovations and experiments including the development of specialist centres and the employment of teachers with special roles, family literacy schemes and literacy summer schools and the exploration of new forms of work-related learning. The government has expressed a willingness to adapt the national curriculum to meet specific local needs. The sums of public money going into these zones are quite slight, but the government is seeking partnership arrangements with local firms and other organizations to try to increase the resources available. By January 1999, 25 zones had been started, with more being planned.

The Education of Ethnic Minorities

Britain has a non-white population of around three million. About 45 per cent of these are British-born. The remainder are predominantly immigrants from the West Indies and the Indian subcontinent. There is thus a substantial non-white school population, concentrated in urban areas. Most of these youngsters are the British-born children of immigrants, since immigration has been tightly controlled since the 1960s. Over 94 per cent of Afro-Caribbean children under fifteen years of age and about 92 per cent of children under fifteen whose parents originate from the Indian subcontinent were born in Britain (figures calculated from 1991 census data).

In the period when many non-white children were themselves immigrants, the system saw their language problems and cultural differences as the main issue. Some of these are still evident. However, many Asian children are encouraged by parents to make the most of educational opportunities, and many have made remarkable progress within the British system. They may face problems, however, in coming to terms with strong contrasts between patterns of home life and those of school life.

Some Asian groups have begun either to make demands for new

developments in the education system in tune with their cultural needs (e.g. appropriate religious education and courses in Asian languages) or to call for separate state-subsidized schools for their children along the lines of Catholic schools. A look across the Irish Sea to Northern Ireland, where a division in education along religious lines has many of the characteristics of a division along cultural lines, and contributes to the division of that community, gives pause for thought regarding this model of education for a culturally diverse society. Such misgivings are reinforced by the extent to which there has also been interest in independence from white parents eager to minimize the Asian influence on certain schools.

At one time in the late 1960s and early 1970s, a number of education authorities bussed children to other areas, to try to prevent certain schools from having high concentrations of Asian children. Since this bussing was a one-way process, applied only to Asians, it was rightly abandoned as discriminatory. Now, the imposition of rules about regard for parental choice means that local authorities cannot even manipulate catchment areas in the interests of any kind of ethnic 'balance'. Parental choices may enhance tendencies towards segregation.

West Indian immigrants come from a society in which European cultural models have a strong influence, and are reinforced through the education process. It is precisely this bias in West Indian society, and in American Negro society, that has been attacked by those concerned about the development of black consciousness. It is argued that this dominance of a white cultural model contributes to the maintenance of a subordinate self-image. Black leaders in Britain have become deeply concerned about the underachievement of children of West Indian origin. They attribute this to a variety of factors, but see the white ethnic and cultural bias in the education system as reinforcing other aspects of disadvantage.

Hence, while the education system continues to see the issues regarding non-white children as issues about their characteristics, it may alternatively be suggested that the central issue is its ethnic and cultural assumptions, the phenomenon described as 'institutional racism'. An official committee, chaired by Lord Swann, reported on its 'Inquiry into the Education of Children from Ethnic Minority Groups' in 1985. In a brief guide to the report, Lord Swann, while not using the expression 'institutional racism', made it very clear that the issue of society and the education system's response was of central importance in explaining the problem of underachievement by non-whites. He argued (Department of Education and Science, 1985, p. 9):

on the evidence so far there is at least a dual problem. On the one hand, society must not, through prejudice and discrimination, increase the social and economic deprivation of ethnic minority families. On the other, schools must respond with greater sensitivity, and without any trace of prejudice, to the needs of ethnic minority children.

Lord Swann saw the latter as to be achieved through the concept of 'Education for All'. This meant that (p. 10):

[t]he fundamental change needed is a recognition that the problem facing the educational system is not just how to educate the children of ethnic minorities, but how to educate all children. Britain has long been an ethnically diverse society, and is now, mainly because of her imperial past, much more obviously one. All pupils must be brought to an understanding of what is entailed if such a society is to become a fair and harmonious entity.

A report by the Office for Standards in Education (Ofsted, 1999) indicated the need for continued attention to 'institutional racism' in schools. It spoke of a lack of attention to explicit strategies to attack these issues and of an absence of monitoring. The crude performance data provides a complex picture of the problems – differences between ethnic groups (with particular grounds for concern about the performances of Afro-Caribbean males) and differences between the various parts of the education system.

Clearly, the central issues now concern the culture of the education system. There is a need to tackle the biases in the system through the encouragement of culturally relevant studies, and a recognition of ethnocentric biases in the curriculum. There needs to be a sophisticated understanding of the issues by all teachers and special efforts to recruit black teachers. There is a need to eradicate ethnocentric biases in the curriculum.

This last problem about the education of black children is very closely linked with the issue of the place which disadvantaged white children find themselves occupying within the system – as discussed in the previous section – and with the quite concrete disadvantages of children from lower-income homes. Inasmuch as black entrants to Britain have generally been forced to accept many of the poorest jobs and worst housing, children find that the 'inferior' stereotype of the black person seems to be reinforced by their, and their parents', experience. Moreover, the fact that many black parents have had relatively little education themselves, and use a dialect form of English very different from that used in the schools, means that, like comparable lower-class white parents, they are ill-equipped to help their children to tackle the education system. There is a web of reinforcing disadvantages here, which makes the development of compensatory education particularly important for this group of children.

Many of the points made here are relevant to other policy areas. In particular, the chapter on the personal social services might have discussed some of the issues about the inadequacies of services for minorities, and explored, in terms not unlike those used about educational separation, the issue of trans-racial adoption, for example. Similarly, the chapter on the health service could have dealt more with the extent to which there is an ethnic dimension to inequalities in health, and explored some of the communication difficulties which arise when white health professionals pay insufficient regard to cultural and language problems. Lack of space prevented those discussions; it has been interposed here because of the particular salience of the issue for education. Readers are urged to think about the relevance of the points made here for those other policy areas.

Special Education and other Welfare Measures

The education of handicapped children requires the system to develop certain special resources. However, the trend is to try to integrate the education of handicapped children as far as possible into the ordinary system. There is a significant group of children in each authority who are classified as experiencing 'learning difficulties', as a result of the possession of various kinds of physical or intellectual handicaps. They are required to be carefully tested, and a 'statement' has to be prepared setting out their needs. Parents have a right of appeal to an independent tribunal if they are dissatisfied with the statement. On the basis of the statement, children with learning difficulties will either secure some extra teaching or support in an ordinary school or be sent to a school where there are special facilities and staffing arrangements. Schools secure enhancements to their budgets to fund these. There are a variety of special schools. In most authorities, there are separate ones designed for children with 'moderate' or 'severe' learning difficulties. There are also some specialized schools, run by private or voluntary bodies, at which local authorities may buy places.

There are a number of non-teaching activities that make contributions to the overall performance of the education system. Schools may provide meals and milk to children. The former may be available free to pupils whose parents are on income support. The extent to which they should be subsidized for others has been something of a political football, and extensive cuts have been made to these services. Means-tested grants may also be available towards the cost of school clothing, and towards support of pupils in the sixteen to eighteen age group who are still at school.

The welfare of schoolchildren is also given attention through the school health service and the education welfare service. Exceptionally, the latter is a social services department responsibility; more typically, it comes under education departments. Historically, the main concern of this service has been truancy. Today, its objectives have been widened to embrace a whole range of problems that may affect educational performance. In this, it has the support of child guidance services.

There are growing concerns about the tendency for schools to use their formal powers to exclude disruptive children. This seems to have been encouraged by the development of competition between schools encouraged by parental choice and the publication of performance data. It is an issue which the government has asked its Social Exclusion Unit (see page 154) to examine.

Conclusions

The state system of education had roots in a mid-nineteenth-century concern with the training of an effective work-force able to operate in an increasingly complex industrial system and society. Its growth has been inextricably entwined with the development of a democratic society. The original view that the newly enfranchized should be literate has been answered by a belief on the part of the electorate that education holds the key to social advancement. Such a view is certainly encouraged by the enormous emphasis put on education by the political parties, particularly Labour and the Liberals. This may be, in part, an illusion. The opportunity structure is determined by the economy and by the political system. Increased education does not, in itself, increase the supply of 'top jobs'; it merely increases the competition for them. The fact that educational qualifications are widely used as a basis for discrimination between applicants for jobs emphasizes the link between education and social and economic advancement, regardless of whether those jobs require education at the level, or of the kind, possessed by those deemed best suited to fill them. Hence, the nature of the education system and the opportunities it provides are of central political importance in Britain.

As job opportunities for young people diminished in Britain in the 1980s and 1990s, a debate about the role of the education system was stimulated. This was linked to a long-standing controversy about the extent to which British economic underachievement can be attributed to defects in the education system – insufficient emphasis on science and engineering, high esteem for a cultural education that has no immediate practical use, and so on. This is a complex issue, involving propositions which are difficult to test empirically. What it does involve is a tendency to assign too much importance to the role of the education system, disregarding the extent to which it has to respond to social and political demands on it. More immediately, this debate seems to encourage a tendency to attribute the shortage of jobs not to deficiencies in the demand for labour but to inadequacies in the supply of labour – to see the education system as failing the youth of this country. This flies in the face of the evidence that competition for jobs is stimulating 'qualification inflation', that the qualifications needed for many jobs are being increased because of the stiff competition for them. It is leading, however, to an ever-increasing demand for vocationally relevant education (particularly for the vast majority of publicly educated boys and girls unlikely to move easily into elite jobs).

Education has become, in the 1990s, perhaps more politicized than ever before. Government are now very clearly unwilling to leave education to the educationalists, or to delegate responsibility for education policy to local authorities or the governors of schools and colleges.

Suggestions for further reading

For a discussion of education policy with a particularly sociological slant readers should look at Finch's *Education and Social Policy* (1984). Ball's *Politics and Policy Making in Education* (1990) deals with some of the changes to the system during the 1980s, and has been supplemented by two good critical research studies: Bowe and Ball's *Reforming Education and Changing Schools* (1992) and Gewirtz et al.'s *Markets, Choice and Equity in Education* (1995). There are no books, at the time of writing, which the author is able to recommend on education developments since the 1997 election.

While it is also now very dated, the literature on education and social class – Douglas, 1964; Floud et al., 1956; Jackson and Marsden, 1962, particularly the last – provides excellent insight into underlying issues that are still with us, despite the near demise of the grammar schools. A more up-to-date edited collection on educational inequality is Dawtrey et al., 1995.

Law's *Racism, Ethnicity and Social Policy* (1996) explores the issues about education, among other topics, while Gillborn's *Race, Ethnicity and Education* (1992) is a rather older examination of these issues.

Chapter 9

EMPLOYMENT POLICY

- Introduction
- Characteristics of the British approach to manpower policy
- The main employment policy measures
- Training
- Conclusions
- Suggestions for further reading

Introduction

In chapter 1, it was pointed out that while the examination of employment policy can, on the one hand, be seen as taking us to, or beyond, the limits of what is conventionally considered to be social policy, on the other hand, issues about the relationship between social policy and the management of the economy are of fundamental importance for our subject. Two extreme political positions may be contrasted. One sees the preservation of a market-based economic system as the main priority, and requires social policy to do as little as possible to interfere with the market. The other gives primacy to social goals and requires that market forces must be managed, and in certain cases eliminated, to ensure those goals are realized. These are, of course, simplified statements of the 'right' and 'left' wing boundaries within which much democratic political discourse takes place. If the right wing position is adopted, there is little place for employment policy *per se*. Market forces impacting on individuals' prospects of finding and retaining work are to be left alone, the only concern is that those state interventions in society that are deemed to be unavoidable have a minimal impact on the labour market. The characteristic social policy of such a regime is the 'poor-law' (see chapter 2, pages 15–16) to provide social aid in exceptional circumstances but designed to ensure that it has no adverse effect on labour market participation. By contrast since the left wing position sees the management of the labour market (and other markets) for social ends to be a perfectly legitimate concern, it regards employment policy as a central concern of public social policy.

The real political discourse, of course, lies between these polar positions. Hence, there are employment policies, which have social effects, to be studied. There are also issues to be considered about the employment effects of other social policies (particularly social security policies). However, it is also the case that there is considerable controversy about those effects, which needs to be seen in the context of different views about the extent to which the labour market can (or should) be subject to manipulation by governments. An analyst of social policy with a comparative perspective, Esping-Andersen (1996), has encapsulated the contemporary controversy about the appropriate relationship between social policy and the labour market (p. 10):

> Since the early 1970s, we can identify three distinct welfare state responses to economic and social change, Scandinavia followed until recently a strategy of welfare state employment expansion. The Anglo-Saxon countries . . . have favoured a strategy of deregulating wages and the labour market, combined with a certain degree of welfare state erosion. And the continental European nations . . . have induced labour supply reduction while basically maintaining existing social security standards. All three strategies were intimately related to the nature of their welfare states.

Britain is put, by Esping-Andersen, clearly into his Anglo-Saxon category, yet, as a member of the EU, it is confronted by the alternative models. Furthermore, within the EU, attempts are being made to develop active labour market policies, with social goals, despite different social security policies that cannot easily be harmonized. 'European social policy' in practice is largely employment or labour market policy. Hence, ever since Britain joined the EEC, there has been a political debate about the shape of employment policy, and Britain has had to respond to measures from that community which may have an impact on the working of the labour market.

There is a developing debate about the most appropriate response to what are seen as increasingly significant 'global' market forces. One side in that debate (what Esping-Andersen might call the Anglo-Saxon side) argues that the only way a nation can compete in the global economy is to adopt labour market deregulation, lowering wages and related employment costs. The other side either disputes the power of the so-called global forces or argues that a large economic bloc like the EU can resist or influence those forces. An in-between position involves the suggestion that an efficient highly trained labour force can enable a nation to compete without at the same time necessarily lowering wages. It will be shown that some of Britain's employment policy responses are premised on the possibility of this 'middle' course; see page 215.

The discussion so far has sought to characterize employment policy in general terms. Once examined in more detail, employment policy is seen to have various aspects, each of which may be given more or less attention. In this sense, the overall perspectives, outlined above, can have various manifestations. Employment policy will be likely to involve attempts to influence four aspects of work or themes:

1   The overall level of labour market participation
2   The characteristics of work
3   The nature of the supply of labour
4   The demand for labour

First, then, Government interventions may aim both to increase and to decrease the overall level of labour market participation. The poor-law approach described above clearly aimed to maximize participation. Conversely, the introduction of pensions and sickness benefits may be seen as enabling some people to withdraw from having to try to participate. However, many other policies influence participation. Women have been explicitly excluded from some forms of labour market participation in the past, whereas more recently efforts have been made to counter discrimination against women and to encourage them to enter the labour force. Education policies may offer opportunities for young people which keep them temporarily out of the labour force. Finally, emigration and immigration policies will have effects on the size of the labour force.

Second, Governments may regulate work – influencing its hours, conditions and rates of pay, i.e. the characteristics of work. They may also enact measures, which influence the security of work. More indirectly they may influence the conditions under which employers and employees are able to bargain about these issues, through rules about trade unions and collective bargaining.

The first point above dealt with the quantity of labour; this third one rather concerns what may be called the 'quality' of labour. Government's education and training policies affect the nature of the supply of labour, so may measures designed to influence attitudes to work. In this category, to simplify the overall taxonomy used here, are also included measures (labour exchanges, etc.) which influence the rates at which employees and employers make contacts (inasmuch as these do not affect the level of labour market participation *per se* but rather its working).

Last, Governments create work – the demand for labour – in many different ways. Attention in discussions of employment policy tend to be focused on explicit job creation measures, or explicit 'Keynesian' demand creating economic policies but, in reality, work may be created by many government initiatives (sometimes without this being a specific intention). In this sense, many social policy innovations – to increase the availability of health or social care or education or to increase the supply of houses – will have employment creating effects. So, of course, as was pointed out in chapter 1, will a decision to wage war.

All of these themes occur in British employment policy, but there has been a tendency for points 1 and 3 to be more evident than the other two. For an understanding of contemporary policy there is a need to explore the way in which policy stances have evolved over quite a long period, with varying emphasis on the four themes. This is done in the next section.

Characteristics of the British Approach to Manpower Policy

Nineteenth-century governments paid little attention to managing the labour market, but they did adopt measures both to maximize the participation of adult males in the labour force and to restrict the participation of women and children. Alongside, and sometimes part of the latter measures, were efforts to control working conditions.

In the early twentieth century, British governments gradually came to reject the view that the economy, and accordingly the labour market, should be left to work 'naturally'. At the end of the nineteenth century, adherents of 'classical' economic theory began to acknowledge that it was perhaps necessary for government to play a role in assisting the market system to operate more smoothly. In particular, the problems of adjustment to changing economic situations in the short run began to be regarded as sufficiently serious to justify intervention. One such problem concerned the linking of 'sellers' of labour with 'buyers'. To this end, after 1909, systems of labour exchanges were created.

Around the turn of the century, attention was given to the

existence of various 'sweated trades' in which marginal workers, often including large numbers of women, were exploited. A measure of protection was enacted for workers in the 1909 Trade Boards Act, and in moves towards the establishment of minimum wages in some industries during World War I. These might have been steps towards much greater regulation of employment. However, a bigger concern of the male-dominated working class movement was to give greater legal protection to trade unions and for these to be the main protectors of wage levels and conditions of employment through negotiated agreements with employers. A voluntary approach to employment regulation became dominant.

Between the two World Wars, continuing evidence that the economy could not readily absorb all who wanted work kept the issue of unemployment on the political agenda. There were strong pressures that forced the erratic development of income maintenance measures for the unemployed (see discussion in chapter 2 on pages 24–5), but manpower policies evolved very little. A few limited job-creation and training schemes were developed, but economic orthodoxy was against the heavy public expenditure on the creation of work that, by the middle of the 1930s, began to characterize the policy response in the USA. Only as preparation for war began to alleviate unemployment did official thinking begin to come to terms with its structural character. This change of approach is primarily associated with the Keynesian revolution in economic thinking that linked unemployment with underconsumption and urged governments to spend, and, if necessary, to unbalance budgets, to pull out of a recession. The primary policy response required was, in this case, a macro-economic one, rather than a form of manpower policy *per se*. However, at the same time, the special problems of certain regions, particularly those where employment had depended on declining heavy industries, also began to be recognized.

As indicated above, the two World Wars could be seen as massive labour demand creation schemes! Indeed, so strong was the need for labour that measures were adopted to draw new participants, particularly women, into the labour force.

The unexpected success of economic policies in preventing high unemployment from 1945 to 1970 enabled British governments to continue to adopt a comparatively passive stance on manpower policies. The trade unions were broadly satisfied with this situation, full employment offered the ideal context for the continuation of working-class advancement by way of collective action. The employment situation, initially at least, did not favour female interests. An expectation that the high female labour market participation of the wartime period would come to an end was reinforced by neglect of attention to the prevention of discrimination against women and an absence of child care provisions. Full employment led, in the 1950s and 1960s, to official acceptance of the recruitment of labour from the countries of the former British Empire. Public employers, including the health service, sought workers from these countries. There were racist campaigns against open entry to Britain from the Caribbean and the Indian sub-continent, and controlling legislation was enacted (a sequence of measures starting with one in 1962). These used need for labour as a crucial test for the grant of an entry permit. Since the enactment and subsequent tightening of immigration controls coincided with the beginning of a fall in labour demand, immigration very quickly ceased to have an impact on the growth of the labour force.

In 1970, the incoming Conservative government, led by Edward Heath, decided to restructure the public employment service as part of its effort to make public administration more dynamic. A consultative document *People and Jobs* (Department of Employment, 1971) declared that the employment service needed to be modernized. The employment exchanges were too identified with a limited service to the unemployed.

It is not irrelevant that this modernizing effort came at the time Britain entered the EEC. In modernizing the service, the government was clearly influenced by German and Swedish concepts of 'active manpower policy', in which the employment service was seen as playing a crucial role in preserving full employment without high inflation. Britain's own problem in swinging rapidly from situations of economic stagnation, when unemployment began to rise, into situations of an 'overheated' economy, bringing inflation and balance of payments difficulties, were seen as, at least in part, attributable to problems of labour supply. Overheating was associated with difficulties in securing adequately trained skilled labour. It was felt that a more sophisticated employment service, dealing with a much higher proportion of the job placements and able to give more expert attention to training problems, would much more effectively match supply and demand in the labour market, and thus contribute much better to the maintenance of a balanced economy. A new, active service would seek to have a real impact on the working of the labour market.

In practice, the British manpower initiatives of the early 1970s were brought into operation in a context not just of high inflation but also of rapidly rising unemployment. The modernized employment services had to operate in an economy about which many economists had abandoned the 'Keynesian' belief that there is a direct, simple relationship between unemployment and inflation.

While *People and Jobs* saw the future of the service in terms of a lesser concern with the unemployed and a greater degree of assistance to those who sought to move between jobs, in fact the stagnation that occurred in the labour market forced the system to give a great deal of attention to the issue of unemployment, and to develop a range of temporary special job-creation and training measures.

On coming to power in 1979, the Thatcher government inherited various special measures to deal with the problem of unemployment from its Labour predecessors. Its initial inclination was to curb these activities as part of its general attack on public expenditure. The main employment policies of the government involved an emphasis on reintroducing the full rigours of the market-place into the labour market. A succession of measures weakened trade unions. At the same time the government was eager to reduce the impact of the meagre employment protection measures still on the statute book, such as the wage regulation which had survived since 1909 for a small number of trades.

It is difficult to separate the impact of Thatcherite measures designed to free the working of the labour market from the changes in the labour market that had already started to occur in the 1970s. It seems likely that the former accelerated the rate at which the latter took effect. It is not appropriate here to go further into these issues. What is relevant, however, is that Margaret Thatcher's government soon decided that they could not entirely discard the special measures developed in the late 1970s. It quickly came to realize that the special programmes, particularly those for the young unemployed, offered the cheapest way of providing a response to the problem of growing unemployment. So, in fact, the early 1980s saw a growth of expenditure on special training schemes and temporary job-creation measures (Moon and Richardson, 1985).

Certainly some of the measures adopted – in particular, job creation and the use of subsidies – seem to have been influenced by the more active manpower policies of countries like Sweden. Ironically, in Sweden in the 1950s and 1960s, such measures were seen as ways of helping the very small minority of the population unable to secure work on the open market when employment was as full as possible. These measures take on a rather different character in an economy characterized by a seriously deficient demand for labour. They were criticized as inadequate alternatives to the effective management of the economy. One distinguished economist, Lord Vaisey, argued (House of Commons, 1977, p. 147):

The sum total of these schemes seems to me to be cosmetic rather than genuine in its economic consequences. What they do in effect is to push employment around a bit without much net effect. They are in no sense a substitute for the substantial regeneration of British industry.

In economic terms, the official answer to Vaisey's argument was that these schemes provided or protected jobs with minimal inflationary effects, by comparison with more direct ways in which the economy might be stimulated. However, there is also a social policy issue here: such policies may be used to influence the impact of a recession on particular groups of people. While they may do little or nothing to change the overall level of employment, they may help to ensure that particular people – the young, the previously long-term unemployed, those resident in certain areas – experience the ill effects of being out of work rather less than other people.

Politicians, when they justify special measures to provide employment, deliberately obfuscate these issues. They want to be able to claim jobs saved or created by government intervention as contributions to the alleviation of unemployment as a whole. The actual macro-economic effect of these interventions is, happily for them, profoundly obscure.

Since 1980, programmes of assistance to unemployed people and training have gone through a large number of changes. Students will find even quite recent books misleading on detailed schemes, and if they try to trace the changes over recent years, they will be bewildered by the 'alphabet soup' of different schemes each generally identified only by its initials. Undoubtedly this complex evolution – and perhaps, indeed, even the government's willingness to persist with such activities – has been influenced by the changing EEC subsidies available from the European Social Fund.

In the early 1990s, the Conservative government's approach to job-creation and training measures became one in which the needs of the existing economic system were stressed, and control was firmly in the hands of private sector employers. There was a strong emphasis on the training of the young. For older, long-term unemployed people, there were special programmes, with an increasing requirement of activities as a condition of financial support (even if these do not readily help the individual back into the regular labour market). Conservative governments blew hot and cold about the desirability of measures of this last kind. One influence was the considerable sums the government was being forced, by the high level of unemployment, to spend on benefits. It spent with great reluctance, and increasingly found ways to reduce benefits and prevent individual access to such help.

Britain moved from a situation in which little was done to try to plan to prevent unemployment in the 1930s, through an era when regional policies were quite prominent, but generally the health of the labour market seemed to make planning unnecessary, between 1945 and 1971, into a brief phase when it was recognized that part of Britain's economic problem stemmed from the lack of an 'active labour market policy', in the 1970s. The rise of unemployment from 1975 onwards then 'hijacked' active labour market policy, concentrating efforts on special measures for the unemployed. Responses to the problem of unemployment have preoccupied the system ever since.

The new Labour government has placed a strong emphasis on employment policy but, in many respects, there is a high level of continuity with the policies of its predecessor. In search of a difference, it is perhaps fair to say that while, as noted above, the Conservatives 'blew hot and cold', Labour is (at the time of writing) blowing very hot indeed. The examination of the history of employment policy suggests that Labour might have been expected to adopt a stance of stressing job creation measures and strengthening the trade union role as the protector of the work-force. That has been rejected as very much an 'old Labour' strategy. Alternatively, Labour might have adopted some of the initiatives of the 1970s again and given them a more distinctly 'continental' European twist, with an emphasis on increasing employment security. That too has been rejected, with the partial exception of the acceptance of a need for a minimum wage. Instead the emphasis of 'new' Labour has been very much on measures to improve and increase the supply of labour. Typical examples of this emphasis are given in the Green Paper on Welfare Reform (HMSO, 1998, p. 31):

> The Government's commitment to expand significantly the range of help available therefore alters the contract with those who are capable of work. It is the Government's responsibility to promote work opportunities and to help people take advantage of them. It is the responsibility of those who can take them up to do so.

Earlier in an election manifesto which emphasized its supply-side programme on youth unemployment, the Labour Party had said:

> Labour's welfare-to-work programme will attack unemployment and break the spiral of escalating spending on social security.

We find the same theme echoed in measures for disabled people and for single parents; these were mentioned in chapter 5 but will be discussed further in this chapter (pages 220–1).

Since this section has emphasized the influence of levels of unemployment on the British policy response, it is appropriate to end with a note on those. Comparison of unemployment levels is made notoriously difficult by the different ways these are measured. There has been a tendency for the published figures to be of those registering for employment, or receiving benefit. These ignore the unemployment of those without benefit entitlements, and can be subject to manipulation as registration and/or benefit systems change. An alternative is a labour force survey, though even in this case care must be exercised as variations in the way people are asked about their desire for work or their job search behaviour influence the figures. Table 9.1 provides data on the percentages of the economically active who were unemployed at various dates, derived from a labour force survey using International Labour Office definitions of unemployment. It shows a falling trend over the 1990s, but with significant differences within the UK. Unemployment rates vary in terms of skill level. Another particularly disturbing difference is that between rates for different ethnic groups. In early 1998 the 'white' rate was calculated to be 6 per cent but that for 'black' people was 19 per cent (Office for National Statistics, 1998, table 4.22, p. 82). By the end of 1998, unemployment had fallen further. The UK rate was about 6.2 per cent compared with a EU average of 9.8 per cent, including a German rate of 9.4 per cent, a French rate of 11.8 per cent and a Swedish rate of 7.6 per cent (Office for National Statistics, 1999a, table C51).

Table 9.1   Percentages of the economically active who were unemployed at survey dates in the spring of various years

	1993	1994	1995	1996	1997
England	10.3	9.5	8.6	8.1	6.9
Wales	9.6	9.3	8.8	8.3	8.4
Scotland	10.2	10.0	8.3	8.7	8.5
Northern Ireland	12.5	11.7	11.0	9.7	7.5
United Kingdom	10.3	9.6	8.6	8.2	7.1

Source: Office for National Statistics (1998b), p. 33.

The Main Employment Policy Measures

Britain's manpower policies are the responsibility of the Department for Education and Employment (DfEE). Local responsibility for services for job seekers is managed by an agency called The Employment Service. Training is the responsibility of 80 separate Training and Enterprise Councils (TECs) in England and Wales, and 22 local enterprise companies in Scotland. These are independent companies set up by the government, with their own boards of directors, which have contracts to administer government grants. In Northern Ireland, there is a training and employment agency responsible to the Department of Economic Development for Northern Ireland.

'Job centres' are the modern successors to the labour exchanges which were set up in 1908 to do just what their name suggests, to link employers seeking workers with employees. In the 1970s, job centres were seen as replacing the large institutional exchanges with modern shop-front offices in commercial and shopping centres. There was an emphasis on self-service, individuals being able to select jobs from open-display advertisements, turning to staff only when advice was necessary. The aim as expressed in 1971 was to counter the problem that 'the Service is regarded by many workers and employers as a service for the unemployed' (Department of Employment, 1971, p. 5). The hopes for this approach have been dashed, however, by the rise in unemployment. The 1990s have seen an explicit acceptance by the government that this is precisely who the service is for – the long-term unemployed in particular. Accordingly, a visitor from the 1930s would find the modern job centre a puzzling place: on the one hand, all the apparatus of modern consumerism – a pleasant office, courteous staff, ample explanatory material – and on the other, a battery of questions and controls which would seem remarkably familiar.

In chapter 5, it was shown that the state financial support for unemployed people is provided by the job seeker's allowance. To qualify, a person has to make a clear undertaking, signing a job seeker's agreement, on the steps he or she will take to try to find work. Even for those who have been contributing to the national insurance (NI) scheme, job seeker's allowance is means-tested after six months. Benefit may also be stopped or reduced if individuals are found to have lost employment unnecessarily or to have failed to take employment opportunities.

The job centres now have a central role to play in relation to the surveillance of the behaviour of the unemployed. The initial job seeker's agreement is subject to regular review (based on an earlier 'restart' scheme). Particular attention is paid to those who have been out of work for six months or more. At the reviews, the individual's efforts to find work are examined, and a variety of other options is explored:

- Referral to a 'job club', where guidance, training and assistance are offered with job search activities
- A job interview guaranteed by an employer who has agreed to see long-term unemployed people in return for an enhanced recruitment service
- Referral to specialized job search assistance which may involve attendance at a seminar or training course (there are a variety of jargon names for these, which change from time to time: 'job-plan', 'workwise', 'restart', etc.)
- Placement on an appropriate training course
- Referral to special courses, focusing not so much on skill deficiencies as on personal attributes and attitudes
- Opportunities to undertake a job while still on benefit, on a trial basis
- Financial assistance to start a business
- A career development loan

Labour, in 1997, made the extension of all this, with particular attention to the issues about the young unemployed, central to its social policy programme. It pledged to give a quarter of a million young people (aged between 18 and 24) six months in either work or training. It funded this scheme from a one-off levy on the windfall profits that had accrued to the newly privatized utilities. The scheme was started experimentally at the beginning of 1998 and brought into full operation in April of that year. It adds three more options to the battery of measures available:

- Work in the voluntary sector or with a new organization called the Environment Task Force
- A job for which employers may be paid a subsidy of up to £60 a week
- Full-time education or training

It was backed up by a further strengthening of the already strict system of benefit withdrawal sanctions against those who do not accept places.

In June 1998, a further special programme was adopted to offer subsidized work and improved access to education or training, for people over 24 who have been out of work over two years.

There is, thus, now a substantial complex battery of measures to help unemployed people to find work. There are many people incorporated into the various schemes. The evidence on the fall in the unemployment rate, and particularly the fall in youth employment looks encouraging. However, it is always difficult to separate the impact of specific schemes from other influences on the labour market. The Trades Union Congress (1999) has suggested that 'the buoyant labour market was the main factor behind' the positive trend. Bennett and Walker (1999, p. 14). stress the need to focus on retention in as well as recruitment to jobs:

> monitoring and evaluation of welfare to work measures must have a longer-term perspective, rather than merely observing the percentage of 'positive outcomes' achieved in the short term. The need to ensure that people are not stuck on the first rung of the labour market ladder, trapped in low-paid jobs, has similar implications.

Most measures seem premised on the view that work is available and that the problem lies in the attitudes and behaviour of unemployed people. An exception to this is the subsidies, which may create extra work. However, since these are time-limited and mostly funded from a one-off levy, the underlying assumption is therefore that they will have a lasting effect on the level of demand. These measures give little or no attention to issues about the quality of work or the level of pay. In fact, the emergence of individual subsidies is some kind of recognition by the government that much of the work on offer to the long-term unemployed is very low-paid.

There has been extensive controversy regarding the impact of the social security system on the behaviour of the unemployed. It is alleged that unemployed people have been deterred from seeking work by the high levels of benefit relative to the lowest earnings levels. This has been used as an argument for making sure that the unemployed gain less than any other group from the benefit system. The introduction of the family credit scheme was seen by the government as seeing to it that people with family responsibilities would be better off in work than on benefit.

The new Labour government has been particularly concerned to attack the issue of in-work benefits. Chapter 5 described the way they are developing a system of tax credits for low-income workers with families, for child care payments by such workers and for disabled workers. In addition, in his April 1999 budget, the Chancellor announced that there would be a wage top-up of a maximum of £60 for people over 50 who returned to work after six months or more on benefits. At the same time, issues about the rewards accruing from work have been tackled in a rather different way by the introduction of a minimum wage. A proposal from a commission set up to make recommendations on this issue has been enacted. The minimum wage (at the time of writing – it is assumed there will be subsequent adjustments to allow for inflation) is £3.60 for people over 21 and £3 for younger workers. These are low figures relative to average wage levels, but do involve a modest shift away from a market approach to wage determination at the bottom.

Since World War II, there have been specialized advice services available for disabled workers. The Employment Service has Disability Employment Advisers. These officials will give specialized advice and can recommend that disabled people go into special employment and training programmes more quickly than other unemployed people. There are also some specific employment schemes for severely disabled people.

Until the implementation of the Disability Discrimination Act of 1995, there was also a quota imposed on all except the smallest employers to take on a small proportion of disabled people. That quota was replaced by procedures for the prevention of discrimination against disabled workers. These included a requirement that employers should make 'reasonable' adjustments to premises to overcome the disadvantages of disabled people. It is difficult, so far, to assess the impact of the changes under the 1995 Act. The quota was poorly enforced, but the new law requires action against discrimination to be activated by disabled people themselves. This may be very difficult to do. It is difficult to assess whether there has been actionable discrimination in a context of stiff competition for jobs.

Throughout the 1980s, the government tolerated – indeed, partly encouraged – a situation in which people with disabilities were able to leave the unemployment register and receive the long-term, higher-rated invalidity benefit. This contributed to a reduction in the apparent size of the unemployed population. There was a steady growth in the numbers on invalidity benefit, particularly men in their fifties and early sixties. Then, in the 1990s, the Department of Social Security became concerned about the cost of supporting this group. In 1995, as shown in chapter 5, invalidity benefit was replaced by incapacity benefit, with its much stricter test of fitness for work. The Labour government has followed up on that measure by further reducing the availability of incapacity benefit (see chapter 5, page

112) and by requiring applicants for it to undergo an interview with an employment adviser to explore work possibilities.

We see, in the government's approach to incapacity benefit, a willingness to increase overall labour market participation, a change driven perhaps by a concern to reduce social security expenditure. A similar approach can be seen with regard to single parent families. A modest sum from the 'windfall levy' (see page 218) has been allocated to help lone parents. There is a network of experimental schemes – so far without compulsion – designed to help lone parents into work. These new schemes have arisen to fulfil a manifesto pledge:

> Today the main connection between unemployed lone parents and the state is their benefits. Most lone parents want to work, but are given no help to find it. . . . Once the youngest child is in the second term of full-time school, lone parents will be offered advice by a proactive Employment Service to develop a package of job search, training and after-school care to help them off benefit.

It may be that compulsory labour market participation by single parents with children over school age will follow. Similarly, childless wives of men who claim the jobseeker's allowance are being required to register for work.

Training

Young people aged sixteen or seventeen who have left school but not obtained work are expected to participate in 'youth training'. With certain special exceptions, the only way in which a youngster in this group can receive financial help from the state is by participating in this scheme. The training is designed to provide both broadly based skills and specific forms of craft training. There is a system of qualifications (NVQs – 'national vocational qualifications') which may be acquired while participating in 'youth training'. In the financial year 1997–8 about 199,000 young people in Great Britain started on training schemes (58 per cent of these on what are called 'modern apprenticeships') (Office for National Statistics, 1999b, p. 67).

Youth training involves public subsidy to a wide range of schemes – provided by private employers, voluntary organizations and public bodies – offering a mixture of work experience and training. The achievement of qualifications is now strongly emphasized within youth training as a whole. These schemes vary enormously in quality, from elaborate skill training at one extreme to what are little more than 'make work' schemes for lower-ability young people in high-unemployment areas at the other. The better the local demand for young workers, the better the quality of the schemes, in terms of both the training they offer and the real labour market opportunities they lead on to. However, three points must be recognized:

- Britain has (by contrast with most of continental Europe) a very high proportion of young people ending their full-time education and training at the age of sixteen.
- Britain used to have a strong pattern of apprenticeship into skilled work in industry, which has now collapsed.
- Before the rise of unemployment in the mid-1970s, the labour market for young people aged sixteen to eighteen was a thriving one, which has now more or less disappeared.

Youth training may be seen as a necessary means of filling a vacuum in the British education and training system, but it has also contributed to the creation of that vacuum by undermining the incentives to employers to provide work or training for young people at their own expense. The state now pays for most of this, through youth training. These comments are also pertinent to the initiatives in relation to eighteen- to twenty-four-year-olds, discussed above.

It is worthy of note at this point that the Education and Employment departments were amalgamated in 1995. In the preceding fifteen years, the two departments had been to some extent competitors in the provision of measures for young people who were not committed to going on to higher education. Experiments were developed within schools to introduce youngsters to the world of work and, for those just out of school, further education and youth training were sometimes competitors, sometimes linked. Inasmuch as there is controversy about the extent to which efforts for this group should be narrowly vocational or have wider educational objectives, the departmental integration may make a difference. At the end of chapter 8, it was observed that, despite the evident shortage of jobs, there has been a strong tendency to blame youth unemployment on the inadequacies of education. The DfEE is certainly intensifying the training emphasis in modern education.

As was shown in the last section, government sponsored skill-training predates the modern rise of unemployment. Since that rise, adult training, like all the other employment services, has gone through a bewildering series of changes. A wide range of training is now available delivered locally by the training and enterprise councils (TECs) or local enterprise companies. Trainees may receive training grants.

Conclusions

This chapter began by setting the issues about employment policy in their wider social policy context and by emphasizing the wide range of ways in which government's may develop policies. Attention was drawn to the fact that employment policies may involve different emphases (which may of course be found in combinations) which attempt to affect four areas of influence:

- The overall level of labour market participation
- The characteristics of work
- The nature of the supply of labour
- The demand for labour

It was then shown that these concerns have all appeared from time to time in British employment policy but that the overall stance has been relatively *laissez-faire*, doing little to intervene directly in the labour market, leaving influences on labour demand to a combination of comparatively accidental effects stemming from other policy decisions and treating unemployment as an issue to be tackled largely through income maintenance policies. Then, the rise of unemployment in the 1970s was met by revitalized public agencies committed to 'active' manpower policy. Initially, this led to exploration of the development of job-creation measures, but these measures were undermined by a reluctance to compete with the 'regular' labour market. This led to a concentration on intervention in the labour market on behalf of specific groups of the unemployed. Such intervention has a strong 'supply side' emphasis, the concern being with 'what is wrong with' the victims of unemployment, rather than on deficient demand. Workers who are either more highly skilled or more willing to work for very low rewards are seen as less likely to be unemployed. Concentration on these issues is expected to reduce unemployment.

The new Labour government has placed a particularly strong emphasis on these supply side solutions, but it has also been prepared to countenance measures which will have the effect of increasing the pool of people seeking work. It has boldly characterized its own efforts in these terms (Department of Social Security, 1998a, p. 23):

> The Government's aim is to rebuild the welfare state around work. The skills and energies of the workforce are the UK's biggest economic asset. And for both individuals and families, paid work is the most secure means of averting poverty and dependence except, of course, for those who are retired or so sick or disabled, or so heavily engaged in caring activities, that they cannot realistically support themselves.

That perspective puts a very high premium on work. It is open to three objections. First, it may be challenged as placing paid work on a pedestal, above all other means of sharing resources in society. That is a philosophical issue which will not be examined here. Second, it presumes that the problems of supplying enough work, for all who are to be forced to need it, can be solved. Third, and closely related to that second point is that, it seems to be silent on the quality of work opportunities on offer. If the government's initiatives can increase the volume of work available, what kind of work will that be?

A more gloomy assessment of this approach is based on the extent to which employment growth in Britain, as opposed to economic growth (these are issues that are not necessarily linked), has involved low-paid insecure and often part-time work. Dex and McCulloch (1995) estimated that around half of all women and a quarter of all men were in what may be called 'non-standard work' contracts, i.e. part-time work, temporary work or self-employment. However, a much higher proportion of new work may be of that kind (Gregg and Wadsworth, 1995; Cousins 1999).

Many people, including not least the Prime Minister, Tony Blair, in his introduction to the Green Paper tell us we have to learn to live in a world in which working lives need to be more flexible. The crucial problem here is, as Wheelock (1999) suggests, whether we are on the 'high road' or the 'low road' to flexibility in the labour market. The low road means that:

> Global competition and the structural shift to services put downward pressure on the wages of the unskilled, wages which are already at the lowest end of the market. (pp. 79–80)

The high road on the other hand:

> relies upon employment based on sophisticated technology and innovation to keep abreast of international competition. Those employed

in this sector – in high tech industries such as petrochemicals, comput-
ing, biotechnology etc. – must be highly trained. They must be
prepared to be 'functionally flexible' in the sense that they undertake
a range of tasks and learn how to do new ones. (p. 80)

In fact, analyses of divisions in labour markets (Piore and Sabel,
1984) suggest that while a lucky minority may be on the 'high road',
the majority, and particularly those people who are likely to have to
apply for benefits and to use state services to help them in the labour
market, are on the low road. This has serious long-run implications
for other social policies, and particularly for contributory approaches
to pension provision; see the discussion on pages 134–5.

When I last revised this chapter, I said that my feeling grows each
time I revise it that much British employment policy is an exercise in
rearranging the deckchairs on the Titanic, with an overriding concern
to increase the discomfort of passengers. The Blair government
strongly asserts this is not the case. However, I will not be convinced
of this until there is better evidence from the government of two
things:

- Serious attention to issues about the supply of jobs as opposed to
  the deficiencies of the labour force
- Interest in the growing EU concerns about job security

Until that is evident, the suspicion will remain that the enormous
emphasis on the future of welfare as lying in labour market participation by all who can do so involves a sophisticated political
exercise at 'blaming the victims', who are perceived as making
insufficient efforts to secure work.

Suggestions for further reading

This is a topic on which recent policy change has rendered many
books rather dated. There have been a large number of books on
unemployment, but few have dealt with the measures for the unemployed in any depth. Quite an old book which nevertheless sets out
the issues about unemployment and policies for the unemployed very
well is Sinfield's *What Unemployment Means* (1981). An examination of contemporary developments in the labour market, in Britain
and elsewhere, can be found in Wheelock and Vail (1998). Christine
Cousins' *Society, Work and Welfare in Europe* (1999), while it is a

comparative study, has a valuable discussion of contemporary British developments.

Up-to-date analyses of policies are contained in the Unemployment Unit's regular bulletin. That Unit also publishes an *Unemployment and Training Rights Handbook* and a *Guide to Training and Benefits for Young People* (there are regular updatings of each).

Chapter 10

HOUSING

- Introduction
- The social housing sector
- Owner-occupation
- The private rented sector
- Homelessness

- Housing and social exclusion
- The selling of social housing
- Conclusions
- Suggestions for further reading

Introduction

In Great Britain in 1996, the housing stock comprised almost 24 million dwellings. Of these, 18.7 per cent were rented from local authorities; 4.6 per cent were rented from housing associations; 9.8 per cent were privately rented; and 66.9 per cent were owner-occupied (Wilcox, 1998. Table 17d, p. 95). It will be shown in this chapter that public policies influence all these sectors, if not directly through public provision, then indirectly through tax subsidies (in the case of the owner-occupied sector) or rent regulation (in the privately rented sector).

From the end of World War I until 1979, the owner-occupier and publicly provided sectors grew dramatically at the expense of the privately rented sector. Since 1979, the growth of owner occupation has continued, but the public rented sector has declined in size as a result of the sale of council houses to their occupiers. Moreover, what was earlier describable as the public rented sector (or 'council housing') is now better described as 'social housing'. It consists of rented housing under a mixture of local authority and housing association ownership. Much of the subsidy for this sector now comes directly to tenants, in the form of housing benefit. This benefit is also available to private tenants, further blurring the private–public distinction.

Developments in the UK housing system have been enormously influenced by government intervention. The department directly responsible for housing policy in England is the Department of the Environment, Transport and the Regions (DETR). In the other countries of the UK, housing policy is one of the devolved responsibilities.

To understand housing policy, there is a need to look at issues about all the housing sectors. There are complex interactions between them; a change in one sector has implications for others. For example, increased opportunities for owner occupation have both diminished the demand for private rented accommodation, and been partly created by landlords' desires to sell houses that seem no longer to offer a satisfactory return if they are let. Later in this chapter, fuller attention will be given to some of the interactions of this kind that have policy implications. However, it is clearly simplest to introduce this discussion of policies by examining each sector separately.

The Social Housing Sector

While a small amount of public housing was built earlier, the effective growth of this sector dates from the enactment of legislation after World War I to enable local authorities to receive central government subsidies towards the provision of housing 'for the working classes'. A long succession of subsequent Acts of Parliament elaborated this initiative, encouraging both the building of large estates designed to meet basic housing needs and the adoption of substantial slum clearance schemes. While the housing no longer has to be specifically 'for the working classes', this sector has become the main provider of houses for those unable to buy their own.

The history of the subsidy system developed in this sector is complicated. There is a need to look at this briefly so as to understand the contemporary situation. For many years the government used, but regularly changed, a system whereby local authorities secured a fixed sum per dwelling annually over a fixed period of years. In the 1960s, the Labour government adopted a new approach, without terminating the older subsidies, whereby percentage subsidies were paid, effectively to subsidize the rate at which authorities borrowed money. However, in the 1972 Housing Finance Act, the Conservatives sought to sweep away all the continuing older systems of subsidy. The objective was to move to a system in which general-purpose subsidies would eventually be eliminated. They recognized the need to continue to subsidize certain particularly expensive forms of development, in particular slum clearance. They also acknowledged a case for subsidizing low-income tenants by requiring authorities to operate rent rebate schemes which received an element of national subsidy. Otherwise, they expected local authorities to move towards balanced housing budgets by raising rents. A national system of 'fair rents', at higher levels than existing rents, was to be developed, which might leave some authorities, those whose housing commitments were particularly costly, with deficits, but these would be met partly out of central government grants. However, most authorities were expected to reach a position at which general subsidies would be unnecessary, and some would achieve surpluses.

Naturally this new scheme was designed to be phased in gradually. Rents were to be increased in stages, and a 'transitional subsidy' was paid. Before the transition could be completed, the Conservatives lost power, and the new Labour administration suspended the operation of the Housing Finance Act. It planned, instead, a modified version of the Conservatives' scheme that did not directly interfere with the authorities' power to fix their own rents, and did not necessarily entail a gradual phasing out of general-purpose subsidies. The general approach offered a potential for manipulation in a variety of ways determined by the ideology of the government operating it. The approach was described by HMSO (1977, p. 83):

1 The starting-point of the calculation of subsidy would be an authority's entitlement to subsidy in the previous year.
2 Each year, a basis for calculation of the extra expenditure admissible for subsidy – including extra costs of management and maintenance assessed on an appropriate formula – would be settled for the coming year in consultation with local authorities.
3 Each year, an appropriate level of increase in the 'local contribution' to costs, from rent and rates, would be determined for the coming year, also in consultation with local authorities.
4 If the extra admissible expenditure of an authority exceeded the increase in the 'local contribution', subsidy entitlement would be increased. If, on the other hand, the extra local contribution exceeded this extra expenditure subsidy, entitlement would be correspondingly reduced.

The Labour government fell in 1979 before it could enact this system, but the Conservatives' Housing Act of 1980 essentially took it over. Then, what became crucial, since the new government was committed to reducing as far as possible the central government subsidy to council house rents, was the annual assumptions made, under point (3) above, about appropriate levels of rent increases.

This was used, particularly after the Local Government and Housing Act of 1989, to drive up rents through reduction of subsidy.

Thus, during the 1980s and 1990s, large numbers of local authorities ceased to be entitled to a subsidy from central government, other than contributions to pay the cost of rent rebates (housing benefit). In England in 1997–8 the subsidy to local authorities, excluding support for housing benefit, was about £696 million (Wilcox, 1998, table 67, p. 160). It has been falling steadily; it had been £1357 million in 1990–1.

Under the arrangements described above, rents could still be subsidized from local resources (at that time, the 'rate fund'). What in fact happened, in the early 1980s, was that there was an increased divergence between authorities. The sharp withdrawal of the central subsidy meant that, in aggregate, local subsidies to rents exceeded national subsidies by 1983. However, it was only in a small number of authorities, mostly in London, that such contributions were of any significant size (Malpass, 1990, p. 168). In around half of all authorities, no contributions were made at all. At the other extreme, an increasing number of authorities were making contributions to the rate fund from rents; that is, council tenants not on housing benefit were subsidizing rate-payers!

In the 1989 Act, the government set out to force local authorities to phase out these exchanges between housing accounts and their general accounts. This measure was widely described as 'ring-fencing' the housing revenue accounts. Local authorities were forced to raise rents to replace local contributions. A further complication was that, in determining the rules for these accounts, the government started taking into account a notional income from housing benefit subsidy. What this implies is that authorities may find that they are, in effect, required to subsidize the housing benefit to low-income tenants partly from the rents of other tenants. This new regime is gradually being phased in; and, as before, the actual situation depends on the government's application to each authority of the formula described above.

As suggested already, as the general subsidy has disappeared and general rents have increased, so housing benefit has tended to become the dominant form of subsidy going to local authority tenants. This is paid not by the DETR, but by the Department of Social Security. Housing benefit expenditure was about £5,539 million in Great Britain in 1997–8 (Wilcox, 1998, table 110, p. 200).

The determination of capital expenditure – that is, primarily the building of new houses – is also based on a system devised in the late 1970s by the Labour government. Before 1977, local councils determined their house-building programmes without consultation with central government. However, to implement those programmes, they had to secure central acceptance, both to enable them to undertake such extensive investment and to obtain subsidies (inasmuch as subsidies were linked to specific building projects). Local government proposed, and central government would dispose. The whole system was relatively haphazard, since central government tried to link its decisions to national and relative local priorities, but was dependent on local initiatives, and did not necessarily have an overall view of national housing needs. Under the system established in 1977, local authorities are required to submit for annual central scrutiny their 'Housing Investment Programmes'. These include not only their plans for the provision of new local authority housing, but also their plans to make loans for house purchase, to give grants for housing improvements, to improve their own stock, to clear unfit houses, to purchase houses and to assist housing associations. Statistical returns from the authorities are required on their own current and future activities, and on their intelligence on local housing needs and problems of private sector building. On the basis of these submissions, the English local authorities then, after a process of negotiation through the regional offices of the DETR (there are similar procedures in Scotland and Wales), receive annual expenditure allocations, not in the form of specific permission for particular projects, but in the form of a broad block.

The impact of the Conservative governments between 1979 and 1997 on this system was simply to limit expenditure, particularly on new building. In the late 1970s, local authorities in the UK built a little over 100,000 dwellings each year. In the early 1980s, it was down to a little over 30,000 a year and, in the 1990s, it has dropped to a very low figure indeed. In 1998, only about 300 public sector houses were completed in England. That figure (under 0.2 per cent of total completions) was dwarfed by the number of completions for housing associations (20,000, or 17 per cent of the total) (DETR, 1999). The new Labour government is, at the time of writing, releasing some more money for local authority building and renovation, from the receipts from council house sales.

The changes in public housing policy in the 1980s, towards the reduction of subsidies and the restriction of new building, need to be seen together with the government's stimulation of the sale of council houses. The role of local authorities in the provision of housing was beginning to be restricted. A Housing Act passed in 1988 aimed to go very much further in marginalizing that role. In a measure misleadingly presented by the government as enabling tenants to choose their landlords, opportunities were presented to housing associations and other independent buyers approved by the government to acquire local authority properties. Initiatives of this kind were bound in practice to come from potential buyers, encouraged by local authorities who wanted to sell their stock, rather than from tenants exercising 'choice'. Such moves could be blocked only if a majority of the tenants concerned vetoed them. Another section of the Act proposed to set up a number of housing action trusts in areas where, according to the government, substantial estate improvements were needed. These trusts would take over local authority properties, spend government money on improvements, and could then pass on the property to new owners.

The housing action trust idea was opposed by tenants in several of the areas where they were planned, and the government backed down or gave pledges that after improvements the properties could be restored to local authority ownership. The 'tenants' choice' proposal led to a limited number of housing association acquisitions from small southern authorities. While the 1988 Act did not work out in the way the government planned, the strict controls over local rent setting and the continuation of limitations on the availability of capital for new building by local authorities have had two effects. One has been the growth of the hitherto small housing association sector, because it has had relatively greater freedom to raise loans for building and rehabilitation work than local government. The other has been the exploration by local authorities of the case for voluntary transfer of their stock to a housing association so as to achieve greater managerial freedom, in particular the freedom to raise money for building and repairs. This latter development is involving not only housing stock transfers to existing housing associations, but also the setting-up of new associations, often formed from the staff of the local authority housing departments. Interestingly, Wilcox (1998) comments on this issue, comparing Conservative and Labour policies, but coming to what may seem an unexpected conclusion (p. 12–13):

> The whole tenor of the CSR [the comprehensive spending review initiated by the new government] has none of the last government's heavy-handed political drive towards stock transfers . . . Nonetheless, for many councils the current capital and revenue financial regimes mean that stock transfers will remain compellingly financially attractive. Stock transfer enables councils to escape from the strongly redistributive net of the council capital finance and subsidy systems to use rental income to fund investment rather than cross-subsidize the cost of housing benefit.

Housing associations were important in the nineteenth century, as voluntary charitable bodies, but declined in relative importance with the growth of the public sector in the first half of the twentieth century. Over the last thirty years, though, housing association growth has begun to be given increasing government encouragement, being seen as an alternative form of social housing to the large, bureaucratic local authority sector. Housing associations in England may receive grants and subsidies from the government through the Housing Corporation. There is a similar, separate body in Wales. In Scotland, Scottish Homes functions both as a lender of government money and as a direct housing provider. In Northern Ireland (where, incidentally, local authority housing functions have been transferred to a single Housing Executive directly responsible to the government), there is no intermediary body for housing associations.

In the 1980s and early 1990s, the government made more money available to housing associations than to local government. Nevertheless, inhibitions on public capital projects have led to curbs on the resources going through the Housing Corporation and related bodies. As suggested above, however, housing associations, unlike local authorities, can raise money on the open market without government permission. Loans from central government have to some extent been replaced in this way, but with inevitable consequences for the rents charged to tenants. The legislation on rents allows new housing association tenants to be charged what are described as 'affordable rents'. What constitutes an 'affordable rent' is not clearly defined by the government, but 'was interpreted by the National Federation of Housing Associations as a rent approximately equal to 20 per cent of the tenant's average net income' (Balchin, 1995, pp. 195–6). Housing benefit is available to low-income tenants, making a formula like this somewhat hypothetical in many cases.

Housing associations vary widely in size, scope and character. Some differ little in their characteristics from private companies; these have grown in size recently, absorbing some smaller associations along the way. Others have distinct charitable aims and objects, and many are specifically local in their coverage. A small number are co-operatives.

Despite the encouragement of housing associations, social housing provision in general has diminished. As was shown at the beginning of this chapter (page 227), local authority and housing association properties amount in 1996 to 23.3 per cent of the total stock (that is 5,583 thousand dwellings). By contrast, in 1981, they were 32.5 per cent of the stock (6,849 thousand dwellings) (Wilcox, 1998, table 17c, p. 94). This has been a product of both council house and housing association sales to tenants (the 'right to buy' legislation extends to housing associations) and the low amounts of new building.

The new Labour government might be expected to be interested in reversing the trend away from social housing. However, the Minister responsible for housing policy in the DETR, Hilary Armstrong (1998) had this to say in a presentation of the principles that were to govern the new housing policy:

> I am agnostic about the ownership of housing – local authorities or housing associations; public or private sector – and want to move away from the ideological baggage that comes with that issue. What is important is not, primarily, who delivers. It is what works that counts.

The policy evolution described above, ending with that statement from Hilary Armstrong, leads to a situation which Liddiard (1998, p. 121) justifiably describes as one in which 'housing is one of the UK's least contested areas of social policy'. Liddiard goes on to say:

> the apparent consensus ... seems incomprehensible given the real problems facing housing in the UK. As we enter the new millennium, one and a half million homes are unfit for human habitation and three and a half million are in urgent need of repair while there is a widely accepted need for some 100–120,000 new social homes a year.

We will return to these issues on page 239, but first we need to look at what is happening in the other two sectors.

Owner-occupation

It has already been suggested that the examination of housing policy raises difficulties for any distinction between social policy and other areas of public policy. It might be imagined that the private market for owner-occupied houses had very little to do with social policy or indeed with government interventions in society. However, such an impression can be readily corrected by examining the attention that housing has been given in the policies of the major parties in the years since World War II. A central issue in the general elections of 1950 and 1951 was the performance of the Labour government in 'building' houses, and the claim of the Conservative Opposition to be able to 'build' more houses. The argument was about the building of houses in general, not just building by public authorities. The

Conservatives came to power in 1951 committed to 'building' 300,000 houses a year, but many of these were to be built by private enterprise for owner-occupation. Indeed, the Conservatives increasingly encouraged the development of this sector during the 1950s. Since then, both parties have been concerned to assist the development of owner-occupation. They see an aspiration towards owner-occupation as having considerable electoral implications.

How, then, do public policies influence the owner-occupied housing sector? What used to be of central importance was the large public subsidy that was given to owner-occupiers through the fact that interest payments on mortgage loans attracted relief from the income tax system. This has been steadily phased out and will disappear in April 2000.

It is not only through tax relief that the government has influenced opportunities for individuals to secure owner-occupied housing. In the period immediately after World War II, the government maintained a tight control over building through control over access to building supplies. As it relaxed these controls, it stimulated private building. Then, in the 1950s, as it began to reduce the amount of local authority building, it thereby encouraged a shift of resources into building for sale. During that period of management of a full-employment economy along Keynesian lines, the government came to realize that one of the ways in which it could most easily influence the economic climate was by influencing the demand for new building. While the direct controls of the immediate post-war period no longer exist, there remain a series of factors that influence the scale of building of houses for sale: the extent to which alternative – particularly public sector – opportunities exist for the building industry, the availability of credit – particularly cheap credit – for building enterprises and land speculators, the availability of mortgage funds for home-buyers, and the availability of land.

Until the 1980s, the main suppliers of finance for house purchase were the building societies. These were comparatively cautious financial institutions, whose activities had grown slowly. Their origins lie in nineteenth-century self-help and charitable ventures, and they remained for a long while in some sense non-profit-making institutions. They depend for their operation on being able to attract money from small investors, influenced by the general range of opportunities open to savers, to lend to house-buyers.

Once the proportion of the population with their own houses was high enough, government encouragement of home ownership naturally entailed a concern to open opportunities for borrowing money to those who were regarded by the building societies, who have naturally been cautious in these matters, as 'bad risks'. Hence, there was governmental pressure on these 'private' organizations to lend to more 'marginal' people or for more 'marginal' properties.

During the 1980s, the government deregulated the financial market. Restrictions on building societies' activities were removed, and other lenders, including banks, discovered opportunities to move into the domestic mortgage business. There was a boom period when lenders saw the housing market as an ideal source of profits. Mortgages were sold aggressively, and the customary caution about the creditworthiness of borrowers was abandoned. This further fuelled the boom to which it was a response: owner-occupation expanded, and house prices rose rapidly. This boom, pushing house prices well beyond the overall rate of inflation, eventually collapsed in the recession at the end of the decade. House prices started to fall; the housing market became exceptionally static; and, with rising unemployment, many recent borrowers were soon in difficulties with their mortgage repayments. Table 10.1 provides some data on levels of mortgage arrears and repossessions in Britain at various dates in the 1990s.

One further complication in this situation has been that houseowners who are out of work and receiving income support secure some help towards the costs of the repayment of mortgage interest. On the other hand, if they have low, earned incomes from full-time work, they are disqualified from income support, and cannot be given any help with their housing costs from housing benefit. In this respect, they differ from workers who are renting, who can be given housing benefit. The government has been concerned about this situation, which forms – in their eyes – a benefits 'trap', which discourages some people from seeking work. They have severely curbed the help available to house-buyers from income support.

During the mid-1990s, the housing market recovered a little. There were fears for a while that a new boom similar to that at the end of the 1980s might be emerging. However, it did not materialize. Both borrowers and lenders may have become more

Table 10.1 Mortgage arrears and repossessions in Great Britain

	1991	1993	1995	1997
Borrowers more than 12 months in arrears	91,740	151,810	85,200	45,200
Repossessions during the year	75,540	58,540	49,410	32,770

Source: Wilcox, 1998, table 47 p. 138

cautious. Without the high levels of tax relief that prevailed in the past, owner-occupied housing is no longer seen as inevitably a safe investment for middle-income people. The overall demand for new owner-occupied houses is less intense than it was in the 1980s – because of the size of the existing housing stock, a fall in the rate of new household formation, and the lower levels of job security enjoyed by young people at the household-formation stage. At the time of writing, nevertheless, there are renewed signs of another housing boom.

Both the new Labour government and its immediate predecessor have seen control over inflation as a key policy to prevent a housing boom. They have also encouraged lenders to develop codes of practice and insurance policies which would prevent the rapid dispossession of people who became unemployed. Until the slump in the late 1980s, housing was a source of widespread capital gains. Of course, few people enjoyed those gains themselves; mostly they expected to pass them on to the next generation. In considering this issue as a whole, there is a connection to be made here with the discussion of the care costs of elderly people (page 169), since capital assets are taken into account in the means-testing process.

The Private Rented Sector

The private rented sector (excluding the housing association sector) now houses about 10 per cent of the British population. This sector has declined to that level from one in which it housed 90 per cent of the population in 1918 and still about 50 per cent in 1951.

There was a political, but now rather academic, argument about the original decline. Was it inevitable, as better outlets for investment opened up? Or was it produced by government-imposed controls? From 1916 onwards, there were rent controls of various kinds, applied with varying degrees of stringency. Controversy raged over the protection of private tenants from both eviction and high rents. Between 1965 and 1988, the fair rent principle was adopted for most forms of private tenure. This represented a political compromise based on a comparatively nonsensical formula according to which rent officers were expected to assume that properties were let in a market in which there was no scarcity. The reality was that rents were determined by a system of comparisons at levels some way below what the market might be expected to bear. At the same time, many landlords sought to evade the rent controls altogether by legal devices such as the granting of a 'licence to occupy' rather than a tenancy. The 1988 Housing Act effectively abandoned rent control, apart from various rather complex measures of protection for tenants with agreements dating from earlier rent control regimes. Since then there has been a slight increase in the size of this sector, by about 200,000 dwellings (Wilcox, 1998, table 17c, p. 94).

In decontrolling this sector, the government argued that returning it to the market-place would arrest its decline, but this depends on the alternative opportunities available to renters. In particular, owning is often a better prospect than renting for most people with the resources to pay market rents and proposing to stay in the same district for some time. Hence, the very slight increase in the sector.

Excluding temporary residents of an area, among whom students figure as a significant group, the superior advantages of owning, means that most private tenants will tend to be low-income earners and recipients of social security benefits. To enable them to pay market rents, the government has had to allow them access to the housing benefit scheme. However, the problem with this scheme is that receipt of benefit removes any incentive to the renter to behave like a free market participant. The cost of the rent falls on the state. To cope with this problem for the social security budget, a complex procedure has been adopted requiring rent officers to rule whether rents should be regarded as excessive for benefit purposes and the hapless tenant (or sometimes the local authority) to find the balance, rather than central government. In other words, a special system of benefit control has replaced rent control.

The private rented sector is unevenly distributed across the country. In some areas, particularly in the north, there are still old, poor-quality houses occupied by elderly tenants who have been in them for many years. With this property, the main public concern has been about conditions. Elsewhere, the private sector may have rather different characteristics. In London, in particular, but also in many other big cities, much of this accommodation is in the form of flats created out of large old houses. These areas tend to accommodate people whom local authorities do not see as their responsibility (or at least place very low on their scales of priorities): in particular, newcomers to the area and the young single. The decline in the rate at which social housing is provided (discussed above) intensifies the pressure on this sector. As other housing problems have been solved, the gap between the good housing conditions of the majority and the often very poor conditions experienced in this part of the private sector has become increasingly evident.

Homelessness

Homelessness has increased as a result of a combination of a decline in the supply of new accommodation with mobility in search of work in the overcrowded south and family breakdown. It also has causes outside the direct control of housing policy, in the unwillingness of the social security system to pay adequate benefits to some groups (in particular, the young). Finally, it must be noted that many among the homeless are in need of health and social care, to assist with problems of mental illness, alcoholism and drug abuse.

In 1977, the Housing (Homeless Persons) Act imposed a duty on local housing authorities to provide accommodation for homeless persons in certain 'priority' groups. These priority groups are, broadly, families with children or elderly or sick persons, together with those made homeless by disasters such as flood or fire. However, authorities need not help families who are deemed to have become homeless 'intentionally'. This controversial provision was added to the Act by an amendment, and may be used to justify refusal of help to someone who has been evicted for not paying rent.

The 1977 Act made it mandatory for an authority to give temporary help, and for more permanent help to be given where a homeless person had a (carefully defined) local connection. It was implicit in the Act that the homeless should be rehoused, except on a very temporary basis, in permanent homes, and not herded into inadequate accommodation. Thus they were in competition with those being rehoused by the housing departments from their waiting lists. In practice, many authorities, particularly in London, used poor-quality temporary accommodation to house homeless people for long periods of time. The Conservative governments of the 1980s and 1990s were unwilling to pressure reluctant local authorities to fulfil their responsibilities better; and, in 1996, enacted amending legislation to limit local authority responsibility in respect of homelessness to the provision of time-limited temporary accommodation (normally for one year).

It must be emphasized that the policy responses described above were principally for the 'priority' groups as defined above. Local authority obligations to the younger single are simply to give advice! It is single homelessness which has grown visibly, particularly in London. It has already been suggested that the roots of this problem lie in a complex of factors, only some of which concern housing policy. Certainly, however, the hard-pressed under-resourced local authority housing departments have been unable to pay much attention to the needs of this group, particularly if the individuals need some combination of housing and social care. It has been left to other special centrally supported initiatives for 'rough sleepers' to try to respond to the problem. The Blair government quickly made this one of their special concerns, referring the issue to the newly created 'Social Exclusion Unit'. This Unit recommended the injection of new resources and the setting up of special programmes on a nationwide basis.

In 1997, local authorities in Britain accepted as their responsibility under the 1988 Act just over 100,000 people (Wilcox, 1998, table 86, p. 179). Wilcox reports from 1991 census data a 'street homeless' figure, that is people sleeping rough, of nearly 3,000 but acknowledges that this is surely an underestimate (Wilcox, 1998, table 91, p. 182).

Housing and Social Exclusion

The government has asked its Social Exclusion Unit to look at housing issues. Its two specific mandates are to look at problem estates and, as noted above, street homelessness. As Lee and Murie (1998) suggest in an essay on this topic, though, the issues about social exclusion are wider ranging than this. In addition to the homeless, it is appropriate to bear in mind that, in 1997, there were about 53,000 people in temporary accommodation in Britain (Wilcox 1998, table 87, p. 180). There was a much greater number in houses deemed to be unfit by the DETR in England, around 1,300,000 and over half of these were owner-occupied. There were also about 300,000 in private rented accommodation and a similar number units of unfit local authority or housing association accommodation (mostly the former) (Wilcox, 1998, table 23b, p. 108).

However, the issues about local authority owned problem estates go much wider than this. The problems of such estates are seen as involving, as well as poor housing conditions, 'crime, disorder, unemployment, community breakdown, poor health, educational underachievement and inadequate public transport and local services' (Social Exclusion Unit, 1998).

A full discussion of the issues about these estates would take us far from the subject of housing. It is important to note that efforts to tackle the physical problems of such estates have often failed, in the face of the wider issues needing to be confronted (Power, 1987). However, what is relevant here is the extent to which the emergence and deterioration of these so-called problem estates has been a consequence of housing policies. This will therefore be explored here.

Allocation of social housing involves achieving a balance between what people want, what they are deemed to need, and what is available. Under conditions of housing scarcity, individuals are in a weak position to assert their wants, unless their co-operation is required with a redevelopment scheme. Housing authorities allocate on the basis of assessments of need, attempting to make the most efficient use of the housing stock. However, in the past, they often gave attention to capacity to pay rent, and many were also disposed to make judgements about potential tenants' suitability for 'good' houses.

There were efforts to move away from such discriminatory allocation of local authority housing, and as the number of families who are desperate for help declined in some areas, the balance of power between housing officers who judge needs and potential tenants who express their wishes inevitably shifted. In some areas, poorer houses were often only easily allocated to, for example, the homeless. Nevertheless, a reshuffling of tenants proceeds all the while, and those allocated the 'bad' houses seek transfers to better ones. Often they secure such transfers only if they have been 'good' tenants and, in particular, if they have been regular rent-payers. The only people who shift in the opposite direction are those who are punished for rent arrears or strikingly non-conforming behaviour, by eviction from 'good' houses and allocation of 'bad' ones.

Local authorities now have stocks of houses and flats of various kinds: in particular, pre-war semi-detached houses, post-war 'semis' built when standards were low, modern houses built to high standards, flats in blocks of various sizes, good old houses acquired from private owners, and patched houses with short lives pending demolition. Of course, these dwellings vary in popularity, with perhaps high-rise flats and short-life houses as the least popular. If, through allocation and transfer policies, there are various forms of segregation within an authority's housing stock, then the 'hierarchy of popularity' will have been influenced by social as well as architectural considerations. Indeed, these social factors may well complicate the hierarchy as certain estates, not necessarily characterized by severe design problems, also acquire reputations as 'rough' or 'respectable', perhaps as a result of some rather complex accidents of history. This can obviously tend to involve differentiation by income, particularly if accessibility to employment opportunities influences tenant choices. Thus the unpopular areas may contain substantial proportions of households dependent on social security benefits. Woods (1999), p. 108 also notes:

In addition to having concentrations of low income people local
authorities have also have to contend with greater movement in and
out of local authority housing. . . . A high turnover of stock makes it
more difficult to develop community spirit and identity and makes it
harder to achieve sustainable and supportive communities.

She goes on to paraphrase a Centre for Housing Policy report (1997)
noting that:

those moving out of the sector were generally couples aged under 45
where one or both people were working. On the other hand, those
moving in to the sector were in the 16–29 age group and unemployed.

One crucial influences on this issue has been the sale of council
houses, which further enhances the social divisions, since houses on
popular estates and on estates in which the more prosperous tenants
live will be more likely to be sold. This is discussed in the next
section.

The Selling of Social Housing

The Conservatives came to power in 1979 determined to stimulate
the sale of local authority and housing association houses to their
tenants. Their Housing Act of 1980 provided a statutory right to
most tenants to buy their own houses, at market prices less a discount
based on length of tenancy ranging from 33 to 50 per cent. Subsequently, the government put pressure on Labour-controlled authorities which dragged their feet in implementing this provision, going
so far in one case, Norwich, as to put in a special commissioner to
do the job. Total sales in England since the inception of the programme had reached nearly 1.7 million by 1997–8 (DETR, 1999).
    Sales gradually fell away from the high numbers seeking to take
advantage of the legislation when it was first enacted. Since social
housing tenants are, generally speaking, low-income people, sales
will have been affected by unemployment. Moreover, the number
with the resources to buy will ultimately be finite, so some falling
away in numbers is to be expected. In the financial year 1997–8 the
number of sales to occupiers in England was down to 44,000 (DETR,
1999).
    There has been a debate about the justification for selling social
housing. This is partly a technical one about the actual effect of such
sales on the housing effort as a whole and partly an ideological one

about tenants' rights. There is a trade-off here between the rights of actual tenants and the interests of potential future tenants whose needs may not be met so easily because public authorities have lost control over some of their stock. The trade-off was made more evident by the refusal of the government to let all the proceeds of sales be recycled into new investment in housing, a policy that Labour is now slowly reversing.

This debate must also be seen in the light of what was said in the last section. The houses that tenants are likely to buy will be in 'good' popular estates. The development within these of a mixture of owner-occupation and renting may be seen as desirable for the future of such estates, in the long run extending social mixing and social diversity to those estates. However, such a development reinforces the growing gap between the 'good' estates and the 'bad'. In this way, it reinforces a future for social housing in which renting (even from a public authority or housing association) will be seen as a much inferior option to ownership. Britain is moving to a situation, like that in the USA, in which social housing is not even 'housing for the working classes', as it was required to be in the original legislation, but housing for the poor. By 1993–4, more than 60 per cent of local authority tenants were on means-tested benefits (Green and Hansbro, 1995, p. 69). This development has been influenced by government policies which push up rent levels, leaving subsidy to the benefit system. This increases the incentive for those required to pay full rents to seek to buy. The problem is that owner-occupation is popular, and its growth seems desirable; but this growth leaves a minority behind in possibly decreasingly satisfactory circumstances.

It is significant that, to enhance the sale of social housing, the government has been forced to provide large discounts. The provision of discounts weakened the economic arguments for sales; older houses that are, perhaps quite reasonably, sold to long-term sitting tenants at low prices still have to be replaced, if there is outstanding housing need, by new, expensive houses. This issue draws our attention to a variation of the same anomaly as exists within the owner-occupied sector: there is a vast gap between the original, 'historic' costs of housing and modern 'replacement' costs. In the owner-occupied sector, someone who bought a house, say in the 1960s, for £2,000 may today be repaying a minute (by modern standards) mortgage. If he or she dies, heirs will receive an asset worth many times the original price. In the local authority sector, a similar house may today, assuming rents have moved in line with prices, be yielding the local authority a 'profit', which it returns to the rent pool to subsidize newer houses. What is a fair rent (in the true sense, not in the sense in which the term is used in the Rent Acts) for such a house? And if the occupier wants to buy, what is a fair price? There are no right answers to these questions; the whole situation is riddled with anomalies. To treat such a tenant well is to give a privilege relative to those who are still seeking local authority accommodation. To treat him or her harshly is to emphasize his or her disadvantage relative to the long-term owner-occupier.

Conclusions

The latter part of this chapter has particularly emphasized the issues that have arisen from the interaction between Britain's various housing sectors with the growth of owner-occupation and the decline of private renting. The interactions here are complex. Studies of housing have given attention to movement between the sectors, examining the filtering hypothesis which suggests that the benefits of new houses, even at the top of the owner-occupier market, filter down to contribute to the reduction of housing need. Superficially, this seems plausible. However, the 'chains' that have been traced resulting from new houses at the 'top' end of the system are often short. Typically, they extend down only to a young new entrant to owner-occupation, perhaps from that part of the private rented sector where the needs of the young mobile middle class are met, perhaps merely forming a new separate household for the first time (Murie et al., 1976; Forrest et al., 1990). The same seems to be true of purchased social housing when it is later sold by the original buyer.

At least three very different kinds of housing 'career' can be detected. One involves movement into or entirely within the owner-occupied sector as described above. Another involves movement, either on separation from a parental home or via the private rented sector, to social housing, but then stops there for the rest of life. A third involves difficulty in moving from the private rented sector to either of the other sectors.

These divisions may have equally serious implications for the allocation of opportunities and for territorial justice in our society. Owner-occupation conveys benefits which are passed on through inheritance, while the other sectors do not. These social divisions may be reinforced across time – this issue is attracting increasing attention; see, for example, Hamnett (1991). However, even owner-occupation is increasingly stratified in terms of the age and quality of the housing and in terms of when individuals achieved that status.

As suggested above, many recent buyers may not have secured appreciating assets comparable to those bought by earlier generations.

Most seriously, though, while it is accepted that the concentration of social problems in certain areas raise policy concerns far beyond those of housing policy, it is important to recognize how housing policy has, and is, exacerbating these problems. Most fundamentally, it is disturbing that council housing which was conceived as housing 'for the working classes', or even 'for everyone' in a brief utopian dream in the 1940s, is now increasingly seen, like the comparable sector in the USA, as welfare housing, where the 'dangerous poor' are segregated and need to be contained. It is not clear that the agnosticism of the new Labour government, as expressed in the quotation above from Hilary Armstrong, offers a solution to this problem. The concerted efforts on the constellations of problems, proposed by the Social Exclusion Unit, is to be welcome, but surely the limitations of this approach are well expressed by Lee and Murie (1998, p. 37). when they say:

> If the situation where only those with no choice move into the social rented sector is to be avoided, a more radical rebuilding of that sector is required. That involves a new look at the structure of housing markets and the range of choice offered in different parts of it.

Suggestions for further reading

Balchin (1995) provides a good general introduction to housing policy. It will be evident that the edited compilation of housing data by Wilcox (1998) is a valuable source. It contains incisive essays on current issues as well as a mine of statistics. It is supported as an annual venture by the Joseph Rowntree Foundation, so hopefully there will be later versions. The many issues about housing finance are well discussed in Malpass's *Reshaping Housing Policy* (1990). Malpass and Murie's *Housing Policy and Practice* (1999) deals with key policies issues. Its fifth edition will be published in 1999. Some up-to-date essays on various issues in housing policy are contained in Williams' *New Directions in Housing Policy: Towards Sustainable Housing* (1997). A thorough account of the 'right to buy' legislation is contained in Forrest and Murie (1991).

Chapter 11

SOCIAL POLICY, POLITICS AND SOCIETY

- Introduction
- Social expenditure in the context of national public expenditure
- Alternative perspectives on social policy and the state

- The quest for efficient and responsive modes of social policy delivery
- Conclusions
- Suggestions for further reading

Introduction

This book has given attention to the major policy areas that are conventionally labelled 'social policy'. It has shown that, within these areas, the state is responsible for a wide range of activities. In the chapters on individual policies, a number of weaknesses were noted in the pattern of provision. Yet it is widely suggested today that the state takes on too much, and that the public service sector, of which the social policy areas account for a large proportion, is too large. We need therefore to look, in this final chapter, at some of the general issues regarding the role of social policy in society and at some of the attempts to make social policy, as a whole, more effective and more responsive to popular needs and attitudes.

Social Expenditure in the Context of National Public Expenditure

Table 11.1 provides figures setting out total public expenditure in Great Britain, with proportions of that expenditure which fall under the four main social policy headings and two others added (to offer a contrast). It uses information on expenditure for the most recent

Table 11.1   Proportions of public expenditure in Great Britain spent on various government functions

Functions	1987	1991	1995	1997
Social protection	34	36	39	39
Health	12	12	13	13
Education	11	11	11	11
Housing and community services	4	4	3	2
Defence	11	10	7	7
Public order and safety	4	5	5	5
All expenditure (£billion at 1997 prices)	280	301	338	337

Source: Office of National Statistics 1999b., p. 116, table 6.22

year for which official information has been published (1997) and for three earlier years to give an idea of recent trends. The figures for the expenditure totals are what are called 'real terms' figures: that is, figures adjusted to common price levels at a single point in time, in this case 1997.

These figures show a rise in expenditure in real terms of 20 per cent. It is important to note that the Conservatives came to power back in 1979 committed to curbing social policy expenditure but failed to do so. It may be quite surprising to readers to see that, at least after 1987, they were able to cut defence but not social protection expenditure. Of the social policy expenditure categories set out in table 11.1, only housing has fallen in proportionate terms; therefore, we may conclude that all the rest have risen in real terms, and that expenditure on social protection (social security and the personal social services) has risen substantially since 1987. The ingredients of this rise were set out in table 5.1 (page 119). Much of it derived from social and economic change – the ageing of the population, the increase in the number of single parent families, the lack of work (in practice having a bigger effect on sickness and disability benefit claims than on those from the unemployed) and the increase of low-wage work (increasing the need for in-work benefits, including housing benefit); see Glennerster and Hills (1998) for a more detailed analysis of these issues.

It is too early to explore the impact of the new Labour government on public expenditure, but it is important to note (a) that they pledged themselves initially to work within the public spending programme of their predecessor and (b) that by 1999 were actually claiming some success in cutting social security expenditure, while at the same time justifying injections of extra money into health and education programmes.

Expenditure on social policy is shown in table 11.1 to be nearly two-thirds of all public expenditure. This means that any government which is concerned to keep levels of taxation and public sector debt under control will be likely to be concerned about pressures (demographic, economic or political) which tend to lead to a rise of social policy expenditure. While social expenditure levels in Britain are quite modest, compared with most of the other EU nations in Northern Europe, a concern about the cost of the British welfare state has come to dominate politics here. The various political perspectives on this issue will be explored further in the next section.

Alternative Perspectives on Social Policy and the State

The account of the development of social policy in chapter 2 showed how, between 1945 and 1979, there was a relatively high level of consensus between the major political parties on the case for high levels of social expenditure, rising with the increase in the prosperity of the nation. In the 1960s and 1970s, some of the complacency about the achievement of the British 'welfare state' was challenged by academics and pressure groups, drawing attention to continuing problems of poverty and weaknesses in the overall policy framework. As Titmuss and his colleagues developed the study of social policy in Britain in the 1950s, they were concerned to attack the complacent belief that the creation of the welfare state, particularly through the social policy reforms of the 1940s, had secured a very much more equal society. It was pointed out that the main beneficiaries of some of the key reforms were the relatively well-to-do. The free health service extended benefits to all, but was used more by the higher social classes. The middle classes could now send their children to grammar schools without having to pay fees. Even the main extensions of the social security system gave the better-off access to benefits from which they were previously excluded. At the same time, while it was true that the tax burden had considerably increased for higher earners, a wide range of concessions and untaxed fringe benefits offset this or provided compensating benefits (Titmuss, 1962; Atkinson, 1975); see also Le Grand (1982) and George and Wilding (1984) for more recent explorations of this issue.

In the early 1960s, researchers, including notably Abel-Smith and Townsend (1965), showed that extensive poverty was still present in Britain. Not only were there large numbers of people dependent on that subsistence level guaranteed by national assistance, but there were also many, a considerable proportion of whom were in families containing a full-time wage-earner, with incomes below or only a little above that level. Hence, it was shown that the welfare state was not either markedly redistributive or particularly effective at eradicating poverty. Where the official response to this was not complacent it did involve, particularly on the part of Labour administrations, efforts to address deficiencies in the pattern of public provision.

However, there were elements in this developing critique of the welfare state which were critical of the institutional arrangements for policy delivery. The medical dominance of the NHS was one of the earliest causes for concern. Later, more and more attention began to be given to the notion that welfare was being delivered in a paternalistic way by professionals and bureaucrats with little attention to the interests and needs of beneficiaries; see Deakin (1994) for a good overview of these issues.

The last three paragraphs outline what may be broadly described as the critique of the welfare state from the Left. While there were always critics of welfare from the political Right, they were relatively lonely voices until the 1970s. The Right wing critique of social policy slowly gained sustenance from the economic problems Britain was facing. The election of the Conservative government headed by Margaret Thatcher in 1979 contributed to moving these critics much more into the political mainstream. They argued that the size of the redistributive exercise via taxation into public expenditure undertaken by the British government has a disincentive impact on private initiative, and has contributed towards low productivity. They suggested that the scale and scope of the state 'bureaucracy' were such that public resources were inevitably used inefficiently. The British people were alleged to be overtaxed and overgoverned (Harris and Seldon, 1979; Minford, 1984).

This Right wing perspective sees the provision of social services as the responsibility of the individual and rejects the idea that such services should be redistributive. The role of the state is merely to alleviate the most extreme forms of hardship, but otherwise to stand back from interfering in the market. It is asserted that, instead of depending on a paternalistic state, people should be free to make choices about amounts and kinds of social benefits, just as they make choices about the purchase of ordinary consumer goods.

These advocates of less government involvement, and of the extension of the role of the market, generally have a stance on social equality too. While it could be the case that bureaucratic rigidity and lack of choice in the present social welfare system might be reduced by an extension of the free market system, changes to such a system might well leave vulnerable low-income groups unprotected. In theory, this might be countered by government interventions to enhance the incomes of the poor and decrease inequality. Hence, the poor would gain both more income and more choice. The difficulty with such compensating changes is that they would entail extensive government intervention to equalize incomes. These would be anathema to those who expound the virtues of free enterprise. They are generally content, instead, to leave the distribution of incomes to be determined by the 'hidden hand' of the market.

In practice, the Conservative governments between 1979 and 1997 moved cautiously towards the Right wing position (Pierson, 1994). They were eager to cut taxation and expenditure, and 'liberate' market forces, but they were also aware of public attachment to many aspects of social policy, particularly the NHS and the education system. They also, as has already been pointed out, had to face the fact that there were social and economic forces driving social expenditure upwards despite their efforts. After the middle 1980s, they came to see institutional change as important both to curb the power of the bureaucrats and professionals who were seen as self-interestedly expanding public social services and to increase the scope for private provision. The 'quasi-market' systems set up in the health, personal social services and education systems came to be the hallmark of the new Conservative social policy.

However, they also countenanced changes in taxation, in the way economic opportunities were distributed and in the rules relating to social benefits which sharply increased inequality in Britain. The official statistics which highlight this most effectively are those which compare households with below average income with the rest of the population. MacDermott (1999) summarizes this evidence as follows, but see also Hills (1998):

> average income grew in real terms by 44 per cent between 1979 and 1996/7, but this growth was far greater among the richest tenth of the population. For the poorest tenth incomes rose by only 10 per cent before housing costs but fell by 8 per cent after housing costs.

This discussion has so far highlighted a critique of the British welfare state from the Left, which has argued that too little is done (particularly for the poor) and a critique from the Right which alternatively asserts that too much is done by the government. Both positions have given some attention to institutional deficiencies, and this theme seems to have been picked up quite strongly by the

Conservatives since 1979. At the same time, the Conservatives proved not surprisingly to be pragmatic politicians who moved cautiously in the direction of their Right wing gurus. Similarly, we find that the Labour party, out of power for a long while, sought to relocate itself in the middle ground rather than simply take its lead from the Left critique outlined above. Tony Blair and his colleagues in the new Labour government have been at pains to try to position themselves in relation to the traditional Left/Right argument in a new way. This involves endeavouring to escape from the uni-dimensional way in which that argument is typically expressed – seeing themselves as adopting a 'third' way rather than a 'middle' way. It is not helpful to discuss here the appropriateness of the imagery: whether there is one dimension, two or more. Readers must, however, make their own judgements as to whether what they are about to read represents a radical repositioning, or as some of the government's critics have suggested, a reformulation of a centre-Right stance (new Conservative rather than new Labour). In making those judgements, readers must bear in mind that political parties and governments are complex institutions in which there is a continuing process of interaction between competing values. The Prime Minister, who will be quoted here, is but the most powerful figure in debates that must be going on within the government on its future direction.

Just before this book was sent off to the publishers, the Prime Minister set out his stance on social policy in a lecture, commemorating William Beveridge. In that lecture, he criticized the Left of the 1970s who 'trapped in a false confusion of means and ends, resisted changing the welfare state on the grounds that to modernize . . . was to undermine it' (Blair, 1999). On the other hand, he argued, the Right, in the 1980s and 1990s, 'were not mistaken about the importance of markets and greater competition. But they failed to see in the modern world that it is not enough' (Blair, 1999).

Tony Blair went on to set out what he saw 'will be' the five necessary characteristics of a modern welfare state:

1   He saw it as tackling 'social exclusion', a fashionable EU notion, mixing a relatively vague concept with the idea of focused attention on particular outsider groups. Tony Blair suggested some causes of social exclusion such as unemployment, poor education and poor housing. There are problems here, discussed in the relevant chapters of this book, as to whether these are symptoms rather than causes of social inequalities. If that is right then very specific interventions to attack them – such as special

zones like Education Action Zones – will have severe limitations in the absence of wider egalitarian policies.

2   He said 'welfare will be a hand up not a hand out' offering a self-help perspective that was very much one of the 'Victorian values' to which Margaret Thatcher wanted to return. The idea of welfare as itself a 'trap' is one that has been widely expressed in US writings (Murray, 1984; Mead, 1986). In chapter 9, the heavy emphasis put by the government on labour market participation was fully discussed. It was argued that the success of that strategy depends not just on what is *done for or to* those who are expected to participate in the labour market but also on what is done to ensure that there are real jobs for them. In the absence of that, this principle may be used as an excuse for doing nothing for those with the greatest difficulties in making use of a 'hand up'.

3   Tony Blair then offered what may be a partial contradiction of his second point, saying 'where people really need security, the most help should go to those with the most need'. He professed an agnostic stance here, as has been the case with various government statements on social security, on the long-standing argument between 'universal and targeted help'. It may be suggested that the government still has some difficult questions to resolve about the relationship between these two. Some of these were discussed in chapter 5.

4   Next came a principle regularly stated by all governments, that fraud and abuse must be rooted out. This is not something on which there is much disagreement, but there is scope for a great deal of argument about the effects of rigorous anti-fraud measures on perceptions of stigma and underclaiming of benefits and services; see the symposium on this in *Benefits* (1998).

5   Tony Blair next reiterated a Conservative stance discussed above about the need to develop new ways of delivering welfare, including partnerships between the public and private sector and the involvement of the voluntary sector. Earlier chapters of this book have identified this theme in various policy areas.

We see here a stance that is very like that of the former Conservative governments on self-help, targeting, the prevention of fraud and new approaches to policy delivery. The concern about social exclusion is rather different, and this was expanded by Blair elsewhere in the lecture to indicate a commitment to the eradication of poverty. Blair criticized his predecessors for the rise in poverty. There are also features of the new government's approach to both 'self-help' and delivery institutions that may perhaps be rather different, these will be discussed in the next section.

The Quest for Efficient and Responsive Modes of Social Policy Delivery

It has been shown above that the view that social policy interventions have not achieved the success that might have been expected from the effort put into them has now been widely accepted. It has been recognized that a complex bureaucracy has been developed to provide social services, and that efforts are therefore needed to overcome the resulting institutional problems with the system.

In the 1960s and 1970s, governments devoted a considerable amount of attention to the organization of both central and local government. There was a search for the most rational form of organization. The search was always made difficult by a wide range of political considerations: reorganization might change the balance of power, and alter opportunities and career prospects of individuals. Moreover, established patterns of organization develop supporting sentiments and loyalties. In any case, the rationalization of government is not an easy process. There are often competing criteria for rationalization which are difficult to assess. For example, there is a conflict between the achievement of uniformity through centralization and the maximization of flexibility through decentralization. The close integration of particular services – for example, health and the personal social services – may weaken links between those services and other related activities – for example, the provision of housing and the achievement of high environmental standards. Rationalization seems to involve a search for the best arrangement, when perhaps, in reality, there are merely alternative arrangements, each carrying costs and benefits. These are difficult to evaluate. Finally, there are informal aspects to organizational arrangements which develop within formal structures. While, in theory, formal arrangements may be sought to maximize effective informal links, these are particularly difficult to predict. Moreover, one of the effects of a formal reorganization is to distort – and perhaps undermine – informal links operating prior to reorganization.

At central government level, there was, between the mid-1960s and the mid-1970s, a move towards super-departments embracing many different policy areas. The 1980s saw some backing away from this approach. The largest of the social policy departments, the Department of Health and Social Security (DHSS) was broken into two. On the other hand, in 1995, Education and Employment were joined together. Probably more important than this has been the 'next steps' initiative whereby policy-making departments delegate their day-to-day policy delivery tasks to executive agencies. The significance of this change for social security and for employment services was discussed in chapter 4. This new model enables the policy departments to set policy output goals and targets to which agencies can be held accountable. The 1960s and 1970s also saw a range of experiments aimed at the more effective co-ordination of public services, both at the central and the local level. At the centre, emphasis was on solving problems that cut across departmental boundaries. A small unit called the Central Policy Review Staff was set up in the early 1970s but was eventually axed by Margaret Thatcher in the 1980s. In relation to the local level, the government's concern was with the co-ordination of policy implementation, particularly in deprived areas. In the 1960s, there were Community Development Projects and Educational Priority Areas. Some of the ideas developed by these special initiatives fed into main stream policies. In the 1980s and 1990s, initiatives like 'city challenge' required local authorities to compete for extra resources to tackle problem areas by putting together bids involving local resources of all kinds. The new Labour government seems to be going back to some of the older ideas. At the central level, the Social Exclusion Unit has been developed to try to secure co-ordinated action on problems like street homelessness, deprived housing estates and truancy. At the local level, there is the idea of the development of zones in disadvantaged areas where, with help from some extra cash from the centre, policy innovation and inter-agency co-ordination may be enhanced. There is thus the setting up of Education Action Zones and Health Action Zones. It is much too early to judge these new initiatives, however the judgements on their predecessors do not encourage high hopes (Higgins et al., 1984; Blackstone and Plowden, 1988). The British system remains one in which, as suggested in chapter 4, innovations in policy implementation alongside the main policy delivery framework have considerable difficulties to overcome.

One of the most significant innovations in respect of accountability developed by the Conservatives in the 1980s and 1990s involved trying to avoid situations in which one agency was the sole provider of a publicly required service. The developments along these lines were discussed in chapter 4 and further explored in the chapters on health, the personal social services and education. The existence of monopoly providers was seen to contribute to inefficiency or to give too much power to key staff (particularly professional staff). In education, the Conservatives tried to increase the range of providers and to use parental choice to produce a 'quasi-market' system. In health and the personal social services, ways of splitting purchasers from providers were developed which, while they did little to empower the ultimate 'customers' seem to offer the possibility of greater controls over providers. The Conservative hope, largely unrealized, was that competition would emerge between providers. This model also allows for the possibility that the providers may be private bodies, even profit-making bodies. The new Labour government has accepted the notion that there may be a range of providers, showing as much suspicion of local authority providers and of professional self-interest as its predecessor. However, it has backed away from the idea that an actual market can be created. The word 'purchasing' is being replaced by 'commissioning', particularly in the NHS.

The Conservative governments between 1979 and 1995 developed two, not necessarily compatible, approaches as important for the control of public services. One of these was a managerialist quest for means of control by creating accountable subdivisions within large organizations and by delegating services to accountable agencies. This process of delegation involved strong budgetary controls and demands for the achievement of specific quantitative outputs; see Pollitt (1990) for further discussion of this. The other involved the search for devices which mimic markets, and thus, as described above, use competition and choice as control devices. After the fall of Margaret Thatcher, the new Conservative regime led by John Major put a strong emphasis on consumerism. Major's approach to consumerism entailed stressing the importance of information about service outputs to enable people to exercise choice and exploring ways to provide financial compensation when services fail to deliver outputs or to deal with problems within a specific time-span. This was central to Major's 'citizens' charter'.

It is important to contrast these approaches to public policy with an alternative which was more popular on the Left. This was to see the key problem for public accountability as not public monopoly *per se*, but rather the absence of devices for popular participation in decision making (Donnison, 1991). The chief characteristic of this approach was to seek to establish ways of decentralizing decision making. In the late 1970s and early 1980s, the lead in this decentralization movement was provided by Labour- (and sometimes Liberal-) controlled local authorities (Gyford, 1985, 1991). Decentralization took the form of the breakdown of some authorities into sub-areas with local offices and local committees, the development of tenants' participation in housing management, and so on.

Arguments for greater participation developed against the back-cloth of the elimination of the smaller organs of local government and an increased centralization of decision making. Accordingly, in those areas where governments, or local authorities, have been willing to countenance the development of participatory devices, there have been grounds for regarding this as tokenism designed to disguise the retreat of the real locus of power.

One of the implications of the abandonment of the quasi-market idea as undesirable or impractical is that it leaves these problems about citizen control unresolved. The idea that public services might become like high street retail shops, in which consumers might make choices between alternatives with their characteristics and their prices reasonably openly displayed, seemed to offer an approach to these issues. Its abandonment brings us back to the conflict about central control. On the one side, there is the argument that centralization offers a uniform approach to standards, the equal treatment of different areas in a relatively homogeneous and compact country and the prevention of particularism and corruption at the local level. On the other side stands the view that there can only be real public accountability if the units of government are small and if local participatory devices can be developed.

It might be expected that, given the critique of the traditional methods of social policy delivery outlined above, the second side in that argument would be winning. Perhaps devolution to the much smaller Scottish, Welsh and Northern Irish societies is a step in that direction. However, that leaves, as was pointed out in chapter 3, much the largest country in the UK undivided. Moreover, effective participation requires much smaller units. Yet the controls over local government are being increased, and most of the experiments on devolution within local authorities have been undermined by resource constraints.

The new government's position on this issue is ambivalent. Pronouncements on local government as a whole, on education and on the personal social services suggest the encouragement of experimentation at the local level, some of which may enhance local participation. On the other hand, there is a deep suspicion of local government – particularly in the light of evidence from some authorities of inefficiency and corruption in a context of long-standing one party control and low levels of electoral participation. The government is making it very clear that local autonomy is something to be earned. It must be questioned both whether independence can be enhanced by such a tutelage system and whether government ministers really want to release control over those issues most likely to be contested.

There is so far no exploration of ways of decentralizing control in the other social policy areas. Arguments for local control over health services fall on deaf ears. Meanwhile, the government's main concern is to increase the accountability of doctors to the NHS hierarchy. Issues about information play an important role in these struggles over control. The citizens' charter ideas presuppose that making information available to citizens will increase their capacity to participate. Here again they sit most comfortable inside the 'high street' model of consumer accountability, helping us to choose our schools, hospitals, etc. In the absence of those choices, their function must be to enable us to participate in political decision processes. Chapter 3 explored some of the difficulties about this. The electoral choice approach to control is a very blunt weapon. Furthermore, inasmuch as data may be used in election campaigns, there are strong temptations for politicians to manipulate it, e.g. numbers on hospital waiting lists, indices of educational achievement, and numbers of places on employment schemes filled. Sophisticated information technology also increases the scope for the collection of data to facilitate central control over local authorities, teachers, doctors and so on.

Fortunately, through all this conflict over local democracy and despite the search for new methods of delivering services, mechanisms have survived that enable citizens to take action over individual grievances. In principle, the two categories into which grievance procedures fall are nearly as old as the nation-state itself: appeals to courts and complaints to elected representatives. In practice, they take modern forms very different from these traditional grievance procedures. In centuries past, litigation vis-à-vis dissatisfaction with an administrative agency depended on an elaborate, costly legal procedure whereby the royal prerogative was invoked on behalf of the aggrieved citizen. These 'prerogative remedies' are still used from time to time and, today, individuals may secure legal aid or the assistance of a voluntary organization to enable them to take grievances against public authorities to the High Court. For everyday purposes, though, what is much more important is that a large number of lower 'courts', generally known as 'tribunals', have been set up to deal with appeals against decisions of public agencies. Furthermore, in many cases, there may be direct appeals to the courts or a supervisory tribunal against the decisions of these bodies.

The area of social policy in which tribunals are most important is social security. Individuals may appeal against most decisions taken by social security officials. There is a two-tier appeal system for social security benefits, with commissioners who operate at the top level, whose decisions are regarded as precedents for lower-tier decisions. Special systems, less detached from day-to-day decision makers, exist to deal with claimants dissatisfied with social fund and housing benefit decisions.

In the housing sector, tribunals deal only with a limited range of disputes over rent levels and security of tenure in the private sector. Disputes between tenants and local authorities are not covered; these have to go to county courts.

There are tribunals to deal with complaints against GPs, but not against other parts of the health service. There are tribunals that review cases of compulsory detention under the Mental Health Acts. There is also a tribunal system to deal with disputes about the licensing of private residential and nursing homes.

Parents may appeal against the refusal of admission of a child to a school and against a child's exclusion from a school. A weakness of these procedures is that the appeal system is run by the very bodies whose decisions are contested. On the other hand, disputes regarding decisions about the appropriate schooling for a child with learning difficulties are heard by an independent tribunal.

The case for tribunals is that they provide for separate (and, in the best cases, independent) review of decisions, particularly those involving official discretion. They are less important for the control of policy itself; it is comparatively rare for tribunal decisions to indicate a significant defect in policy. To aggrieved individuals, they offer not so much a chance to change policy as an opportunity to check a controversial application of policy. The system of tribunals in Britain has been improved considerably in recent years. As a result of the Franks Committee (HMSO, 1957), attempts have been made to make tribunal proceedings more consistent and impartial. A Council on Tribunals maintains an oversight of tribunal arrangement, and reports (if necessary, publicly) its observations to the government. There is still, nevertheless, a suspicion that some tribunals are too closely identified with the government agencies whose decisions they are expected to examine. For example, the committees that adjudicate on complaints against GPs have been seen as rather too closely identified with the administration of the family practitioner services. There is scope both for attacking these problems and for extending the range of issues which may be taken to tribunals.

There is a number of Commissioners, popularly called 'ombudsmen', who are able to investigate complaints against the administration. There is a Parliamentary Commissioner who investigates individual public grievances about central government departments and agencies. There is a small team of Local Government Commissioners who investigate complaints about local government. There is also a Health Service Commissioner for the NHS. These Commissioners are concerned solely with maladministration. They do not deal with policy, so long as that policy has a clear statutory foundation. Nor do they deal with decisions that involve statutorily legitimate discretion or professional judgement. They provide, therefore, like the tribunals, only a limited protection for citizens against the worst abuses of administrative behaviour, not an opportunity to participate in policy formulation or to comment on its overall implementation.

The underlying issue throughout this section concerns the extent to which Britain has a political and administrative system which tends to exclude meaningful participation, except through representative political institutions or through very specific devices to deal with individual grievances for consumers of social services. There has been a failure to make a coherent case for quasi-market controls over social policy, except by way of the wholesale privatization favoured by some Right-wing ideologues. The case for better public control over public services is widely accepted. Inasmuch as the policies of the new Labour government have a new philosophical underpinning, it seems to come from those who see the issues about more responsive government as of central importance (Giddens, 1998). Yet, outside the devolution policies, which may of course have 'knock on' implications for other approaches to decentralization, there is little sign that a shift in this direction is occurring. In many ways, the big preoccupations of ministers are about how to extent their 'reaches' deeper into local authorities, hospitals and schools. Meanwhile, the older more individualistic approaches to citizen control through appeals and complaints remain very important.

Conclusions

This chapter has looked at the general issues about social policy and society by first considering the overall picture of social policy expenditure, and then by looking at the various political perspectives on offer. It showed how the new Labour government has sought to provide a distinctively new approach, turning its back on a perspective which saw the central issue for social policy development to be to improve on the task initiated by Labour in 1945–51. In doing so, it has picked up the emphasis of the Right on self-help, targeting and the use of mixed approaches to policy delivery.

The acceptance by a Labour government of so much of the social policy agenda that was seen in the early 1980s as a new and discordant approach to social policy has reinforced the shift in the terms of the political debate. The issue now, for those with a critical perspective on social policy, is whether the more progressive elements in the Labour agenda – the concern about social exclusion, for example – can be sustained, despite a context in which so much of the social and economic *status quo* is accepted. The crucial issues are about the firm adoption of a perspective which stresses labour market participation. This involves a strong ideological emphasis on paid work, privileging it over other forms of social participation. It also involves a faith in the long-run capacity of the market to deliver acceptable jobs, and to solve the problems of poverty and social exclusion. This is linked with a view of the key role to be played by education and training, which seems alarmingly dependent on a growth of opportunities for skilled workers.

This is the 'high road' to the future of work outlined by Wheelock (1999) and discussed in chapter 9. Yet, as suggested there, the evidence on the way the labour market is developing at the moment gives little scope for optimism.

Hutton has persuasively described Britain as a 30/30/40 society, in which 30 per cent are seriously deprived and another 30 per cent insecure (Hutton, 1995). The 'comfortable' 40 per cent are inclined to look the other way. Labour's political strategy involves a positive sum game in which the aim is to add to their numbers without at the same time provoking their resistance. This is both a difficult strategy and one that tends to give lower priority to the immediate needs of many of the seriously deprived.

Britain's situation, as Tony Blair and Gordon Brown are only too eager to remind us, needs to be seen in a global context. On the one hand, comparisons with nations close by (in the EU) suggest that the performance of the British welfare state could be better. On the other hand, the economic forces which make full employment difficult to sustain and low-wage sectors endemic are creating problems for even the most progressive welfare states. Economic elites – through international organizations like the Organization for Economic Co-operation and Development (OECD) and the World Bank – warn governments that high public expenditure levels will have adverse consequences for competitiveness.

I end this edition of this book as I ended the last edition by stressing again, despite the change of government since then, that the struggle for better social policy is an increasingly difficult one. Great gains were made when humanitarian aspirations and political and economic forces were moving in the same direction. This is no longer the case. In this book, I have tried to explore what has been achieved and the complex edifice of social policy institutions which is in place and which does a great deal to advance welfare. However, I would be dishonest if I tried to end on an upbeat note. There is much still to be done, in an economic and political environment which makes social policy advance very difficult.

Suggestions for further reading

A collection edited by Glennerster and Hills (1998) provides a most authoritative examination of the impact of the Conservative governments on public expenditure. Hills has also produced an admirable guide to the case against those who see social policy growth as impossible in his *The Future of Welfare: A Guide to the Debate* (1997). The book by Hutton cited in the text and the report of the Commission on Social Justice (1994) offer progressive agendas for social and other public policy. Jones and Macgregor's book, recommended at the end of chapter 2, is an early example of what will surely soon be a flood of assessments of social policy under the Blair government.

The two sides in the debate on social policy provision have been well put together in a collection edited by Loney (1987); other important contributions are Deakin's *The Politics of Welfare: Continuities and Change* (1994), George and Wilding's *Welfare and Ideology* (1994), and Donnison's *A Radical Agenda* (1991).

Recommendations on the emergent literature on institutional change were included at the end of chapter 4.

There is a growing literature which puts Britain's welfare state in a wider context: notably Ginsberg's *Divisions of Welfare* (1992) and Gould's *Capitalist Welfare Systems: A Comparison of Japan, Britain and Sweden* (1993). My own contribution to this literature is *Social Policy: A Comparative Analysis* (Hill, 1996).

REFERENCES

Abel-Smith, B. 1976: *Value for Money in Health Services*. London: Heinemann.

Abel-Smith, B. and Townsend, P. 1965: *The Poor and the Poorest*. London: Bell.

Acheson, D. 1998: *Inequalities and Health*. London: HMSO.

Alcock, P. 1997: *Understanding Poverty*, 2nd edn. Basingstoke: Macmillan.

Alcock, P. and Pearson, S. 1999: Raising the poverty plateau: the impact of means-tested rebates from local authority charges on low income households, *Journal of Social Policy*, 27(3) 497–516.

Alcock, P., Erskine, A and May, M. (eds) 1998: *The Student's Companion to Social Policy*. Oxford: Blackwell.

Argyris, C. 1960: *Understanding Organisational Behaviour*. London: Tavistock.

Armstrong, H.1998: Principles for a new housing policy. *Housing Today*, 83.

Ashford, D. E. 1986: *The Emergence of the Welfare States*. Oxford: Blackwell.

Atkinson, A. B. 1975: Income distribution and social change revisited. *Journal of Social Policy*, (41), 57–68.

Atkinson, A. B. 1994: *State Pensions for Today and Tomorrow*. London: Welfare State Programme Discussion Paper 104.

Audit Commission 1986: *Making a Reality of Community Care*. London: HMSO.

Bachrach, P. 1969: *The Theory of Democratic Elitism*. London: University of London Press.

Balchin, N. 1995: *Housing Policy: An Introduction*. London: Routledge and Kegan Paul.

Baldwin, P. 1990: *The Politics of Social Solidarity*. Cambridge: Cambridge University Press.

Baldwin, R. 1995: *Rules and Government*. Oxford: Oxford University Press.

Ball, S. J. 1990: *Politics and Policy Making in Education*. London: Routledge.

Barclay, P. 1982: *Social Workers: Their Roles and Tasks* (Report of a Working Party). London: Bedford Square Press.

Bardach, E. 1977: *The Implementation Game*. Cambridge Mass: MIT Press.

Barr, N. A. 1981: Empirical definitions of the poverty line. *Policy and Politics*, (1), 1–21.

Becker, S. and Macpherson, S. 1988: *Public Issues, Private Pain*. London: Social Services Insight Books.

Becker, S and Silburn, R. 1990: *The New Poor Clients*. Nottingham: Benefits Research Unit.

Beer, S. H. 1965: *Modern British Politics*. London: Faber & Faber.

Benefits 1998: The politics of fraud: a symposium, *Benefits*, 21, January, 2–19.

Bennett, F. and Walker, R. 1999: Will work work? *Poverty*, 102, 12–15.

Beveridge, W. 1942: *Social Insurance and Allied Services*. Cmnd 6404. London: HMSO.

Blackstone, T. and Plowden, W. 1988: *Inside the Think Tank*. London: Heinemann.

Blair, T. 1999: *Beveridge Lecture*, http://www.number10.gov.uk/public . . . s/uktoday_right.asp?

Booth, C. 1889–1903: *Life and Labour of the People in London*. 17 vols. London: Macmillan.

Bosanquet, N. 1983: *After the New Right*. London: Heinemann.

Bottomore, T. B. 1966: *Elites and Society*. Penguin: Harmondsworth.

Bowe, R. and Ball, S. J. 1992: *Reforming Education and Changing Schools*. London: Routledge.

Braybrooke, D. and Lindblom, C. E. 1963: *A Strategy of Decision*. New York: Free Press.

Brittan, S. 1971: *Steering the Economy*. Penguin: Harmondsworth.

Bryson, L. 1992: *Welfare and the State*. Basingstoke: Macmillan.

Butcher, T. 1995: *Delivering Welfare: The Governance of the Social Services in the 1990s*. Buckingham: Open University Press.

Butler, D., Adonis, A. and Travers, T. 1994: *Failure in British Government: The Politics of the Poll Tax*. Oxford: Oxford University Press.

Byrne, T. 1994: *Local Government in Britain*, 6th edn. Penguin: Harmondsworth.

Cahill, M. 1994: *The New Social Policy*. Oxford: Blackwell.

Cairncross, A. 1985: *Years of Recovery: British Economic Policy 1945–51*. London: Methuen.

Campbell, C. and Wilson, G. K. 1995: *The End of Whitehall: Death of a Paradigm*. Oxford: Blackwell.

Castle, B and Townsend, P. n.d.: *We CAN afford the Welfare State*. London.

Central Advisory Council for Education 1954: *Early Leaving*. London: HMSO.

Central Advisory Council for Education 1959: *Fifteen to Eighteen* (Crowther Report). London: HMSO.

Central Advisory Council for Education 1963: *Half Our Future* (Newson Report). London: HMSO.

Central Advisory Council for Education 1967: *Children and their Primary Schools* (Plowden Report). London: HMSO.

Central Statistical Office 1995a: *Population Trends*, Winter issue. London: HMSO.

Central Statistical Office 1995b: *Public Finance Trends*. London: HMSO.

Central Statistical Office 1996: *Social Trends 26*. London: HMSO.

Central Statistical Office 1998: *Social Trends 1998*. London: HMSO.

Centre for Housing Policy 1997: *Contemporary Patterns of Residential Mobility in Relation to Social Housing in England*. York: Centre for Housing Policy.

Clark, B. R. 1956: Organizational adaptation and precarious values. *American Sociological Review*, 21, 32–6.

Clarke, J., Cochrane, A. and McLaughlin, E. (eds) 1994: *Managing Social Policy*. London: Sage.

Cole, D. and Utting, J. 1962: *The Economic Circumstances of Old People*. London: Codicote.

Commission of the European Communities 1993: *European Social Policy: Options for the Union*. Luxembourg: Official Publications of the European Communities.

Commission on Social Justice 1994: *Social Justice: Strategies for National Renewal*. London: Vintage.

Cousins, C. 1999: *Society, Work and Welfare in Europe*. Basingstoke: Macmillan.

Crossman, R. H. S. 1975, 1976, 1977: *Diaries of a Cabinet Minister*. 3 vols. London: Hamish Hamilton and Jonathan Cape.

Crozier, M. 1964: *The Bureaucratic Phenomenon*. Chicago: University of Chicago Press.

Cutler, T. and Waine, B. 1997: *Managing the Welfare State*. Oxford: Berg.

Dahl, R. A. 1961: *Who Governs?* New Haven: Yale University Press.

Dale, J. and Foster, P. 1986: *Feminists and State Welfare*. London: Routledge and Kegan Paul.

David, M. 1998: Education, education, education. In H. Jones and S. MacGregor (eds), *Social Issues and Party Politics*. London: Routledge, 74–90.

Davies, M. (ed.) 1997: *The Blackwell Companion to Social Work*. Oxford: Blackwell.

Dawtrey, L., Holland, J. and Hammer, M. (eds) 1995: *Equality and Inequality in Education Policy*. Buckingham: Open University Press.

Deacon, A. 1976: *In Search of the Scrounger*. London: Bell.

Deacon, A. and Bradshaw, J. 1983: *Reserved for the Poor*. Oxford: Martin Robertson.

Deakin, N. 1994: *The Politics of Welfare: Continuities and Change*. Hemel Hempstead: Harvester Wheatsheaf.

Deakin, N. and Parry, R. 1998: The Treasury and new Labour's social policy. In E. Brunsdon, H. Dean and R. Woods (eds), *Social Policy Review 10*. London: Social Policy Association, 34–56.

Dearlove, J. and Saunders, P. 1991: *Introduction to British Politics*, 2nd edn. Cambridge: Polity Press.

Department of Education and Science 1985: *Education for All* (a brief guide by Lord Swann to the Report of the Committee of Inquiry into the Education of Children from Ethnic Minority Groups). London: HMSO.

DfEE (Department for Education and Employment) 1997: *Excellence in Schools.* London: HMSO.

DfEE 1998a: *Education and Training Statistics for the United Kingdom.* London: HMSO.

DfEE 1998b: *Teachers: Meeting the Challenge of Change.* London: HMSO.

Department of Employment 1971: *People and Jobs.* London: HMSO.

Department of Employment 1988a: *Employment for the 1990s.* Cmnd 540. London: HMSO.

Department of Employment 1988b: *Training for Employment.* Cmnd 316. London: HMSO.

Department of the Environment 1996: *Housing and Construction Statistics.* London: HMSO.

Department of Health 1995: *Health and Personal Social Services Statistics.* London: HMSO.

Department of Health 1997: *The New NHS.* London: HMSO.

Department of Health 1998a: *A First Class Service: Quality in the NHS.* Consultation Document. London: HMSO.

Department of Heath 1998b: *Health and Personal Social Services Statistics for England,* 1997 edn. London: HMSO.

Department of Health 1998c: *Modernising Social Services.* Cm. 4169, London: HMSO.

Department of Health 1999: *A New Approach to Social Services Performance.* London: HMSO.

DETR (Department of the Environment Transport and the Regions)1998: *Modern Local Government in Touch with the People.* Cm4014, London: HMSO.

DETR 1999: *Housing: Key Figures.* http://www.housing.detr,gov.uk. information. key figures.htm www.housing.detr,gov.uk.information

DHSS (Department of Health and Social Security) 1967: *The Future Structure of the National Health Service.* London: HMSO.

DHSS 1968: *The Administrative Structure of Medical and Related Services in England and Wales.* London: HMSO.

DHSS 1976: *Priorities for Health and Personal Social Services.* London: HMSO.

Department of Social Security 1997: *Social Security Statistics.* London: HMSO.

Department of Social Security 1998a: *A New Contract for Welfare.* Cm 3805, London: HMSO.

Department of Social Security 1998b: *Children First: A New Approach to Child Support.* London: Department of Social Security.

Department of Social Security 1998c: *Jobseeker's Allowance Quarterly Enquiry.* May, London: HMSO.

Department of Social Security 1998d: *Partnership in Pensions.* London: HMSO.

Dex, S. and McCulloch, A. 1995: *Flexible Employment in Britain: A Statistical Analysis.* London: Equal Opportunities Commission.

Dicey, A. V. 1905: *Lectures on the Relations between Law and Public Opinion*. London: Macmillan.

Donnison, D. 1991: *A Radical Agenda*. London: Rivers Oram.

Dorey, P. 1999: *The Major Premiership*. Basingstoke: Macmillan.

Douglas, J. W. B. 1964: *The Home and the School*. London: Macgibbon and Kee.

Dunleavy, P. 1981: *The Politics of Mass Housing in Britain*. London: Oxford University Press.

Dunleavy, P. (ed.) 1997: *Developments in British Politics*. New York: St Martins Press.

Eardley, T., Bradshaw, J., Ditch, J., Gough, I. and Whiteford, P. 1996: *Social Assistance in OECD Countries: Synthesis Report*. London: HMSO.

Eckstein, H. 1960: *Pressure Group Politics*. London: Allen and Unwin.

Edgell, S. and Duke, V. 1991: *A Measure of Thatcherism*. Glasgow: HarperCollins.

Esping-Andersen, G. 1990: *The Three Worlds of Welfare Capitalism*. Cambridge: Polity Press.

Esping-Andersen, G. (ed.) 1996: *Welfare States in Transition*. London: Sage.

Etzioni, A. 1961: *A Comparative Analysis of Complex Organisations*. New York: Free Press.

Etzioni, A.1969: *The Semi Professions and their Organization*. New York: Free Press.

Field, F. 1996: *Stakeholder Welfare*. London: Institute of Economic Affairs.

Field, F. 1998: Keith Joseph Memorial Lecture. Press release.

Fimister, G. 1986: *Welfare Rights in Social Services*. London: Macmillan.

Fimister, G. 1995: *Social Security and Community Care in the 1990s*. Sunderland: Business Education Publishers.

Finch, J. 1984: *Education and Social Policy*. London: Longman.

Finer, S. E. 1958: *Anonymous Empire*. London: Pall Mall.

Floud, J., Halsey, A. H. and Martin, F. M. 1956: *Social Class and Education Opportunity*. London: Heinemann.

Ford, J. 1969: *Social Class and the Comprehensive School*. London: Routledge and Kegan Paul.

Forrest, R. and Murie, A. 1991: *Selling the Welfare State*. London: Routledge.

Forrest, R., Murie, A. and Williams, P. 1990: *Home Ownership: Fragmentation and Differentiation*. London: Unwin Hyman.

Foster, P. 1983: *Access to Welfare*. London: Macmillan.

Fox, A. 1974: *Beyond Contract: Work, Power and Trust Relations*. London: Faber.

Fraser, D. 1984: *The Evolution of the British Welfare State*. London: Macmillan.

Friedman, M. 1962: *Capitalism and Freedom*. Chicago: University of Chicago Press.

Friedman, M. 1977: *Inflation and Unemployment: A New Dimension of Politics*. London: Institute of Economic Affairs.

Friedson, E. 1970: *Professional Dominance*. New York: Atherton.

Friend, J. K., Power, J. M. and Yewlett, C. J. L. 1974: *Public Planning: The Inter-corporate Dimension*. London: Tavistock.

George, V. and Wilding, P. 1984: *The Impact of Social Policy*. London: Routledge and Kegan Paul.

George, V. and Wilding, P.1994: *Welfare and Ideology*. 2nd edn. Hemel Hempstead: Harvester Wheatsheaf.

Gewirtz, S., Ball, S. J. and Bowe, R. 1995: *Markets, Choice and Equity in Education*. Buckingham: Open University Press.

Giddens, A. 1998: *The Third Way: The Renewal of Social Democracy*. Cambridge: Polity Press.

Gilbert, B. B. 1970: *British Social Policy 1914–39*. London: Batsford.

Gillborn, D. 1992: *Race, Ethnicity and Education*. London: Unwin Hyman.

Ginsberg, N. 1992: *Divisions of Welfare*. London: Sage.

Glennerster, H. 1992: *Paying for Welfare*. Oxford: Blackwell.

Glennerster, H. 1995: *British Social Policy Since 1945*. Oxford: Blackwell.

Glennerster, H and Hills, J. (eds) 1998: *The State of Welfare*. Oxford: Oxford University Press.

Glennerster, H., Matsaganis, M. and Owens, P. 1994: *Implementing Fundholding*. Buckingham: Open University Press.

Glennerster, H., Power, A. and Travers, T. 1991: A new era for social policy: a new enlightenment or a new Leviathan? *Journal of Social Policy*, 20(3), 389–414.

Gold, M. (ed.) 1993: *The Social Dimension*. Basingstoke: Macmillan.

Gordon, D. and Pantazis, C. 1997: *Breadline Britain in the 1990s*. Aldershot: Avebury.

Gough, I. 1979: *The Political Economy of the Welfare State*. London: Macmillan.

Gould, A. 1993: *Capitalist Welfare Systems: A Comparison of Japan, Britain and Sweden*. London: Longman.

Green, H. and Hansbro, J. 1995: *Housing in England 1993–94*. London: HMSO.

Gregg, P. and Wadsworth, J. 1995: A short history of labour turnover, labour tenure and job security 1975–93. *Oxford Review of Economic Policy*, 11(1), 73–90.

Griffiths Report 1983: *NHS Management Enquiry*. London: Department of Health and Social Security.

Gyford, J. 1985: *The Politics of Local Socialism*. London: Allen and Unwin.

Gyford, J. 1991: *Citizens, Consumers and Councils*. London: Macmillan.

Hall, P. 1976: *Reforming the Welfare*. London: Heinemann.

Hallett, C. and Stevenson, O. 1979: *Child Abuse: Aspects of Interprofessional Communication*. London: Allen and Unwin.

Halsey, A. H. (ed.) 1972: *Educational Priority*, vol. 1. London: HMSO.

Ham, C. 1999: *Health Policy in Britain*, 2nd edn. Basingstoke: Macmillan.

Hamnett, C. 1991: A nation of inheritors? Housing inheritance, wealth and inequality in Britain. *Journal of Social Policy*, 20(4), 509–36.

Harris, J. 1972: *Unemployment and Politics*. London: Oxford University Press.

Harris, J. 1977: *William Beveridge: A Biography*. Oxford: Oxford University Press.

Harris, R. and Seldon, A. 1976: *Pricing or Taxing*. London: Institute of Economic Affairs.

Harris, R. and Seldon, A.1979: *Overruled on Welfare*. London: Institute of Economic Affairs.

Harrison, S., Hunter D. J. and Pollitt, C. 1990: *The Dynamics of British Health Policy*. London: Unwin Hyman.

Hawkins, K. (ed.) 1992: *The Uses of Discretion*. Oxford: Clarendon Press.

Heclo, H. H. 1974: *Modern Social Politics in Britain and Sweden*. New Haven: Yale University Press.

Heclo, H. H. and Wildavsky, A. 1981: *The Private Government of Public Money*. London: Macmillan.

Hennessy, P. 1992: *Never Again: Britain 1945–51*. London: Cape.

Higgins, J. 1988: *The Business of Medicine: Private Health Care in Britain*. London: Macmillan.

Higgins, J., Deakin, N., Edwards, J. and Wicks, M. 1984: *Government and Urban Poverty*. Oxford: Blackwell.

Hill, M. 1972: *The Sociology of Public Administration*. London: Weidenfeld & Nicolson.

Hill, M.1993: *The Welfare State in Britain*. Aldershot: Edward Elgar.

Hill, M. 1996: *Social Policy: A Comparative Analysis*. Hemel Hempstead: Harvester Wheatsheaf.

Hill, M. 1997a: *The Policy Process in the Modern State*. Hemel Hempstead: Prentice Hall/ Harvester Wheatsheaf.

Hill, M. (ed.) 1997b: *The Policy Process: A Reader*, 2nd edn. Hemel Hempstead: Prentice Hall/ Harvester Wheatsheaf .

Hill, M. (ed.) 2000: *Local Authority Social Services*. Oxford: Blackwell (forthcoming).

Hills, J. 1997: *The Future of Welfare: A Guide to the Debate*, 2nd edn. York: Joseph Rowntree Foundation.

Hills, J. 1998: *Income and Wealth: The Latest Evidence*. York: Joseph Rowntree Foundation.

HMSO 1957: *Report of the Committee on Administrative Tribunals and Enquiries* (Franks Report). Cmnd 218. London: HMSO.

HMSO 1968: *Report of the Committee on Local Authority and Allied Personal Social Services* (Seebohm Report). Cmnd 3703. London: HMSO.

HMSO 1972: *Proposals for a Tax-credits System*. Cmnd 5116. London: HMSO.

HMSO 1977: *Housing Policy: A Consultative Document*. Cmnd 6851. London: HMSO.

HMSO 1979: *Report of the Royal Commission on the National Health Service* (Merrison Report). Cmnd 7615. London: HMSO.

HMSO 1989: *Caring for People: Community Care in the Next Decade and Beyond*. Cmnd 849. London: HMSO.

HMSO 1998: *The Government's Annual Report 97/98*. London: HMSO.

Holme, A. and Maizels, J. 1978: *Volunteers in Social Work*. London: Allen and Unwin.

Hood, C. 1991: A public management for all seasons. *Public Administration*, 69(1), 3–19.

House of Commons 1977: *Seventh Report from the Expenditure Committee: The Job Creation Programme*. London: HMSO.

Hudson, B. 1994: *Making Sense of Markets in Health and Social Care*. Sunderland: Business Education Publishers.

Hudson, B. 1997: Michael Lipsky and street level bureaucracy: a neglected perspective. In M. Hill (ed.), *The Policy Process: A Reader* 2nd edn. Hemel Hempstead: Prentice Hall/ Harvester Wheatsheaf , 393–403.

Hutton, W. 1995: *The State We're In*. London: Cape.

Jackson, B. and Marsden, D. 1962: *Education and the Working Class*. London: Routledge and Kegan Paul.

Jenkins, W. I. 1978: *Policy Analysis*. London: Martin Robertson.

Johnson, N. 1990: *Reconstructing the Welfare State*. Hemel Hempstead: Harvester Wheatsheaf.

Jones, B. et al. 1998: *Politics UK*. Hemel Hempstead: Harvester Wheatsheaf.

Jones, C. 1997: Poverty. In M. Davies (ed.), *The Blackwell Companion to Social Work*. Oxford: Blackwell, 118–25.

Jones, H. and MacGregor, S. (eds) 1998: *Social Issues and Party Politics*. London: Routledge.

Jordan, A. G. and Richardson, J. J. 1987: *British Politics and the Policy Process*. London: Unwin Hyman.

Jordan, B. 1974: *Poor Parents*. London: Routledge and Kegan Paul.

Jowell, J. 1973: The legal control of administrative discretion. *Public Law*, 178, 178–220.

Judge, K. 1982: The public purchase of social care. *Policy and Politics*, 10(4), 397–416.

Judge. K 1987: *Rationing Social Services*. London: Heinemann.

Keynes, J. M. 1936: *The General Theory of Employment Interest and Money*. London: Macmillan.

Klein, R. 1995: *The Politics of the NHS*. London: Longman.

Kohli, M., Rein, M., Guillemard, A-M. and van Gunsteren, H. 1991: *Time for Retirement: Comparative Studies of Early Exit from the Labour Force*. Cambridge: Cambridge University Press.

Land, H. and Rose, H. 1985: Compulsory altruism for some or an altruistic society for all. In P. Bean, J. Ferris and D. Whynes (eds), *In Defence of Welfare*. London: Tavistock, 74–96.

Law, I. 1996: *Racism, Ethnicity and Social Policy*. Hemel Hempstead: Prentice Hall.

Le Grand, J. 1982: *The Strategy of Equality*. London: Allen and Unwin.

Le Grand, J.1990: *Quasi-Markets and Social Policy*. Bristol: School for Advanced Urban Studies.

Le Grand, J., Mays, N. and Mulligan J-A. 1998: *Learning from the NHS Internal Market*. London: Kings Fund.

Lee, P. and Murie, A. 1998: Social exclusion and housing. In S. Wilcox (ed.), *Housing Finance Review*. York: Joseph Rowntree Foundation, 30–37.

Liddiard, M. 1998: Home truths. In H. Jones. and S. MacGregor (eds), *Social Issues and Party Politics*. London: Routledge, 132–8.

Lindsey, A. 1962: *Socialised Medicine in England and Wales*. Chapel Hill: University of North Carolina Press.

Ling, T. 1994: The new managerialism and social security. In J. Clarke, A. Cochrane and E. McLaughlin (eds), *Managing Social Policy*. London: Sage, 32–56.

Lipsky, M. 1980: *Street-Level Bureaucracy*. New York: Russell Sage.

Loney, M. (ed.) 1987: *The State or the Market*. London: Sage.

Lowe, R. 1999: *The Welfare State in Britain since 1945*, 2nd edn. London: Macmillan.

Lynes, T. 1962: *National Assistance and National Prosperity*. London: Codicote.

Lynes, T. 1997a: *Supplementary Pensions in Britain: Is there still a Role for the State?* Paper given at European Institute for Social Security seminar in Dublin.

Lynes, T. 1997b: The British case. In M. Rein and E. Wadensjö (eds), *Enterprise and the Welfare State*. Cheltenham: Edward Elgar, 309–51.

MacDermott, T. 1999: Poverty: Labour's inheritance. *Poverty*, 102, Spring, 16–19.

Mack, J. and Lansley, S. 1985: *Poor Britain*. London: Allen and Unwin.

Malpass, P. 1990: *Reshaping Housing Policy*. London: Routledge.

Malpass, P. and Murie, A. 1999: *Housing Policy and Practice*, 4th edn. London: Macmillan.

Marsh, D. and Rhodes, R. A. W. 1992a: *Implementing Thatcherite Policies*. Buckingham: Open University Press.

Marsh, D. and Rhodes, R. A. W. 1992b: *Policy Networks in British Government*. Oxford: Oxford University Press.

McCarthy, M. 1986: *Campaigning for the Poor*. Beckenham: Croom Helm.

Mckay S. and Rowlingson, K. 1999: *Social Security in Britain*. Basingstoke: Macmillan.

McKeown, T. 1980: *The Role of Medicine*. Oxford: Blackwell.

Mead, L. 1986: *Beyond Entitlement: The Social Obligations of Citizenship*. New York: Free Press.

Means, R. and Smith, R. 1994: *Community Care: Policy and Practice*. Basingstoke: Macmillan.

Minford, P. 1984: State expenditure: a study in waste. *Economic Affairs*, (April–June), supplement.

Moon, J. and Richardson, J. J. 1985: *Unemployment in the U.K.* Aldershot: Gower.

Moran, M. and Wood, B. 1993: *States, Regulation and the Medical Profession.* Buckingham: Open University Press.

Morgan, K. O.1984: *Labour in Power 1945–51.* Oxford: Oxford University Press.

Mukherjee, S. 1972: *Making Labour Markets Work.* London: PEP.

Murie, A., Niner, P. and Watson, C. 1976: *Housing Policy and the Housing System.* London: Allen and Unwin.

Murray, C. 1984: *Losing Ground.* New York: Basic Books.

O'Connor, J. 1973: *The Fiscal Crisis of the State.* New York: St Martin's Press.

Office for National Statistics 1998: *Regional Trends.* London: HMSO.

Office for National Statistics 1999a: *Labour Market Trends.* London: HMSO.

Office for National Statistics 1999b: *Social Trends.* London: HMSO.

Ofsted 1999: *Raising the Attainment of Minority Ethnic Pupils.* London: Ofsted.

Packman, J. 1975: *The Child's Generation.* Oxford: Blackwell.

Parker, H. 1989: *Instead of the Dole.* London: Routledge.

Pater, J. E. 1981: *The Making of the National Health Service.* London: King's Fund.

Peters, T. and Waterman, R. 1982: *In Search of Excellence.* New York: HarperCollins.

Phillimore, P., Beattie, A. and Townsend, P. 1994: Widening inequality in health in Northern England 1981–91. *British Medical Journal,* 308, 1125–8.

Pierson, P. 1994: *Dismantling the Welfare State.* Cambridge: Cambridge University Press.

Piore, M. and Sabel, C. 1984: *The Second Industrial Divide.* Oxford: Blackwell.

Piven, F. F. and Cloward, R. A. 1972: *Regulating the Poor.* London: Tavistock.

Pollitt, C. 1990: *Managerialism and the Public Services.* Oxford: Blackwell.

Power, A. 1987: *Property before People.* London: Allen and Unwin.

Pressman, G. and Wildavsky, A. 1973: *Implementation.* Berkeley: University of California Press.

Ranade, W. 1997: *A Future for the NHS.* Harlow: Longman.

Rao, N. 1996: *Towards Welfare Pluralism.* Aldershot: Dartmouth.

Ridley, F. 1988: *The Local Right: Enabling not Providing.* London: Conservative Political Centre.

Roberts, D. 1960: *Victorian Origins of the British Welfare State.* New Haven: Yale University Press.

Roberts, G. K. 1970: *Political Parties and Pressure Groups in Britain.* London: Weidenfeld & Nicolson.

Robins Committee 1963: *Higher Education.* Cmnd 2154. London: HMSO.

Robinson, R. and Judge, K. 1987: *Public Expenditure and the NHS: Trends and Prospects*. London: King's Fund Institute.

Rose, H. 1981: Rereading Titmuss: the social division of welfare. *Journal of Social Policy*, 10(4), 477–502.

Rowntree, B. S. 1901: *Poverty: A Study of Town Life*. London: Macmillan.

Royal Commission on Long Term Care 1999: *With Respect to Old Age*. London: HMSO.

Sanderson, M. 1991: Social equality and industrial need: a dilemma of English education since 1945. In T. Gourvish and A. O'Day (eds), *Britain Since 1945*. London: Macmillan, 159–82.

Savage, S. P., Atkinson, R. and Robins, L. (eds) 1994: *Public Policy in Britain*. London: Macmillan.

Scally, G. and Donaldson J. 1998: Clinical governance and the drive for quality improvement in the new NHS in England. *British Medical Journal*, 317, 61–5.

Schattschneider, E. E. 1960: *The Semi-Sovereign People*. New York: Holt, Rinehart and Winston.

Schumpeter, J. 1950: *Capitalism, Socialism and Democracy*. New York: Harper and Row.

Semmel, B. 1961: *Imperialism and Social Reform*. London: Oxford University Press.

Sinfield, R. A. 1978: Analysis in the social division of welfare. *Journal of Social Policy*, 7(2), 129–56.

Sinfield, R. A. 1981: *What Unemployment Means*. Oxford: Martin Robertson.

Smith, B. C. 1976: *Policy Making in British Government*. London: Martin Robertson.

Smith, M. J. 1993: *Pressure, Power and Policy*. Hemel Hempstead: Harvester Wheatsheaf.

Social Exclusion Unit 1998: *Consultation on Deprived Urban Neighbourhoods*. http://www.cabinet-office.gov.uk/seu/1998/depneigh.htm

Stacey, M. 1988: *The Sociology of Health and Healing*. London: Unwin Hyman.

Stanworth, P. and Giddens, A. 1974: *Elites and Power in British Society*. Cambridge: Cambridge University Press.

Taylor-Gooby, P. 1985: *Public Opinion, Ideology and State Welfare*. London: Routledge and Kegan Paul.

Thane, P. 1996: *Foundations of the Welfare State*. London: Longman.

Timmins, N. 1996: *The Five Giants: A Biography of the Welfare State*. London: Fontana.

Titmuss, R. M. 1958: *Essays on the Welfare State*. London: Allen and Unwin.

Titmuss, R. M. 1962: *Income Distribution and Social Change*. London: Allen and Unwin.

Townsend, P.1979: *Poverty in the United Kingdom*. Harmondsworth: Penguin.

Townsend, P., Davidson, N. and Whitehead, M. (eds) 1988: *Inequalities in Health*. Harmondsworth: Penguin.

Trades Union Congress (TUC) 1999: *Labour Market Briefing*. London: TUC.

Unemployment Unit 1992: *Working Brief*. London: Unemployment Unit (issued monthly).

Urry, J. and Wakeford, J. (eds) 1973: *Power in Britain*. London: Heinemann.

Walter, J. A. 1988: *Basic Income: Escape from the Poverty Trap*. London: Marion Boyars.

Webb, A. 1985: Alternative futures for social policy and state welfare. In R. Berthoud (ed.), *Challenges to Social Policy*, Aldershot: Gower, 46–71.

Weber, M. 1947: *The Theory of Social and Economic Organization*. Trans. A. M. Henderson and T. Parsons. Glencoe, Ill.: Free Press.

Webster, C. 1998: *The National Health Service: A Political History*. Oxford: Oxford University Press.

Wheelock, J. 1999: Fear or opportunity: insecurity in employment. In J. J. Vail, J. Wheelock and M. Hill (eds), *Insecure Times*. London: Routledge 75–88.

Wheelock, J. and Vail, J. (eds) 1998: *Work and Idleness: The Political Economy of Full Employment*. Boston MA: Kluwer.

Wilcox, S. (ed.) 1998: *Housing Finance Review*. York: Joseph Rowntree Foundation.

Wilding, P. 1982: *Professional Power and Social Welfare*. London: Routledge.

Williams, F. 1989: *Social Policy: A Critical Introduction*. Cambridge: Polity Press.

Williams, P. (ed.) 1997: *New Directions in Housing Policy: Towards Sustainable Housing*. London: Chapman.

Willis, P. 1977: *Learning to Labour*. Westmead: Saxon House.

Woods, R. 1999: No place like home?: Insecurity in housing. In J. J. Vail, J. Wheelock and M. Hill (eds), *Insecure Times*. London: Routledge, 105–18.

Wootton, G. 1970: *Interest Groups*. Englewood Cliffs, NJ: Prentice-Hall.

INDEX